ALSO BY RIC EDELMAN

The Truth About Money

Ordinary People, Extraordinary Wealth

Discover the Wealth Within You

The New Rules of Money

What You Need to Do Now

What You'll Learn in This Book

The Most Proven, Successful Investment Strategy There Is. 7

Why brain-damaged people are good investors. 20

Why women are better investors than men. 22

Why you have only a 0.0000000000000000000000000000000000000000 00000000000000000000000000000000000000000000000000000000000000 00000000000000000000000000000000000000000000000000000000000000 000000000000000000000000000000000000000000000022883557% chance of getting it right only half the time 23

How to get *all* the profits of the stock market. . . . . 11 and 26

How your car's thermostat explains investor behavior. 29

Why investment returns differ from investor returns 48

Widows of Western Europe are a lot prettier than you'd guess 89

Why you must sell all your retail mutual funds 93

How to beat the retail mutual fund industry at its own game 167

The greatest invention since mutual funds. 179

How to create the investment portfolio that's right for you. 185

How to invest the money in your retirement plan at work 205

Why 20-somethings are acting like little old ladies. 208

The dangers of investing in L Funds 211

How to avoid missing out on some of your employer's match. 218

Why parents are in la-la land when it comes to college planning 223

Why grandparents should <u>not</u> save for college for the grandkids 228

How to generate lots of stable, predictable income from your investments. . . . 231

A really bad pitch from insurance salespeople 257

What You'll Discover Inside

Your Own Personal Investment Portfolio Is Inside — Find it Using Ric's Fun and Simple Guide to Portfolio Selection

Ric's guide is fun and easy to use! By answering just a few simple questions, you'll discover which of Ric's forty-three portfolio models is best for you. Turn to page 192 to get started!

Are Your Mutual Funds Ripping You Off? Discover the Shocking Revelations in Ric's *Mutual Fund Scandal Timeline*

Deceptive marketing practices. Illegal market timing and late trading. Excessive charges. Hidden fees. Are *your* mutual funds among those implicated in the scandal? Find out inside — Ric names names and shows you what's really going on at the biggest mutual fund and brokerage firms in the country. Turn to page 93 for the gory details.

Learn Advanced Investment Concepts — You, Too, Can Master the Academics Thanks to Ric's Clear Explanations

Investing doesn't have to be a black box. Beta, the Sharpe Ratio and the Fama-French 3-Factor Model sound intimidating at first, but Ric makes it all quite simple and easy to understand. Instantly, you'll learn how to benefit from the most brilliant minds in academia — using their proven methods for achieving long-term investment success. You'll look incredibly smart at that next cocktail party, too! Turn to page 41 for Ric's speed-course.

Beware Those Who Tout Life Insurance as an Investment

Insurance is important, but not when it comes to investing — and anyone who says otherwise is a liar. If you've been pitched the idea of buying life insurance as an investment, go no further until you read Ric's expose! Turn to page 257 to learn the facts.

Will Baby Boomers Cause the Stock Market to Nose Dive?

Will the stock market crash as the Baby Boomers retire? Turn to page 283 to find out what the Age Wave means for your investment strategy.

THE
LIES
ABOUT
MONEY

**Achieving Financial Security
and True Wealth by Avoiding
the Lies Others Tell Us —
and the Lies We Tell Ourselves**

Ric Edelman

*f*P

New York   London   Toronto   Sydney

*f*P

Free Press
A Division of Simon & Schuster, Inc.
1230 Avenue of the Americas
New York, NY 10020

First Free Press hardcover edition October 2007

FREE PRESS and colophon are trademarks of Simon & Schuster, Inc.

For information about special discounts for bulk purchases, please contact Simon &
Schuster Special Sales at 1-800-456-6798 or business@simonandschuster.com.

Designed by Ric Edelman and Suzi Fenton

Manufactured in the United States of America

10 9 8 7 6 5 4

Library of Congress Cataloging-in-Publication Data

Edelman, Ric.
  The lies about money : achieving financial security and true wealth by avoiding the lies
others tell us—and the lies we tell ourselves / by Ric Edelman.
      p. cm.

 1. Portfolio management—United States. 2. Stocks—United States. 3. Mutual funds—Corrupt
practices—United States. 4. Finance, Personal—United States. 5. Financial security—United
States. I. Title. II. Title: Achieving financial security and true wealth.
  HG4529.5.E34 2007
  332.6—dc22   2007029286

ISBN-13: 978-1-4165-4311-4
ISBN-10:   1-4165-4311-2

NOTE TO READERS

This publication contains the opinions and ideas of its author. The strategies outlined in this book may not be suitable for every individual, and are not guaranteed or warranted to produce any particular results. Presentation of performance data herein does not imply that similar results will be achieved in the future. Any such data is provided merely for illustrative and discussion purposes; rather than focusing on the time periods used or the results derived, the reader should focus instead on the underlying principles.

This book is sold with the understanding that neither publisher nor author, through this book, is engaged in rendering legal, tax, investment, insurance, financial, accounting, or other professional advice or services. If the reader requires such advice or services, a competent professional should be consulted. Relevant laws vary from state to state.

No warranty is made with respect to the accuracy or completeness of the information contained herein, and both the author and the publisher specifically disclaim any responsibility for any liability, loss or risk, personal or otherwise, which is incurred as a consequence, directly or indirectly, of the use and application of any of the contents of this book.

To Ed Moore

Seventeen and a half years ago, an offhand remark led to a blessing.

His dedication to our cause, his unwavering support,
his ceaseless work, his outstanding judgment,
and most importantly his warm friendship
mean everything to Jean and me.

Acknowledgments

I learned long ago that you must do two things when you set out to write a book. First, you must say something important. Second, you must be right.

There's no question that this book is important — the revelations it contains about the retail mutual fund industry offer profound implications for tens of millions of Americans. But is the information correct, and is the advice valid? I spent four years diligently researching the material for this book, but that wasn't enough. So I asked a few people to assist me.

Okay, I asked 50. After completing the manuscript, I asked all the financial advisors at Edelman Financial to review it. I also asked a dozen or so other staff members, some of whom has expertise in insurance and mortgages, others who are not directly in the financial field — to make sure that the technical aspects of the book make sense to those not immersed in the jargon of personal finance. They all did an outstanding job: The manuscript was 550 double-spaced pages, and when I received their comments, they had redlined every page except five. The book in your hands reflects all their comments, and bears little resemblance to my original manuscript.

Thus, I am indebted to financial advisors James Baker, Jack Bubon, Alfonso Burgos, Scott Butera, Kristine Chaze, Brandon Corso, Marty Corso, John Davis, Mary Davis, Patrick Day, Alan Facey, Joe Gilmore, David Heinemann, Ed Jenkins, Diane Jensen, Jan Kowal, JB Liebstein, Andrew Massaro, Ed Moore, James Negley, Denise Neuhart, Betty O'Lear, Doug Rabil, Darrell Reynard, Rey Roy, Valentino Taddei, Christine Wessinger, Tom Wood, and Anderson Wozny, and to staff members Fabio Assmann, Mike Attiliis, Mark Bagley, Christine Cataldo, Sharon Deaver, Tim Goode, Jerry Mason, Matt Nichols, Kala Payne, Carol Roberts, Carol Rowane, Evy Sheehan, Ryan Singer, Deborah Smith, Mary Jane Spradlin, Garrett Stokes, Katie Tracy, Shirley Traversy, Jan Wilson, Jo-Anna Wilson, and Denise Zuchelli.

The most challenging aspect of the book was creating the Edelman Guide to Portfolio Selection. With 64 possible combinations, it was crucial that each path maps to the correct portfolio. The programming was completed by my IT department's software developer Paul Loftus, and it was converted to static (book) form by Project Leader Mike Attiliis and VP of Communications Will Casserly. Verification of their work was completed by financial advisors Alfonso Burgos, Alan Facey, David Heinemann, James Negley, Denise Neuhart, David Sheehan, and Christine Wessinger, as well as staffers Mike Attiliis, Christine Cataldo, Catherine Caceres, Dale Tison, Adam Epling, Jo-Anna Wilson, and Stacy Burleson. Software developer Louis Innaci designed the programs that created the forty-three pie charts. Compliance and accuracy reviews were provided by Eraine Parker, Sue Harpe and Jackie Prensky.

Acknowledgments

Once again, I tip my hat to my graphic designer, Suzi Fenton. Unlike authors who merely write books, we actually design and produce the layout, too — giving the publisher finished, camera-ready pages ready for production. This was no easy task, considering the huge numbers of charts, graphs, quotes, page and line sidebars, cartoons, and footnotes — not to mention the Guide's questions that pepper pages throughout the book. Every visual element had to fit in precise locations, and Suzi masterfully executed this ballet — and tolerated my many changes throughout the pagination process. And she did it all under short deadlines. Many thanks, too, to Will Casserly, who oversaw the design work and created the book's front and back cover.

The Mutual Fund Scandal Timeline, which took me four years to research and write, underwent a complete review by Simon & Schuster's crack legal team, led by Jennifer Weidman. We provided multiple independent sources so they could verify the timeline line-by-line. The effort to collect these sources was led by Jo-Anna Wilson, ably assisted by Mark Bagley and Ryan Singer.

Important thanks go to my Executive Assistant, Stacy Brosnahan. She not only makes sure I'm doing what I need to be doing, but she stepped in several times to assist with myriad details on the book (such as collecting hundreds of pieces of data for me, for a single chart). People often ask how I'm able to do so much; she's a big part of the reason.

This is my first book with Free Press, an imprint of Simon & Schuster, and I am very happy to have found this new home. Everyone has been terrific, from my editor, Dominick Anfuso (and his assistant, Wylie O'Sullivan), to the publicity team led by Carisa Hays and Nicole Kalian. The high level of attention provided by Associate Publisher Suzanne Donahue and Executive Vice President & Publisher Martha K. Levin is everything a writer could desire. They all took me on faith, and I am grateful for their can-do spirit. For all of them, I say Thank You — with special thanks to my agent, Gail Ross, who piloted me through the process in style.

Most important of all, of course, is my wife Jean. Her willingness to let me devote every weekend to the book for seven straight months is a true testament to both her endless patience and her shared commitment of providing consumers with valuable financial education they can't get elsewhere. I am humbled by her love and devotion, which I try hard but never quite succeed to match.

And finally, let me mention my second cousins, Jill, age 12, and Jenna, 10. They didn't help with the book, but they each gave me a dollar in exchange for seeing their names in print. Sorry, but last names would have required two dollars.

Contents

Introduction 1

Chapter 1

The Most Proven, Successful Investment Strategy There Is ... 7

The Importance of Saving Regularly 8

Why We're Long-term Investors 10

Why We Diversify 25

Why We Rebalance Periodically 33

Chapter 2

The Academics Behind the Strategy 41

Concept #1: Actual Return 43

Concept #2: Rate of Return 43

Concept #3: Average Returns................................... 44

Concept #4: Risk 47

How to Measure the Risk of an Investment......................... 49

How to Compare the Risks of Different Investments.................... 52

The World is Round — And Why That Matters to Your Investments.... 55

Concept #5: Terminal Wealth Dispersion........................ 62

Chapter 3

Why You Should Use Mutual Funds........................... 83

Less Filling, *and* Tastes Great 87

Scotch, Golf, and . . . Mutual Funds 89

Chapter 4

The Demise of the Retail Mutual Fund Industry 93

THE MUTUAL FUND SCANDAL TIMELINE 119

The Three Key Abuses 120

A Different Point of View? 164

Turn Your Outrage Into Action 165

Chapter 5

How to Beat the Retail Mutual Fund Industry at Its Own Game 167

The Best of Both Worlds: Active Selection
Combined with Passive Management 174

Chapter 6

The Greatest Invention Since Mutual Funds 179

Chapter 7

Creating the Investment Portfolio That's Right for You 185

Follow the GPS with Three Points In Mind 186

Can a Book Eliminate the Need for an Advisor? 188

Introducing Ric's GPS *Building and Managing an Investment Portfolio Using the Edelman Guide to Portfolio Selection®* 192

Chapter 8

Three Important Insights to Insure Your Investment Success 199

Insight 1: Never Let Your Investment Decisions
Be Determined by Taxes 199

Insight 2: Never Let Investment Decisions Be Determined by Fees 202

Insight 3: Keep Your Portfolio Consistent with
Your Current Circumstances 203

Chapter 9

Applying This Strategy to Your Employer Retirement Plan 205

What to Do with Your Retirement Account
after You Leave Employment 215

If You're Not Saving for Retirement 217

Chapter 10

Applying This Strategy When Saving for College 221

If You're Not Saving for College 223

Why Grandparents Should *Not* Save for College for Their Grandchildren 228

Chapter 11

Applying This Strategy When Investing for Income **231**

Should You Adjust Your Portfolio Model Due to a Pension? 235

Chapter 12

**Three More Important Insights to
Insure Your Investment Success** **241**

Insight 4: You *Will* Retire One Day, and Probably
Sooner than You Anticipate, No Matter How Much You Protest 241

Insight 5: Do Not Underestimate the Amount
of Income You'll Need in Retirement 242

Insight 6: Do Not Overestimate Your Investment Returns 253

Chapter 13

Implementing This Strategy with Life Insurance **257**

Chapter 14

Implementing This Strategy with Variable Annuities **269**

Are Principal Guarantees Worthwhile? 272

Is Tax Deferral All That Valuable? 274

Should You Invest in a Variable Annuity in
Your Retirement Plan at Work? 280

What to Do If You Want to Get Rid of Your Variable Annuity 281

Chapter 15

**Should You Adjust Your Portfolio
Because Baby Boomers Are Retiring?** **283**

Epilogue

Lessons Learned **289**

Sources **293**

For Further Reading **295**

About the Author **303**

Index **307**

THE
LIES
ABOUT
MONEY

Introduction

"Why are you calling *me*? These children are only ten years old. You should be calling the high schools."

The year was 1986, and I was beginning my career as a financial advisor. Because I wanted to teach people about personal finance — more about that later — my wife, Jean, and I began offering college planning seminars to elementary-school PTA groups.

Every time I telephoned a PTA president, I got the same reply. "Why are you calling *me*?" he or she would say. "These children are only ten years old. You should be calling the high schools."

Back then, parents of young children never thought about college. The only issue pertaining to college was choosing one, a decision easily avoided until the child was a junior in high school. It never occurred to parents that college costs were skyrocketing and that they'd need many, many years to accumulate sufficient savings. It might be obvious to us now, but in the 1980s, college planning was a revolutionary idea. In fact, it wasn't just revolutionary — it was unheard of.

So too were the other aspects of investing and personal finance. For example, in 1989, as my reputation as a financial educator grew, I was invited for the first time to appear on the radio. After a brief introduction, the host presented me with a thoughtful question. "What's a mutual fund?" he asked.

My, how far we've come. Just two short decades ago, few people had ever heard of financial planning. Employers (not workers!) picked the investments for 401(k) plans; Individual Retirement Accounts were still fairly new (and when surveyed, most people said IRA meant the Irish Republican Army). Nobody worried that Social Security might go broke, and no one had ever heard of long-term care. College planning, retirement planning, estate planning — none of these concepts was a part of mainstream America.

Today, of course, all of this is well known, and everyone, it seems, knows the importance of saving for the future. This year's newborns will spend more than $250,000 to obtain a college degree, while today's middle class must accumulate millions of dollars if they want to retire in comfort and financial security.

Americans are rising to the challenge. They are spending more attention to personal finance than ever, and the marketplace has responded. When I started offering financial advice and education in 1986, the only consumer resource was *Money* magazine. Today there are dozens of magazines, two daily newspapers, an entire television news network, many radio programs, and literally thousands of books devoted to the subject. Personal finance peppers the general media as well — even sitcoms feature story lines around household finance issues. All this demonstrates an unprecedented level of consumer awareness.

And that awareness has led to action. Nearly 60% of all working Americans now contribute part of their paycheck to a retirement plan at work, and tens of millions have an IRA account. Section 529 College Savings Plans are very popular (for reasons you'll read about in this book), and at cocktail parties, people are as likely to talk about mutual funds as sports.

Retail mutual funds are, by far, the most popular investment vehicle in the country — more than half of all American families, or 54 million households — own them. With more than 8,400 funds holding $10 trillion in assets, it's not a stretch to say that retail mutual funds are almost as common and indispensable as automobiles.

So. You now understand the need to engage in financial planning, and you're investing to meet your long-term goals of college and retirement. That's great news.

But a new problem has developed, and this is why I've written this book — a book I never imagined writing. Just as I gave you the truth about money in my first book, I must now alert you to the lies that are placing your financial security in jeopardy. Some of these are lies you tell yourself, while others are lies thrust upon you by those in the financial services industry: the retail mutual fund industry, the brokerage community and its stock brokers, and even some in the media. You need to become aware of these lies so that you can avoid the pitfalls they create.

And there's no greater pitfall than the one created by the retail mutual fund industry. There's no other way to say it: The retail mutual fund industry is ripping you off. You are incurring greater risks, lower returns, and higher fees than you realize, and as a result, you are in danger of not achieving your financial goals.

The situation is shocking — and no one is more astonished than me. My firm, one of the largest and best-known investment advisory firms in the nation, has placed $4 billion of our clients' assets into retail mutual funds. On my radio and TV shows, through my books, newsletter, website, and seminars, I've been the retail mutual fund industry's biggest proponent. For more than twenty years, I've said that retail mutual funds are the best way to save for college, retirement, and every other important financial goal you can name.

No longer. Jean and I have now sold all our investments in retail mutual funds. All my colleagues at Edelman Financial have done likewise, and our clients are following our advice. You need to sell all your retail mutual funds, too.

All this is painful to say and will certainly be distressing for you to read, but you need to know what's happening with your investments. So excuse me for being blunt, but the fact is that the retail mutual fund industry is now flush with liars, crooks, and charlatans. Daily business activities include deceit, hidden costs, undisclosed risks, deceptive trade practices, conflicts of interest, and fundamental violations of trust — all at your expense. Since September 2003, the retail mutual fund industry has paid out more than $5 billion in fines, and more than eighty executives have been barred from the industry or thrown in jail. Despite this, state and federal regulators say that investors are still being abused.

The disgrace of the retail mutual fund industry poses a huge challenge for everyday investors like you and me. You're struggling to get your kids through college and provide yourself with a comfortable retirement, and you've been counting on retail mutual funds to help you achieve these goals. Your needs haven't changed, but your strategy must.

And so, in this book I'll reveal exactly how Jean and I have changed the way we manage our own money and how our firm now manages our clients' investments. You'll get complete behind-the-scenes details of our investment strategy — why we invest with a long-term focus, the importance of diversification, and the crucial need for (and methods of) portfolio rebalancing. Our investment strategy is simple, yet comprehensive and remarkably effective. I'll show you how to develop, implement, and maintain your own portfolio step by step. You'll be surprised at how straightforward it is, and the advice and information in this book makes it easy.

You'll also take a tour of the academics behind the world of investing, to show you that proper money management has nothing to do with "hot tips" and everything to do with scientific analysis bolstered by historical facts. Your fears of investing will melt away as you discover how easy it is to invest successfully, and your enthusiasm will build as I show you how to create your own highly detailed portfolio in sync with the latest academic research — just like we do for our own clients.

To understand the mess created by the retail mutual fund industry, we'll go back in time to the beginning of the industry, from Alexander Hamilton and Scottish sea merchants all the way to today's "bad boys" who are operating today's retail mutual funds.

Along the way, you'll learn how to invest the money in your employer retirement plan and how to save for college (with a special note for doting grandparents). And for those who are retired, I'll show you how to generate more income than is possible from bank CDs, without sacrificing stability. You'll also see the role insurance and annuities play in the investment game — watch out for more surprising lies! — and you'll get my six insights that are essential to your investment success.

And we won't stop there. Not only will you learn everything you need to know about building an investment portfolio, *this book will actually build one for you.* The Edelman Guide to Portfolio Selection that weaves through these pages — it starts on page 193 — will take you on a journey that ends at one of forty-three portfolios. Each one is based on the investment strategies and guidelines used by the Edelman Managed Asset Program, one of the largest and fastest-growing investment services in the country. You'll be able to use this portfolio on your own or in conjunction with your financial advisor, secure in the knowledge that you are enjoying the advantages of highly sophisticated portfolio modeling based on the latest academic research, delivered to you in a completely objective manner.

By the time you're finished reading, you'll know how to avoid the lies about money that are hurting your efforts to achieve your goals, so that you can regain control of your investments and return to the path of financial success quickly, easily, and cheaply, just as we have done for ourselves and our clients.

As astonishing as it is to read that we are completely abandoning the investments offered by the retail mutual fund industry — investments that we have long admired and endorsed — our doing so (and my telling you about it) is consistent with how we've always handled our investments.

You see, Jean and I founded Edelman Financial out of self-interest. Like you, we were ordinary consumers and investors, and, just like you, we had been subject to the bad investment advice that is all too pervasive throughout the industry. And, probably like you, we became fed up.

Finally, we said to each other, "Let's figure out how to make the right investment decisions for ourselves. Then we can build our own financial planning practice to share what we've learned." In other words, we went looking for investments that we could buy personally, and then we began to share what we learned with other consumers. Today we provide investment advice to more than eight thousand families.

This explains one of the most unique aspects of our firm: The investments that our clients own are the very same ones that Jean and I and all the financial advisors in our organization own. This approach has always struck us as common sense: If it's good enough for our clients, it ought to be good enough for us, and vice versa.

So, Jean and all the advisors of Edelman Financial, join me in inviting you to read, learn, and benefit from this book.

Chapter 1
The Most Proven, Successful Investment Strategy There Is

In the old days, people bought investments to make money. That seems like an odd statement — why else would anyone buy an investment? — but today's approach is a fundamental change from the old style.

Sure, you want to make money from your investments. But why? Old-timers invested simply because they knew that doing so would enable them to accumulate more money, and having more money is certainly better than having less money. Thus, they wanted to pick investments that made more money than other investments — and soon, the mantra of "beating the market" became the goal.

We now know that this approach doesn't always work. First of all, merely making money from your investments doesn't mean you're making *enough* money. That's why smart investors now evaluate their investment results in the context of goals. Are your investments earning *enough*? Without goals, you can't possibly know.

And smart investors have also come to realize that "beating the market" is pointless. This was made painfully clear in 2002, when the S&P 500 Stock Index fell 22%. If your investments fell only 20% that year, congratulations! You beat the market!

This is why you should consider investments to be mere tools. Do not choose them because you think they will beat the market but because they will help you achieve a goal.

This book will show you, therefore, how to assemble a wide array of investments into a cohesive package; a sophisticated portfolio that properly reflects your circumstances, objectives, and tolerance for risk. You'll learn my philosophical basis for portfolio composition and see how to apply it to your situation. Best of all, the approach laid out in these pages will work for you no matter what your goal is.

So let's talk about investing in that context. Most people have three primary long-term financial goals. They want to be able to pay for college for their children (and/or grandchildren), retire comfortably and in financial security, and help care for or support elderly parents and other family members as needed.[1]

Whether your goals are these or something else, you'll enjoy the highest possible assurance of achieving them by following four simple steps. These steps offer you, without question, the most effective approach to virtually guarantee long-term financial success:

1. Save regularly.

2. Hold your investments for very long periods.

3. Build a highly diversified portfolio.

4. Periodically rebalance that portfolio.

That's all there is to it. This is how we've always managed our investments and our clients' investments. This is how we do it today, and it is how we'll continue doing for decades to come.

The Importance of Saving Regularly

Companies often invite me to speak to their employees. At one recent seminar on financial planning, one worker raised his hand.

"Can you tell me how to get rich?" he asked.

His question evoked laughter among his coworkers, but he wasn't kidding. I pondered his question for a moment, and considered telling him about semicovariance or the harmonic mean (both of which you'll learn about later on[2]).

Instead, I gave him a simpler, more direct answer.

---

[1]What about home ownership? Home ownership is typically not a long-term goal. If you don't already own a home, it's either not a goal or you want to buy one as soon as possible. Thus, the investment strategies for home ownership are not the same as those for college and retirement. To learn how to buy a home, read Part 8 of *The Truth About Money*.
[2]Oh boy! Bet you can't wait!

"Get some money," I replied.

My answer is a sad truth that most financial advisors are not willing to admit. If you don't have any money, there's not much that an investment advisor can do for you. All our strategies and methods begin with one assumption: that you have money to invest.

I don't mean to sound glib, and I don't want you to mistake my answer as dismissive.[3] But the truth is that your financial success begins with your *willingness* to save. You already have the ability; you merely need to be willing to do so. Many people who tell me they can't afford to save are spending $50 a month or more on cable TV.[4]

Don't blame your income for the fact that you're not saving money. Making more money has nothing to do with it. You earn more than you did ten years ago — back then, you longed for the money you're complaining about today! It's a common occurrence: A study by the National Bureau of Economic Research shows that high-income households have just as much trouble saving money as low-income households; both groups save pretty much the same amount.

So don't blame your poor savings on your income. Don't wait for your income to rise. Just start saving, and save every month.

In *Ordinary People, Extraordinary Wealth*, I revealed that five thousand ordinary Americans became wealthy simply by saving small amounts of money on a regular basis. You'll find four ways that you can easily create savings in chapter 49 of *The Truth About Money*.

> **Here are three more ways: Stop smoking, stop drinking coffee, and lose weight. If you buy a pack of cigarettes and a café latte every day, you'll enter retirement with $2.8 million *less* than you'd have otherwise.[5]**
>
> **And a study at Ohio State University found that people thirty pounds overweight spend more on health care, earn less money, get promoted less often, and enter retirement with smaller amounts of savings and only half the assets**

---

[3] I also told him to "marry up." Okay, that was a little glib.
[4] Go ahead, tell your kids, "Sorry you won't be able to go to college. But tonight we're watching HBO!"
[5] It's true: A pack and a latte each costs $5. You need to earn $7.14 to spend those five bucks, assuming a 30% combined federal and state tax bracket. If you instead invested that money in a retirement plan for your forty-year career, earning 10% per year, you'd accumulate $2,792,084.

of slimmer people.[6] **Cornell University says that women who are sixty-four pounds overweight earn 9% less than average, and Michigan State University found "consistent evidence of weight discrimination" that reduces the incomes of overweight people. The data also showed that as individuals lost weight, they significantly gained wealth.**

So if you want to improve your personal finances, quit drinking coffee, stop smoking, and lose weight.

If you want to become rich, marry up — I mean, start saving money. Begin by joining your retirement plan at work (see chapter 9). Once you're contributing the maximum, divert all additional cash to paying off credit cards.[7] Once that's done, build cash reserves.[8] Then, and only then, are you ready to begin your long-term investment program.

Why We're Long-term Investors

We approach investing with a long-term view, and for one simple reason: It's the only way you can be sure that you'll capture the profits produced by the financial markets. Consider the ten-year period ending December 31, 2006. If you had owned the S&P 500 Stock Index[9] for the entire 2,516 days that the stock market was open for business, you would have earned 8.4% per year.

But as Figure 1.1 shows, if you missed the ten days that the stock market did best, your return would have fallen to 2.2%. It's true: 74% of the total profits earned in the entire decade occurred in just ten days. And if you had missed the fifteen best days, you actually would have missed the entire profit of the whole ten years!

---

[6]They also found that slimmer people get bigger inheritances. They speculate that slimmer people live longer and thus are more likely to receive inheritances. They also hypothesize the possibility of discrimination within families.

[7]Don't accelerate the payoff of mortgages, car loans, or student debt; simply make those monthly payments on time. But do get rid of your credit card debt as soon as possible. To learn how, read chapter 51 of *The Truth About Money*. Sorry for all the references to *TAM*, but it's either that or reprint those chapters here.

[8]To learn how, read *What You Need to Do Now*. (At least I didn't reference *TAM*.)

[9]You can't. Indexes are not real investments but a theoretical portfolio of specific securities — common examples are the S&P, the Dow Jones Industrial Average (DJIA), NASDAQ — the performance of which is often used as a benchmark in judging the relative performance of certain asset classes and market sectors. Indexes are unmanaged portfolios, and investors cannot invest directly in an index. Past performance is not indicative of future results. You can, though, invest in mutual funds designed to replicate the holdings of an index, so it's sort of the same thing. But the NASD says that I have to insert sentences two, three, and four whenever I talk about the S&P 500 or any other index.

Figure 1.1

If you want all the profits,
you must be invested all the time

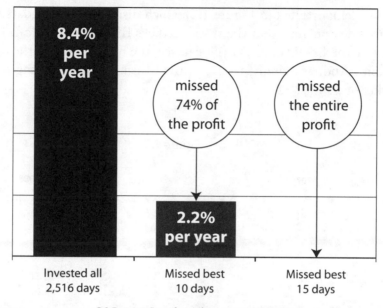

S&P 500 Stock Index 1997–2006

I hope you didn't buy this book expecting to learn when to buy or sell. No one is able to tell you that, but I'm one of the few willing to admit it.

But even some of my own clients expect me to have a crystal ball. During the three-year bear market of 2000 through 2002, as the S&P 500 declined 43%, I'd get an occasional call from a client, saying, "Hey! My account is going down! I thought you were watching it!" And I'd reply, "I *am* watching it. I'm watching it go down!"

Did the caller really think I knew that prices were going to drop? Or that I knew when prices would *stop* dropping? If the client sold merely because prices were down, the only thing we'd know for sure is that the client would be out of the market when prices returned to former levels.

And, of course, a return to former levels is precisely what happened next. Sure, the Dow Jones Industrial Average was 11,287 on April 11, 2000, and it fell to 7,286 by October 9, 2002. But by May 2007 it had risen to 13,200, and everyone who remained invested throughout the entire period enjoyed the entire 17% gain; that short-term decline had no lasting impact on their portfolio.

Many people don't realize that stock market returns gyrate. This is quite different from bank CDs (certificates of deposit), where the rate of return is the same from day to day. And not only do stock returns vary constantly, there's no way to predict *when* the good returns will occur.

This is demonstrated in Figure 1.2, which displays the calendars for 1997 through 2006. The dots represent the stock market's fifteen best-performing days, as measured by the S&P 500.[10] As you can see, the occurrences of the dots are quite random. And, amazingly, twelve of the fifteen occurred during the three-year bear market of 2000–2002!

Figure 1.2

---

[10]See footnote 9.

2001

2002

2003

2004

2005

2006

This is question #2. If you haven't answered question #1, STOP! and turn to page 185.

Q **Will you be adding money to this account on a regular basis?**

a) Yes ....turn to page 77

b) No ....turn to page 54

Obviously, investors want to own stocks when stocks make money, but these charts show that you cannot predict when those times will occur. Therefore, we're forced to conclude (admit, really) that the only way to be certain that we'll be invested when the profits occur is to simply be invested *all the time*.

If you need proof that the stock market produces profits in short bursts, look no further than 2006. As everyone knows, 2006 was a fine year for the stock market.

Wait a moment. Did I say "fine year"? That's not really true. Oh, sure, the Dow Jones Industrial Average[11] gained 16.3% in 2006. And the S&P 500 Stock Index[12] gained 13.6%, according to Ibbotson Associates. Still, these gains are not what they appear to be.

You see, on January 1, 2006, as shown in Figure 1.3, the S&P 500 stood at 1,248. And that's where it was on July 20, nearly seven months later! But then the stock market skyrocketed, with the S&P 500 reaching its high for the year on December 5. And that's where the gains ended.

Figure 1.3

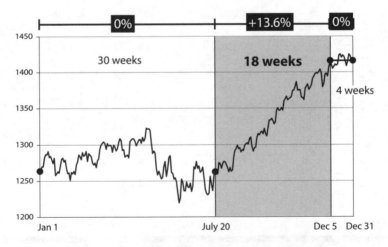

2006 gain for the S&P 500 Stock Index: 13.6%

---

[11]See footnote 9.
[12]See footn — enough already!

Indeed, the S&P 500's entire 13.6% gain for the year occurred from July 20 to December 5 — which means you were treading water through the holiday season, just as you had for the first seven months of the year! So, it's more accurate to say, "We had a great four and a half months!" rather than, "We had a great year!"

What's really amazing is that this really *isn't* amazing. In fact, it's common for the stock market to behave this way. Shown in Figures 1.4–1.12, my analysis of the S&P 500 is quite revealing:

In 2005 the entire year's profit was earned in an eight-week period.

Figure 1.4

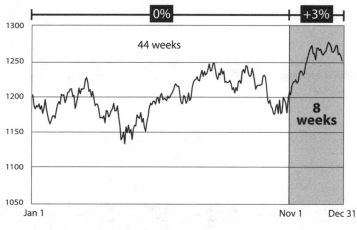

2005 gain for the S&P 500 Stock Index: 3%

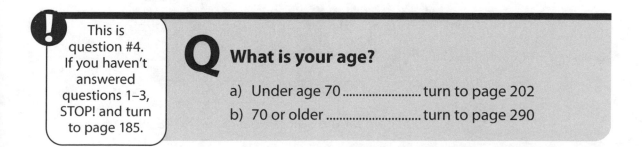

! This is question #4. If you haven't answered questions 1–3, STOP! and turn to page 185.

Q **What is your age?**

a) Under age 70 .... turn to page 202

b) 70 or older .... turn to page 290

In 2004 the entire year's profit was earned in a seven-week period.

Figure 1.5

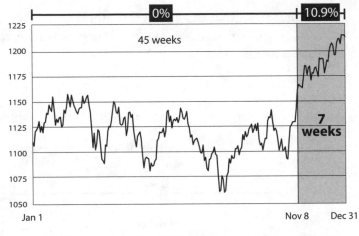

2004 gain for the S&P 500 Stock Index: 10.9%

In 2003 the bulk of the year's profit was earned in two periods —
one four weeks long, the other twelve weeks long.

Figure 1.6

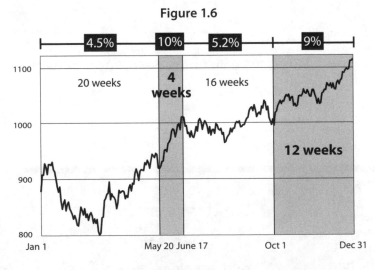

2003 gain for the S&P 500 Stock Index: 28.7%

In 1999 half of the year's profits was earned in the first fourteen weeks,
and the other half was earned in the final eight weeks of the year.
Virtually nothing was earned in the middle thirty weeks.

Figure 1.7

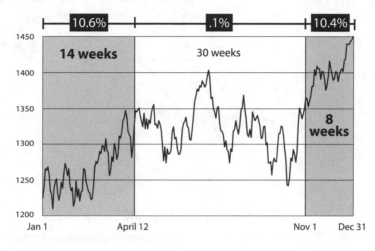

1999 gain for the S&P 500 Stock Index: 21.1%

In 1998 the entire year's profit was earned in an eleven-week period.

Figure 1.8

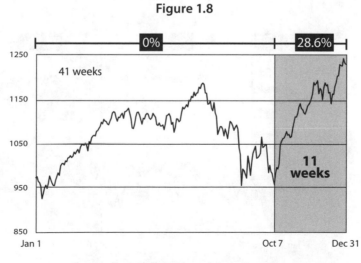

1998 gain for the S&P 500 Stock Index: 28.6%

In 1997 the entire year's profit was earned in a fifteen-week period.

Figure 1.9

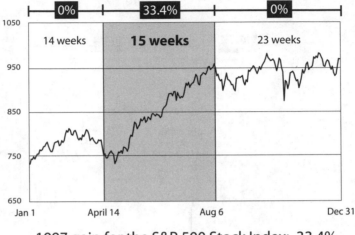

1997 gain for the S&P 500 Stock Index: 33.4%

In 1996 a third of the year's profit was earned in the first six weeks; the remainder was earned in a second fourteen-week period.

Figure 1.10

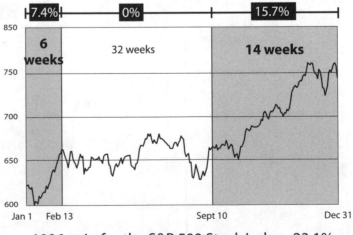

1996 gain for the S&P 500 Stock Index: 23.1%

In 1992 the entire year's profit was earned in a six-week period.

Figure 1.11

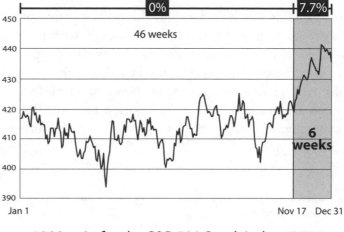

1992 gain for the S&P 500 Stock Index: 7.7%

In 1991 60% of the year's profit was earned in the first fourteen weeks.
The other 40% was earned in the last seven weeks, and no profit
at all was earned in the middle thirty-one weeks.

Figure 1.12

1991 gain for the S&P 500 Stock Index: 30.6%

This is why it's essential that you remain invested throughout the year. Although it's common for the gains to occur in short, dramatic spurts, we never know when they will happen. Thus, being invested *all the time* is the only way to be certain that you'll capture all those gains.

This also explains why it's important that you be patient when investing. People who bought stock mutual funds in January 2006 were probably frustrated as Presidents' Day came and went with no real profits to speak of. Then came St. Patrick's Day, Memorial Day, and the Fourth of July — and still nothing! But if you think that's frustrating, imagine how you'd feel if you sold in July, only to watch stock prices climb 13% in the next few months! Remember that investing is all about staying focused on the long term. Don't let short-term activity (or inactivity!) distract you.

Are you brain damaged?

As far as investing is concerned, you might wish you were. People who have suffered brain damage are better investors than healthy people. So says a 2006 study published in *Psychological Science*. Researchers at Stanford University, Carnegie Mellon University, and the University of Iowa evaluated how emotions affect investment decision making. The scientists examined the investment decisions of individuals whose injuries prohibited their brains from processing emotional impulses and, therefore, responses to those impulses. Researchers then compared the decisions of this group with people who have no brain damage, to see which set of subjects made better investment decisions.

The study showed that the group of emotionally impaired patients made better investment decisions than those who were healthy.

My colleagues and I consider these findings quite understandable. In our experience, investors routinely base investment decisions on emotions rather than logic. Instead of carefully and dispassionately evaluating important data through a systematic due-diligence process, many investors simply respond to gut instinct. If they are worried about the economy or current events, they want to sell; if they are happy or confident, they want to buy.

The result, not surprisingly, is that investors buy when prices are high and sell when prices are low — which is the exact opposite of how you're supposed to invest. Thus, people whose brain damage prevents them from acting emotionally have a distinct advantage.

This is not to suggest that you should hope for brain damage. But it does make me wonder who the brain-damaged people really are.

Indeed, short-term unpredictability should not dissuade you from owning stocks and stock mutual funds. Instead, you should simply conclude that making money in the stock market is a matter of "time in" not "timing." If you're always invested in stocks, you're sure to capture whatever gains the market offers.

This is why we believe very strongly that you must invest for the long term; it is the only way to capture the gains.

The buy-and-hold approach offers substantial benefits over the alternative strategy of market timing. Timers want to be invested only when profits occur. But no timer has ever succeeded in doing that over any long period. Nonetheless, they try, and in the course of doing so, they incur lots of problems that buy-and-holders avoid:

- **Timers pay more than twice as much in taxes as buy-and-holders because their short-term moves don't qualify for long-term capital gains tax rates.**
- **Timers incur higher transaction costs because every move generates expenses, and**
- **Timers lead boring lives. They're stuck sitting in front of their computer terminals for hours on end, watching the market for signs that it's time to make a move. Life's too short for that nonsense.**

I once met a guy who said he's a long-term investor because he's owned mutual funds for twenty-five years. But he's never owned a single fund for more than a year or two.

Owning investments for short periods, but doing that for a long time, does not make you a long-term investor. This guy was actually a short-term investor, and he's been a short-term investor for a *looooooong* time.

Don't assume that *long term* merely refers to being invested for an entire year. Rather, it means that you need to buy your investments and hold them for many, many years — hence the common phrase "buy and hold." This point is well illustrated by a 2007 study of Morningstar data by the financial firm DiMeo Schneider & Associates, which examined the performance of the top 25% of all stock funds for the ten-year period ending December 31, 2006. Although these funds posted the best ten-year track records, 90% of them suffered below-average returns for at least three consecutive years during the ten-year period. And more than half of them generated below-average returns for five consecutive years.

Women are better investors than men.

That's the conclusion reached by Terrance Odean, professor of banking and finance at the University of California, Berkeley, after analyzing 150,000 accounts at a major discount brokerage firm.

Odean wanted to study the trading patterns of ordinary investors, so he focused on the clients of a discount firm because such investors make their own decisions rather than following the recommendations of stockbrokers and financial advisors. By skipping advice, discount brokers charge lower commissions, which attract do-it-yourself investors.

Odean studied the trading activity and annual returns over a six-year period and concluded that women earn 1.5% more per year in the stock market than men. Single women do even better, earning nearly 2.5% more per year than single men.[13]

These results are a big deal. But they have nothing to do with stock picking; according to Odean's data, women are not better than men at picking good stocks. (His data show that men and women have equally poor abilities at picking stocks.)

So if it isn't stock picking, what is it?

The answer is based on the amount of trading they do. Both men and women, according to the study, detract from their profits by trading actively — and men trade more often than women. In other words, Odean's study shows that the more you buy and sell, the worse you'll do. And since men buy and sell more frequently, they do worse, on average, than women.

Like many others, this study (titled "Boys Will Be Boys: Gender, Overconfidence, and Common Stock Investment") confirms that **buy and hold** is far better than *market timing,* which is the practice of buying and selling in an attempt to capture short-term profits or avoid short-term losses. Odean discovered that women turn over their portfolios an average of 53% a year, while men sell 77% of their stocks within a year. Thus, men are flipping their portfolios nearly 50% more often than women.

Odean says men trade more than women because men are more confident in their stock-picking ability. Men believe they have some secret that's going to help them pick the right stock at the moment it's going to rise. This false feeling of competency causes them to trade excessively. Since they're often wrong, their overconfidence hurts them.

Conversely, according to Odean, women tend to feel intimidated by the market, and so they are more likely to hold their investments for longer periods. And the longer they held, the more money they made.

The lesson is clear: The more you trade, the worse you'll do over long periods.

---

[13]If you think this doesn't sound like much, consider that after twenty years, the woman who earns 12% per year on a $100,000 account will accumulate $291,879 more than a man who earns 10% per year.

Would you be willing to hold on to an investment that might be performing poorly (relative to peers) for five years in a row?

It's a daunting question. Most people would become frustrated. They'd sell, and switch their money into…

…into what, another fund that also has been underperforming for the past several years? Not likely. If you're upset that your fund has performed poorly for the past three or five years, you'll replace it with something that has been performing well. Since 90% of the top performers have long stretches of underperformance, that means you're likely selling your "bad" fund just as it's about to zoom in performance, and you're likely to buy a "good" fund just as it is about to enter its own period of underperformance. In other words, by switching midstream, you're probably locking in your bad returns!

> **Think you're good enough to figure out when you should get in or out of the stock market? Anyone is good enough to guess correctly once. The problem is, you must guess correctly *twice*. Indeed, you must know when to get in *and* out (or out and then in) — for doing only one or the other will lead to disastrous results.**
>
> **So can you correctly move in *and* out, and can you do it correctly on a consistent, long-term basis? The academics say you can't. In a series of studies from 1994 to 2002, scholars[14] have shown that from 1926 to 1993, you had a 0.0022883557% chance of correctly timing the stock market just half the time.**

Thus, it is crucial that you maintain a long-term perspective. Buy your investments and hold them for year after year. Now, I've been saying this for years — that the buy-and-hold strategy always beats that alternative, which is market timing. One form of market timing is selling a "bad" fund to buy a "good" fund, as we've just discussed. Another form is to try to buy stocks before they rise and sell them before they fall. That, too, is doomed to failure, and I've said so for years. To be more exact, what I've said is that buy-and-hold *always* beats market timing.

---

[14]"Stock Market Extremes and Portfolio Performance" by H. Nejat Seyhun, 1994; "A Nonparametric Test of Market Timing" by Wei Jang, 2003; and "Sequential Optimal Portfolio Performance: Market and Volatility Timing," by Michael Johannes, Nicholas Polson, and Jon Stroud, 2002.

But I must be honest with you. It doesn't *always* win. This fact was revealed to me by a study published in the February 2001 issue of *Financial Analyst Journal.* This study tests and compares — once and for all — the results between the market-timing and buy-and-hold strategies. The authors studied data from 1926 through 1999, in an examination that included six major U.S. asset classes. The objective: to determine whether market timing was effective compared to the buy-and-hold strategy.

They analyzed a variety of monthly, quarterly, and annual market-timing strategies, producing more than one million possible market-timing sequences with, as you'd expect, more than a million different outcomes. Each of these outcomes was compared to the buy-and-hold strategy for the same time period.

> **If you could correctly time the market, how much money could you make?**
>
> At the request of *BusinessWeek* magazine, Ibbotson Associates designed a computer simulation to see how much money you'd have if you had invested $1,000 on January 1, 1926, placing your money into stocks (as measured by the S&P 500 Stock Index) in any month that enjoyed a rise in stock prices and shifting to U.S. Treasury Bills in each month that stocks fell.
>
> By December 31, 2006, your $1,000 would have been worth $30 trillion! (The entire U.S. federal debt is only $8 trillion.) By comparison, if you had maintained your investment in stocks throughout the entire eighty years, you would have accumulated $3 million.
>
> So it's your choice: You can try to time the market in a desperate and futile effort to amass trillions of dollars. Or you can simply buy and hold, and be content with millions.

Now, my position has always been that the buy-and-hold strategy wins 100% of the time against market timers. Yet, to my shock and dismay, this massive, authoritative, and indisputable study concluded that the buy-and-hold strategy did not beat market timing 100% of the time. Imagine my shock. Imagine my shame.

Buy-and-hold wins only 99.8% of the time.

It's true. The study's authors determined that market timing works better in only 0.2% of the back-tested real-data simulations. So while I've always said that market timers will *never* beat those who buy and hold, the truth is that this is true only 998 times out of 1,000. Imagine my embarrassment.

Why We Diversify

We diversify because winners rotate. You see, investing is not just about the stock market. Rather, there are sixteen major asset classes and market sectors (depending on who's counting), so the phrase "stock market" tells only part of the story. Figure 1.13 shows how the sixteen performed over the ten year period from 1997 through 2006. In any given year, some asset classes and market sectors outperform others. But there's no pattern.

Figure 1.13

The Randomness of Returns

Pick any asset class listed in the year 1997, and then track it through years 1998–2006. You'll see that returns gyrate wildly from year to year.

Rank	1997	1998	1999	2000	2001	2002	2003	2004	2005	2006
1- best	Small-Cap Value	Large-Cap Growth	Emerging Markets	Real Estate	Small-Cap Value	Gold	Small-Cap Value	Real Estate	Emerging Markets	Real Estate
2	Mid-Cap Value	Mid-Cap Growth	Small-Cap Growth	Long Govt Bonds	Long Corp Bonds	Long Govt Bonds	Emerging Markets	Emerging Markets	Gold	Foreign Stocks
3	Large-Cap Growth	Foreign Stocks	Large-Cap Growth	Mid-Cap Value	Real Estate	Long Corp Bonds	Small-Cap Growth	Small-Cap Value	Foreign Stocks	Emerging Markets
4	Large-Cap Value	Large-Cap Value	Mid-Cap Growth	Mid-Cap Growth	Inter.Corp. Bonds	Interm Corp Bonds	Foreign Stocks	Foreign Stocks	Mid-Cap Growth	Gold
5	Mid-Cap Growth	Long Govt Bonds	Foreign Stocks	Long Corp Bonds	High-Yield Bonds	Real Estate	Mid-Cap Growth	Mid-Cap Value	Real Estate	Small-Cap Value
6	Real Estate	Long Corp Bonds	Small-Cap Value	Interm Corp Bonds	1-yr Treasury	1-yr Treasury	Real Estate	Mid-Cap Growth	Mid-Cap Value	Large-Cap Value
7	Long Govt Bonds	Interm Corp Bonds	1-yr Treasury	1-yr Treasury	30-day T-bill	30-day T-bill	Mid-Cap Value	Large-Cap Value	Large-Cap Value	Mid-Cap Value
8	Small-Cap Growth	1-yr Treasury	Large-Cap Value	30-day T-bill	Long Govt Bonds	High-Yield Bonds	Large-Cap Value	Small-Cap Growth	Long Govt Bonds	High-Yield Bonds
9	Long Corp Bonds	30-day T-bill	30-day T-bill	Large-Cap Value	Mid-Cap Value	Emerging Markets	High-Yield Bonds	High-Yield Bonds	Long Corp Bonds	Small-Cap Growth
10	High-Yield Bonds	Mid-Cap Value	High-Yield Bonds	Small-Cap Value	Gold	Mid-Cap Value	Large-Cap Growth	Long Corp Bonds	Small-Cap Growth	Large-Cap Growth
11	Interm Corp Bonds	Small-Cap Growth	Gold	Gold	Small-Cap Growth	Small-Cap Value	Gold	Long Govt Bonds	1-yr Treasury	Mid-Cap Growth
12	1-yr Treasury	High-Yield Bonds	Interm Corp Bonds	High-Yield Bonds	Emerging Markets	Foreign Stocks	Long Corp Bonds	Large-Cap Growth	Small-Cap Value	1-yr Treasury
13	30-day T-bill	Gold	Mid-Cap Value	Foreign Stocks	Mid-Cap Growth	Large-Cap Value	Interm Corp Bonds	Gold	30-day T-bill	30-day T-bill
14	Foreign Stocks	Small-Cap Value	Real Estate	Large-Cap Growth	Large-Cap Value	Mid-Cap Growth	Long Govt Bonds	Interm Corp Bonds	High-Yield Bonds	Long Corp Bonds
15	Emerging Markets	Real Estate	Long Corp Bonds	Small-Cap Growth	Large-Cap Growth	Large-Cap Growth	1-yr Treasury	1-yr Treasury	Interm Corp Bonds	Interm Corp Bonds
16-worst	Gold	Emerging Markets	Long Govt Bonds	Emerging Markets	Foreign Stocks	Small-Cap Growth	30-day T-bill	30-day T-bill	Large-Cap Growth	Long Govt Bonds

Relative Performance of Asset Classes 1997–2006

You've already seen what happens if you invest in the stock market only part of the time. Now see what happens if you invest in only some parts of the total financial marketplace. Figure 1.14 shows that if you had invested in all sixteen major asset classes and market sectors for the entire ten-year period ending December 31, 2006, your average annual return would have been 11.1%. But if you omitted the *one* market per year that made the most money, your profit would have been 12% less. And if you missed the top *two* markets of each year, you would have missed 50% of the returns!

This is why we invest pretty much everywhere. Just as my colleagues and I are not good enough to tell you *when* to invest, we're also not good enough to tell you *where* to invest. So by being invested everywhere, all the time, our clients are assured that they'll enjoy the profits, no matter when they come or where they are found.

This is why my definition of diversification is probably quite different from yours.

Figure 1.14

If you want all the profits, you must be invested in all the markets

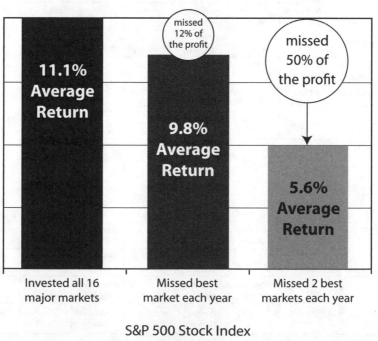

S&P 500 Stock Index
1997–2006

When we ask people to explain what it means to have a diversified portfolio, they often reply that it means owning both stocks *and* bonds, something like this:

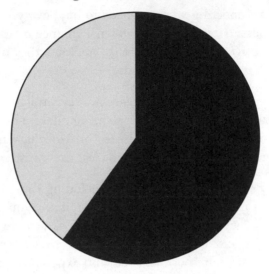

In fact, that's not at all what I mean. Here's an example of what I would say is a diversified portfolio:

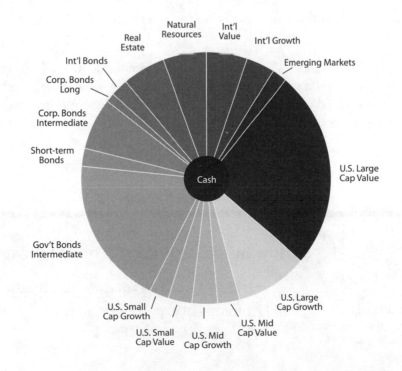

Do You Really Need to Be Fully Diversified?

You might be wondering why you need to buy "everything" when you can instead just buy the best. After all, every personal finance magazine, from *Money* to *SmartMoney* to *Kiplinger's Personal Finance*, touts the "best" funds in each issue. So why not just buy the top-rated funds?

Because mutual funds are unable to sustain their track records. In fact, if you ever want to test an investor's knowledge about mutual funds, just ask him or her if mutual fund ratings, such as those issued by Morningstar, are important: The more important the investor says they are, the less the investor knows about mutual funds.

Indeed, every study ever conducted — including those published by Morningstar itself — shows that fund ratings have no predictive quality. You're as likely to make lots of money investing in 1-star funds as you are by investing in 5-star funds. That's because the ratings simply reflect past performance. Ratings are not predictions about future performance, and experienced investors know this; that's why they disregard fund ratings.

But neophytes think ratings matter. You can't blame them, really. After all, ratings are common. Cars, consumer electronics, even movies get ratings. Consumers have learned that ratings are reliable — everyone agrees that a 5-star hotel is a great place to stay, and a 1-star movie isn't worth seeing. Why, then, can't you rely on fund ratings?

The answer is simple. When you open a refrigerator door, a light comes on. Every time. When you watch a favorite movie, the ending is the same. Every time. Products are identical and can be expected to produce the same results every time. For example, use a toaster ten times the same way, and you'll get the same results every time.

! This is question #3. If you haven't answered questions 1–2, STOP! and turn to page 185.

Q How much cash do you have in reserves?

a) Less than 12 months of expenses.........turn to page 82

b) 12 months of expenses or more...........turn to page 51

But on the eleventh try, while the toaster is on, turn the electricity off. Think your results will be the same as before?

This explains why mutual funds can't replicate their past performance: Their environment constantly changes. If next year's economic environment is different from last year's — and it will be — you can't expect a given investment to perform next year like it did last year. Every year is different from the last, with changes in interest rates, inflation, corporate profits, employment levels, political and social issues, and on and on. Neophytes don't understand this.

Which explains an argument I had with my wife, Jean, last summer. It was one of those funny arguments that only husbands and wives can have. You know the kind I mean.

We were running errands on an extremely hot afternoon. It's never fun getting into a car that's been sitting in the summer sun; the car's thermostat read 115 degrees. So I started the engine, and Jean quickly reached for the knob on the air conditioner and dialed the thermostat all the way down to 65 degrees.

"Whoa, Jean," I said. "We don't need to lower the thing all the way down to sixty-five degrees. Just set it at seventy-two." While I was saying this, I turned the dial back up. At 72, I said, "This is the temperature you want."

Jean's response was measured and thoughtful. *"Are you crazy!?!?!?!"* she shrieked. (OK, she didn't really shriek. But, hey, this is my story, and I'll tell it like I want.) "It will take *forever* to cool off the car if it is set at only seventy-two." As she dialed the knob back down to 65, she explained, "The car will cool down faster if you set it at sixty-five!"

"You're nuts!" I protested, grabbing the knob while narrowly avoiding two parked cars. "Think about this, Jean," I explained. "In order for the car's temperature to drop from one hundred fifteen degrees to sixty-five, the temperature must first reach seventy-two degrees. Therefore, you're not accomplishing anything by setting it at sixty-five."

Jean returned the setting to 65, then stared out the window, giving me a great view of the back of her head. I dialed it back up to 72 and tried again to persuade her. "Look," I said, "the car is now at one hundred degrees. You want it to be seventy-two. The fan is already on maximum. If you set the temperature at sixty-five, the fan will simply blow longer. Instead of stopping at seventy-two, the fan will continue to blow hard until the temperature reaches sixty-five. That's too cold!"

Jean disagreed. I know this because she'd turned the knob back to 65 degrees. "It's too hot in here," she said. I accepted defeat the way husbands do in situations like this.

Eventually, the temperature dropped to 65. The two of us were now freezing. So what did Jean do? She turned the knob up to 85.

"Whoa, Jean," I said, sounding like a broken record. "Slow down! Just set it at seventy-two, because . . ." Well, we replayed our conversation, but somehow the dial stayed at 85 degrees. So the temperature began climbing. It passed 72 and approached 80 degrees. Now we were sweating. So Jean cranked the control knob back down again to 65. I felt like I was playing ping-pong in the car. It's too hot, then it's nice and comfortable, then it's too cold, then it's nice and comfortable, then it's too hot — you get the picture.

Not that many years ago, automobiles lacked thermostats; you had to adjust the fan to reach the desired temperature from the car's cooling and heating systems. But today's cars have thermostats control air-conditioning systems, enabling you to set the temperature you want quickly and efficiently. Left alone, the car will reach its target and stay there without human intervention. But Jean overrode the technology, so the car spent most of the time above or below the target, and we spent most of the time in an uncomfortable environment. Jean thinks I'm crazy, and not necessarily about this topic.

Do you behave like Jean when it comes to your investment portfolio? If you're unhappy with your current return, do you switch into more aggressive, speculative, high-profit-seeking investments in an effort to earn more? And then, when those investments fall in value (as high-risk investments invariably do), do you sell until prices start rising again, whereupon you plow right back into the investments you had previously sold?

Guess what? You are treating your portfolio like the temperature gauge in your car. You're bouncing back and forth, wondering why you're either making too little or losing too much. Stop playing ping-pong with your investments. Build a diversified portfolio instead and hold onto it for decades.

In my next book, I'll tell you about the clocks in our house. Jean has set them all five minutes fast.

Too Much of a Good Thing Isn't Good

One of the latest studies showing that past performance does not predict future results was released in 2006 by Standard & Poors.[15] The firm measured the performance of mutual funds for the five years ending June 30, 2006, and found that, of the funds that were ranked in the top half of all mutual funds in 2001, only 9% were still in the top-half ranking five years later. Only 1% maintained their top-quartile ranking.

The study showed that one fund, which in 2001 was among the top 1% of all mutual funds, was in the bottom 100th percentile in 2005. Another that was in the top 1% of all funds in both 2003 and 2004 fell to the 100th percentile in 2005. (Yep, it literally went from best to worst in a single year!) And another fund — the only one to outperform the S&P 500 Stock Index every year for fifteen years through 2005 — was among the bottom 100th percentile in 2006, making it among the very worst of all mutual funds.

You must never choose an investment based solely on past performance, and that is why you must never, but never, buy a mutual fund based on its rating.

And for goodness' sake, don't buy or sell merely because that's what everyone else is doing!

Investors are notorious for buying high and selling low. They buy when prices are rising, and they sell when prices are falling — because investors act emotionally.

---

[15]I've written about dozens of others in my earlier books, as well as in my monthly newsletter.

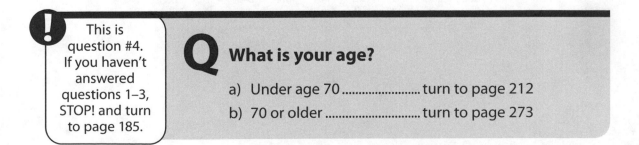

! This is question #4. If you haven't answered questions 1–3, STOP! and turn to page 185.

Q What is your age?

a) Under age 70 ....turn to page 212

b) 70 or older ....turn to page 273

Take a look at Figure 1.15 which plots mutual fund cash flows alongside the S&P 500 Stock Index.

The cash flow data are provided by the Investment Company Institute, the trade association of the mutual fund industry. Each month fund companies tell the ICI how much money investors are depositing in and withdrawing from stock mutual funds. These cash flows show that investors place money into stock funds when prices are rising, and they withdraw money when prices are falling.

Figure 1.15

Most people buy when prices are rising and sell when prices are falling — and they wonder why their account values don't grow

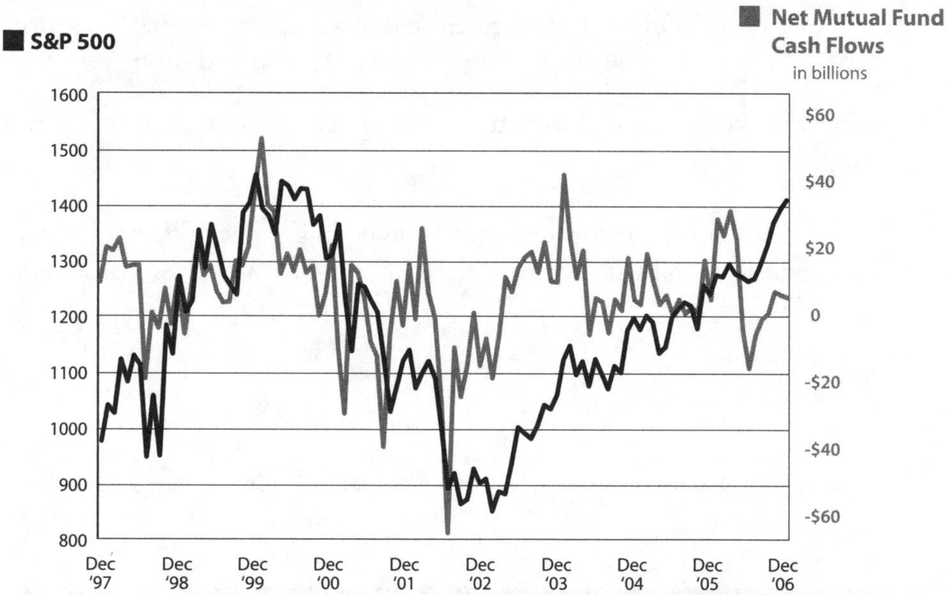

In other words, investors do the exact opposite of what you're supposed to do! You make a profit by buying low and selling high — but investors do it the other way around. And they do it together, like a herd of buffalo stampeding off a cliff.

This is confirmed by a 2006 study by professors at Cornell University and the University of Texas at Austin. They examined 1.85 million retail stock transactions from 1991 through 1996 and found that the trades are "systematically correlated — that is, individuals buy (or sell) in concert." The study found no macroeconomic news or analyst earnings forecasts to explain the trading pattern, and said that "investor sentiment" was behind all the trading.

Your mother told you not to do things just because your friends were doing them. But you still don't listen.

Why We Rebalance Periodically

Imagine you're driving on a highway. Do you take your hands off the steering wheel? Of course not; you know that if you do, the car will drift into another lane. So you not only keep your hand on the wheel, you make small periodic adjustments — in order to avoid *massive* occasional ones.

Managing your portfolio is a lot like steering your car. It's not enough to build a long-term, highly diversified portfolio. You must also maintain it. Otherwise your portfolio will become far riskier than you want and less likely to achieve your goals. Allow me to show you why this occurs and how you can easily solve the problem.

As you've already seen, you should build a portfolio featuring as many as sixteen major asset classes and market sectors. But to make the lesson of rebalancing easier to understand, let's assume we build a portfolio that features only two asset classes: A and B. We'll also assume that we want equal amounts of each. Turn the page to see what our portfolio looks like.

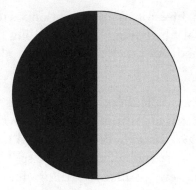

Naturally, these two asset classes and market sectors perform differently. (If they were identical, we wouldn't need to invest in both of them.) So over some period of time, asset B grows in value while asset A declines. Here's how our portfolio now appears:

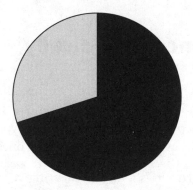

Clearly, our portfolio no longer matches our original design. We don't want a 70-30 portfolio — if we did, we would have started that way. No, what we want is a 50-50 allocation. Thus, we must rebalance the portfolio.

It's obvious what we must do: We must sell some of asset B and buy some of asset A, to restore the model to its original allocations.

Well done, you say. *That's quite simple and easy and — hey, wait a minute! You want me to sell the asset that* <u>made</u> *money and buy the asset that* <u>lost</u> *money?!?!*

Exactly.

But you don't want to. The last thing any investor wants to do is sell an investment

A day doesn't go by before a client or a friend mentions something in the news that he thinks can drive his long-term portfolio to instant success. One tells me that a company is coming out with a cure for a disease, while another argues that a certain market sector is the place to be this year. Meanwhile, someone else says the market will or won't do well because of some recent or upcoming event.

These conversations occur regularly, as even the most intelligent people try their best to outguess not only the pros but their peers — and even themselves! It doesn't matter whether stock prices are moving up, down, or sideways, there are always those who say they know what the market will do next, and where specifically they ought to invest.

Just as regularly, these people incur devastating failure. It is always interesting to review how their predictions panned out, and I've yet to meet anyone who has consistently made the right call at precisely the right time. Most interesting is the fact that the least likely sectors always seem to do the best.

That's why we continually tell our clients that the most prudent course of action is to diversify and not let your predictions turn into big bets. And never, never make investment decisions based on what's happened recently. After all, driving your car by looking in your rearview mirror is certain to lead to bad results.

To illustrate this point, we looked back at 2005 to see what the results would have been if we had invested each month in the one market sector that had performed the best for that month. Yes, with the benefit of hindsight (our rearview mirror), we were assured of being right every time! Here are the top-performing market sectors for each month in 2005:

January	Natural Resources
February	Latin American Stocks
March	Ultra Short Bonds
April	Real Estate
May	Technology Stocks
June	Precious Metals
July	Emerging Market Stocks
August	Japanese Stocks
September	Precious Metals
October	Financial Stocks
November	Precious Metals
December	Japanese Stocks

Would you have guessed that Latin American Stocks were the best performers in February, or that they would have been eclipsed by Ultra Short Bonds in March? Do you think you could have predicted these monthly results?

For the five-year period ending September 30, 2001, according to the mutual fund research firm Lipper Analytical Services, the three *worst*-performing mutual fund categories were gold, emerging markets, and Latin America.

For the next five-year period , the three *best*-performing mutual fund categories were — you guessed it — gold, emerging markets, and Latin America.

that has made a lot of money or buy an investment that has lost a lot of money. Imagine the conversation with your spouse: *"Hey, honey, you know that investment of ours that lost ten grand? I just bought more of it!"*

Even worse: *"Oh, and honey, to buy more of it, I just sold that other investment that's done really well!"*

Yes, that conversation sounds wacky, but it's exactly the conversation you need to have. I really do want you to sell your winner and buy your loser.

Portfolio rebalancing forces you to do the opposite of what you think you should do. Emotionally, you're likely to want to buy more of the asset that rose the most, and you'll want to sell the asset that underperformed. But that's extraordinarily dangerous, for two reasons.

First, you're assuming that investments which have done well will continue to do well. But as we've seen, investing based on past performance is not a reliable way to invest — which is why we're diversifying in the first place.

Second, if you don't rebalance, you'll eventually have all your money in just one asset class: you won't be diversified at all. For example, our hypothetical portfolio started 50-50, and we watch it morph into 70-30. At this rate, it will eventually become 95-5 or even 100-0! Instead of having a low-risk, highly diversified portfolio, we'll have a highly concentrated portfolio — all our money will be in one place!

To get an idea of how dangerous that would be, imagine someone who placed his entire portfolio into the stock market in 1989 at the age of fifty-four. Over the next ten years, his portfolio more than doubled in value. Now sixty-four, he retired, cocky that his investments would sustain his lifestyle for the rest of his life. But he entered retirement just as the bear market began in 1999. Over the next three years, the value of his stock-filled portfolio fell 38%, and by 2002 — at age sixty-seven — he probably wasn't retired anymore.

! This is question #3. If you haven't answered questions 1–2, STOP! and turn to page 185.

Q **How much cash do you have in reserves?**

a) Less than 12 months of expenses ...... turn to page 284

b) 12 months of expenses or more .... turn to page 175

To prevent this from happening — to prevent you from losing the money you've accumulated just at the moment you need it most — you must periodically rebalance your portfolio.[16]

Reinvest Dividends or Pay Them in Cash?

If you're already a mutual fund investor, you know that mutual funds periodically pay dividends and capital gains. Most investors automatically reinvest these distributions instead of taking them in cash. This is smart, because reinvesting actually constitutes a purchase of additional shares. That, in turn, increases the amount of the next distribution — resulting in long-term compounding, which is the key to wealth.

However, when creating a portfolio as diversified as those I'm offering you in this book, and by strategically rebalancing that portfolio as described in these pages, automatically reinvesting those dividends is *not* the best strategy. Instead you should pay all dividends and capital gains into your cash position (usually a money market fund associated with the portfolio).

Here's why: Some asset classes and market sectors pay more in dividends and capital gains than others. For example, bond funds routinely pay monthly or quarterly dividends in large amounts, while many funds in the equity sector pay only one distribution per year (if any). By reinvesting the distributions back into the funds from which they came, you could be placing money that (based on your target allocation) properly belongs in a different fund.

By instead placing all distributions into your cash position, you can then reallocate those distributions into the other funds that need them, via rebalancing. Interestingly, this can reduce the need for rebalancing; our experience has taught us that rebalancing is often needed after a client makes a withdrawal (such withdrawals reduce the balance of the money market fund, triggering a rebalance of the entire portfolio). But by placing all fund distributions into the money market fund, it is better able to remain at proper levels, potentially reducing the need to rebalance even when you make occasional (or even monthly) withdrawals.

---

[16]Of course, you might not want to reallocate back to your original model. Changes in your circumstances could warrant a change in your asset allocation. But that's quite different from saying you'd never want to rebalance.

By reducing the need to rebalance, you avoid any transaction costs that rebalancing incurs.[17] And best of all, you enjoy quicker access to the funds if you need to make a withdrawal. That's because securities regulations require three days to disburse money from accounts that hold securities, while money market assets can be distributed the same day you request the funds.

So instruct the firm handling your account to pay all distributions in cash. But please note that this means they should pay the distributions into your money market account — not send you a check![18]

> In addition to serving as the conduit for rebalancing efforts, it should be noted that the money market fund has as rightful a place in your portfolio as any other asset class or market sector. Too often, investors consider cash to be the place they put money when they are "out" of the market. In fact, cash is itself an investment — with its own features, benefits, and limitations, just like any other investment. (In this case, it is safe from market volatility but subject to tax risk and inflation risk.) So don't begrudge having some of your assets in cash any more than you'd begrudge having some of your money in any other investment.

Does Rebalancing Conflict with the Goal of Long-term Investing?

A long-term investor is supposed to own investments for decades, so it might appear that rebalancing, which causes you to buy and sell periodically, conflicts with that strategy. Actually, there is no conflict at all. In fact, rebalancing supports your long-term strategy.

As a long-term investor, you don't merely want to have a portion of your money in a given asset class for decades; you want to have *a specific portion* of your money in that asset class. If you don't rebalance, you'll often have too much or too little in that investment — thwarting your efforts. Thus, rebalancing helps you preserve your long-term investment objective.

---

[17]Actually, you shouldn't have to pay costs for rebalancing. Our clients, for example, pay no such fees.
[18]But you knew that, right?

When Should You Rebalance?

The most common way investors rebalance their portfolios is by calendar: Every quarter or every year, they rebalance the portfolio. Academic research has shown that it doesn't really matter how often you rebalance, provided you do so consistently.[19]

Because rebalancing involves buying some assets and selling others, you might incur transaction expenses, brokerage commissions, or other fees. Also, selling assets could trigger capital gains or income taxes. Therefore, rebalancing less often might lower these costs. (However, you should maintain an account that doesn't charge you any expenses to rebalance, and if your money resides in an IRA, annuity, or retirement plan, you'll incur no tax liability, either.)

But there's a second, better way to rebalance, and it's the method we use for our clients. It's more cumbersome and time consuming, which is why most investors reject it in favor of calendar rebalancing, but it offers superior results (which is why we use it). It's called *rebalancing by percentage*.

Through this method, you rebalance whenever an asset class or market sector deviates beyond a preset allocation limit. For example, you might allocate 10% of your assets to a certain market sector. You might then say that you'll rebalance if that sector's allocation rises or falls 20%. In this example, you'll rebalance if this market sector falls below 8% of your total assets (20% less than 10%) or if it rises above 12% of your total assets (20% more than 10%).

As you can imagine, it's impossible to predict when that market sector will exceed your preset limits. Therefore, you have no choice but to monitor your entire portfolio every day and be ready to immediately rebalance whenever a trigger is hit. You can rely on software to help with this, but you're still required to check daily and take action. It is indeed cumbersome and time consuming, and this is why most consumers prefer to simply rebalance quarterly or annually.

But percentage rebalancing can be far more effective. Recall from page 12 that all of the stock market's total ten-year profit occurred in just fifteen days. This means that the market generally moves slowly, but sometimes there are dramatic, short-lived movements. If you're rebalancing only quarterly, you'll miss these movements.

---

[19]And when I say *consistently*, I mean it: Maintain the same interval for decades, regardless of current events or market activity.

But if you're prepared to rebalance at any time, you'll be in a far better position to capture these anomalies — enabling you to quickly buy while prices are momentarily depressed or sell while they're suddenly high. Calendar rebalancers miss these opportunities.

In our experience, rebalancing by percentage involves one to four rebalances per year. But unlike calendar rebalancing, you never know when they will occur. Sometimes they occur within weeks of each other; in other times, we might go many months without the need to rebalance.

This chapter has taught you the fundamental approach to achieving financial goals: Engage in long-term investing through a highly diversified portfolio, supported by strategic rebalancing. Now you know what we do for ourselves and our clients.

In the next chapter, you'll explore the academic research that serves as the basis for our approach. Then you'll see why we use mutual funds — essential background that you'll need before reading about the mess created by the retail mutual fund industry. Only then will you be ready to discover our solution to the problem.

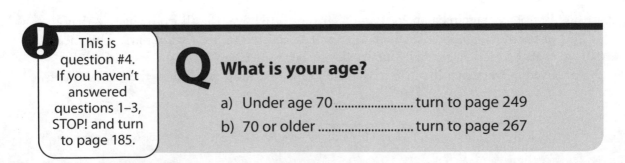

This is question #4. If you haven't answered questions 1–3, STOP! and turn to page 185.

Q What is your age?

a) Under age 70 .... turn to page 249

b) 70 or older .... turn to page 267

Chapter 2
The Academics Behind the Strategy

Now that you understand my approach to investment management, you're ready to explore the reasons why Jean and I and our colleagues at Edelman Financial do it this way.

It's important for you to know that we didn't begin with a decision to invest in mutual funds. We arrived at that conclusion only after examining every conceivable investment strategy — those that were available when I started my career in the 1980s as well as the ones that have been introduced since then. I've read hundreds of books on investing, talked with countless money managers, economists, and analysts, and carefully considered every conceivable choice: day trading, market timing, sector rotation, momentum investing, trend following, technical analysis, data mining, and more. I've even evaluated firms that pick stocks based on astrology!

In the end, my colleagues and I concluded that the best answers are revealed by science and proved through history. Through meticulous and rigorous research over many decades, the most brilliant minds in academia have provided us — you, me, and the entire investing community — clear, proven methods for achieving long-term investment success. This explains why we are disciples of, among others:

- Karl Pearson, who introduced the concept of standard deviation in 1894;

- Harry Markowitz, inventor of Modern Portfolio Theory in 1952;

- William Sharpe, inventor of the Capital Asset Pricing Model in 1964;

- Gary Brinson, Randolph Hood, and Gilbert Beebower who determined the causes of volatility in investment portfolios in 1986; and

- Eugene Fama and Kenneth French, who developed the Fama-French Three-Factor Model in 1992.

You need to understand this academic research in order to understand why we invest through mutual funds, for that research serves as the foundation of our philosophy. Therefore, in this chapter, you will learn five fundamental concepts:

- Actual Return

- Rate of Return

- Average Returns

- Risk

  - How to measure the risk of an investment

  - How to compare the risks of different investments

- Terminal wealth dispersion

With this foundation, you will be able to effectively evaluate all investment strategies, not just mine. And you'll see why the investment strategy described in this book is the best approach.

> **This chapter might get a little dense, but such is the nature of academia. Try to hang in there — it's really worthwhile.**

Warning:
Do not read this
chapter in bed!!!

Concept #1: Actual Return

Our first exploration is the easiest: When you make money from an investment, the profit is your *actual return*. If you invest $100 and later sell for $120, your actual return is $20.

Ta-dah!

But actual returns can be misleading. Say your investment makes $10 while my investment makes $50. You might conclude that I had the better investment. But you could be wrong.

Concept #2: Rate of Return

You see, we must consider the amount we each invested. If you started with $10 while I started with $1,000, we'd have to conclude that your investment was superior.

$$\$10 \times \underline{\textbf{100\%}} = \$10$$

$$\$1{,}000 \times \underline{\textbf{5\%}} = \$50$$

In other words, you don't merely want to know the *actual return;* you want to know the *rate of return*. This is shown by the formula below:

$$F = -P(1+i)\verb|^|n - [p(1+i)\,((1+i)\verb|^|n - 1)\,/\,i]$$

This is why smart investors don't focus on *actual return*. But many people are satisfied with it: They earn interest from a bank CD, and they're thrilled! They have no clue that their *actual return* (the dividend or interest) might represent a very low *rate of return*.

Concept #3: Average Returns

But *rate of return* is flawed too: It assumes a constant figure. That's not a problem if you own a five-year bank CD, where the amount of interest you earn each year remains the same, but *rate of return* doesn't work with investments that fluctuate in value. That's why knowledgeable investors are more interested in the *average return* than the more elementary *rate of return*.

But calculating the *average return* can be tricky. For a demonstration, look at the performance of the S&P 500 Stock Index from 2001 through 2004:

2001	-11.9%
2002	-22.1%
2003	28.7%
2004	10.9%

Using basic arithmetic, you could easily conclude that the stock market's four-year average return is 1.4%.

© United Feature Syndicate, Inc.

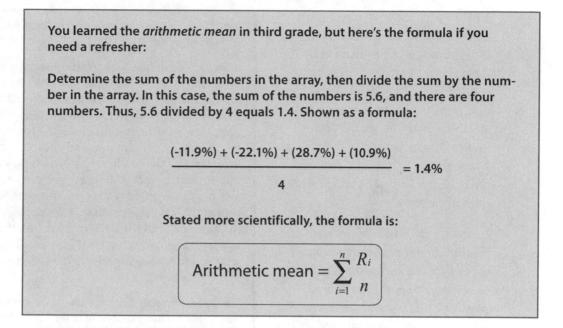

You learned the *arithmetic mean* in third grade, but here's the formula if you need a refresher:

Determine the sum of the numbers in the array, then divide the sum by the number in the array. In this case, the sum of the numbers is 5.6, and there are four numbers. Thus, 5.6 divided by 4 equals 1.4. Shown as a formula:

$$\frac{(-11.9\%) + (-22.1\%) + (28.7\%) + (10.9\%)}{4} = 1.4\%$$

Stated more scientifically, the formula is:

$$\text{Arithmetic mean} = \sum_{i=1}^{n} \frac{R_i}{n}$$

But you'd be wrong, as anyone who owned stocks during that four-year period painfully knows. If you had invested \$10,000 in the S&P 500 on January 1, 2001, you would have lost 11.9% that year; your \$10,000 would have been worth only \$8,812 by December 31. The following year, you'd have lost another 22.1%, further reducing your account to \$6,865. But in 2003 your account rose 28.7%, to \$8,835, and it rose again in 2004 by 10.9%. Thus, you'd have ended the four-year period with \$9,795. That's a *loss*, not a 1.4% average gain!

Is this math a bit too elusive for you? That can happen when we use real historical numbers. So let's create a fictitious set of figures that are a bit more extreme to help you see the point.

Say you invest \$10,000, and you immediately lose 50% of your money. In the second year, you gain 50%, and in the third year you gain 33%. If you do the math, you'll discover that you're back to where you started.

In year one, your ten grand fell to five grand. It then grew to \$7,500 (a 50% gain), which then grew by a third (\$2,500) to bring you back to ten grand.

The arithmetic mean says that your three-year average return is +11%. Did your ten grand really grow 11% per year? Of course not — but that's what the math says it did.

This is why the *arithmetic mean* must never be used when calculating investment returns. The formula can convey inaccurate results, so be very careful if anyone ever tries to convince you to buy an investment because its prior rate of return is such and such. Liars often claim high "average returns" by using *arithmetic mean* inappropriately.

Instead, rely on the *geometric mean*, which enables us to determine that we suffered a $205 loss in our above example. Indeed, *geometric mean* shows an average return of -0.52%, compared to the +1.4% suggested by the *arithmetic mean*.

For you diehards, the formula for geometric mean is:

$$\text{Geometric mean} = \left[\prod_{i=1}^{n} (1 + R_i) \right]^{1/n} - 1$$

There's nothing wrong with earning 5% from an investment. It just shouldn't take you a whole year to do it.
~Unknown

Would you prefer an investment that earns 15% or one that earns 2%?

If that seems like a silly question, watch out — because you're setting yourself up for failure. Indeed, when it comes to investing, the consumer is often his own worst enemy. That's because he has no idea how to properly select investments, and he doesn't know it. Instead he thinks all he has to do is pick an investment based on its past performance. Not only is it unlikely that investments will repeat their past performance (as explained in chapter 1), but the performance he's chasing so lustily isn't what he thinks it is. That's why you must be careful when dealing with average returns.

To demonstrate, let's try to pick mutual funds by looking at those that have done well for the period ending December 31, 2005. But *which* period?

One fund, for example, posted a three-year average annual return of 11.6%. But its five-year record was just 6.7%. Another had a 12.5% annual gain for the three years, but an 8% return for the five-year period. A third fund's three-year average was 10%, compared to 4.6% for the five years. There are dozens such examples.

Many stock funds that post good records for three years have bad records for five years. For example, the stock market did well in 2003, 2004, and 2005 (the S&P 500 Stock Index earned, respectively, 29%, 11%, and 5% in those years) while the S&P was -12% in 2001 and -22% in 2002. The three-year data ending December 31, 2005 don't include those bad years, but the five-year data do.

So be careful when examining average returns. If you review only one time period, you may very well obtain a distorted view.

Concept #4: Risk

OK, so *arithmetic returns* aren't the same as *geometric returns*. But does that mean all geometric returns are the same?

Sadly, no. Consider the following two investments:

Year	Investment A	Investment B
1	10%	20%
2	10%	0%

As you can see, both investments produced an average return of 10%. But investment A earned 10% each year, with no deviation from one year to the next, while the annual returns of investment B deviated substantially. Would you consider these investments to be the same?

Of course not. That is why it's not enough that you examine *average returns*. You must also evaluate the extent to which an investment's returns vary from year to year, because the more that returns vary, the greater the risk that *your* return will be much lower than the *average* return.

And, indeed, that is exactly what happens to most investors. Although the S&P 500 Stock Index gained an average of 11.9% per year for the twenty-year period from 1986 through 2005, the average stock fund investor made only 3.9% per year, according to "Quantitative Analysis of Investor Behavior," a study by the financial research firm Dalbar.

Why the disparity? Dalbar showed that investors did much worse than the market because they shifted their money in and out of funds at the wrong times: They bought when prices were high and sold when prices were low. As a result, they missed 77% of the profits offered by the stock market. If investors had just sat still, they would have made a lot more money.

Dalbar's conclusions were confirmed by John Bogle, founder of Vanguard Funds and a leading advocate for investor education. His analysis of the two hundred stock funds that attracted the most investor money for the ten-year period ending December 31, 2005, shows that the typical investor earned just 2.4% per year, while the funds themselves posted average gains of 8.9% per year. Investors pay "a terrible penalty for their market timing and their fund selections," Bogle told the *New York Times*.

So prevalent is the fact that many investors fail to earn the returns generated by mutual funds that Morningstar in 2006 introduced dollar-weighted performance data. This is a major acknowledgment that a huge portion of investors fail to own investments long term, and they fail to consider risk (volatility) when they choose investments.

Traditionally, the returns of mutual funds and other investments are time weighted, meaning their returns are measured from date to date (most commonly, January 1 through December 31 of the same or subsequent year). But time-weighted returns ignore the fact that nobody invests exactly on January 1 and sells on December 31. That's why Morningstar now shows fund returns data based on cash flows. The differences can be striking, as Figure 2.1 shows. By prominently showing the differences between dollar-weighted returns and time-weighted returns, Morningstar is giving investors something else to think about. The bad news is that, well, investors now have something else to think about — as if investment management isn't hard enough already.

Figure 2.1

Fund	10-Year Annualized Total Return	10-Year Annualized Investor Return	Portion of Return Investors Received
AIM Basic Value A	11.42%	6.61%	58%
BlackRock Mid-cap Growth Inv A	8.86%	2.80%	32%
Dreyfus Mid-cap Value	13.19%	6.05%	46%
Eaton Vance Tax-Mgd Growth 1.1 A	8.68%	3.99%	46%
Federated International Small Co. A	14.88%	2.61%	18%
Fidelity OTC	7.11%	2.61%	37%
MFS Mass. Investors Gr. Stk A	8.00%	0.06%	1%
Munder Internet A	6.88%	−15.65%	−227%
SSgA Core Opportunities	7.85%	0.87%	11%
Vanguard Growth Index	7.15%	1.37%	19%

How to Measure the Risk of an Investment

So, as much as I hate to do this to you, we need a new formula — one to help us measure the variation in annual returns. That measurement tool is called *variance*, shown below.

$$\sigma^2 = \sum_{i=1}^{n} \text{prob}(x_i)\left[x_i - \bar{x}\right]^2$$

> **Even if you've never heard of it, you understand variance. It's the reason you always ask yourself, "Should I stay out and watch it go up, or get in and make it go down?"**

For reasons not worth delving into here, *variance* is too abstract a tool to provide meaningful data.[20] To solve the problem, some genius came up with a solution that he called *standard deviation*.[21] The concept: If it's common for an investment's annual return to vary, or deviate, from its average return, this deviation becomes a standard element of the investment.[22] As its formula below shows, standard deviation is merely the square root of variance. Quite elegant when you think about it.[23]

$$\sigma = \sqrt{\sigma^2} = \sqrt{\sum_{i=1}^{n} \text{prob}(x_i)\left[x_i - \bar{x}\right]^2}$$

---

[20]If you really want to know why, invite some statisticians over for dinner; they'd love to explain it to you.
[21]I mean "genius" literally. Standard deviation was first described by Karl Pearson (1857–1936), who founded the world's first university statistics department, at University College London. Albert Einstein said Pearson's book *The Grammar of Science* is the first book a scientist should read. Many of the book's themes became a part of Einstein's theories.
[22]I explained standard deviation in *The Truth About Money* and *Discover the Wealth Within You*, so I'll spare you the drudgery here. I mean, this chapter is already ugly enough. Let's move on.
[23]Like I said, the guy was a genius.

When applied to our example of investment A versus investment B, we see that the standard deviation of investment A is 0 (because the *annual return* never deviates from the *average return*). This means that you can expect to earn 10% from this investment every year — which is exactly what you'd expect if investment A happened to be a bank CD.

Meanwhile, the standard deviation of investment B is 13. To save you from a semester's course in applied statistics, let me just say that investment returns can be expected to fall within 1 standard deviation about two-thirds of the time, and within 2 standard deviations almost[24] all the time. So for investment B — an investment whose average return is 10% and whose standard deviation is 13 — you can expect that:

- about 67% of the time, the returns of investment B can be expected to be between -3% and 23%, and

- about 95% of the time, the returns of investment B can be expected to be between -16% and 36%.

The conclusion is obvious: High average returns are good, and low standard deviations are good. Therefore, ideally, you want an investment that offers both. Unfortunately, in the real world, such investments don't exist — investment A and investment B are fictional. So let's look at real investments, below:

Year	10-Year CD	S&P 500
1997	6.0%	33.4%
1998	6.0%	28.6%
1999	6.0%	21.0%
2000	6.0%	–9.1%
2001	6.0%	–11.9%
2002	6.0%	–22.1%
2003	6.0%	28.7%
2004	6.0%	10.9%
2005	6.0%	4.9%
2006	6.0%	13.6%
Average Annual Return	6.0%	9.8%

[24]That's *almost*! Not *always*!

As you can see, a ten-year bank CD purchased in 1997 would have paid interest of 6% per year, which was less than two-thirds of the average return of the S&P 500 for the same period. But the CD's standard deviation was zero, while the S&P 500's standard deviation was a whopping 19. Which would you prefer?

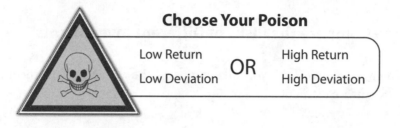

Choose Your Poison

Low Return		High Return
Low Deviation	OR	High Deviation

At this point, you're probably feeling pretty satisfied with yourself. You've just learned that risk is as important as return, and you've learned that standard deviation and its root *variance* enable you to evaluate investment risk.

So you'll probably be pretty annoyed when I tell you that *variance* is flawed. And if that doesn't annoy you, the fact that *variance* is flawed *twice* probably will.

> I remember the time a lady called my radio show. She said, "I want an investment that offers a high return with no risk."
>
> I said, "Me too!"

> **Stop. Put the book down. Take a break. Come back later.**

Welcome back!

The first problem with variance is that it lives in a cocoon. It assumes you own only one investment. But in the real world, you're likely to own many investments.

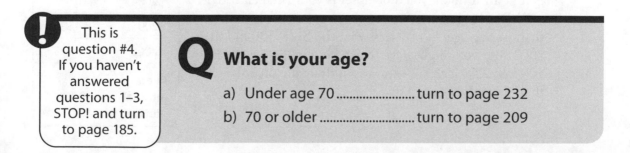

This is question #4. If you haven't answered questions 1–3, STOP! and turn to page 185.

Q What is your age?

a) Under age 70 .... turn to page 232

b) 70 or older .... turn to page 209

This is why it's not enough to determine that an investment has returns that tend to rise and fall. After all, if you own two investments, and each has returns that rise and fall, you don't want them to rise and fall together. You'd rather have one that rises while the other falls, to reduce your overall risk. Therefore, we need a measurement that compares the variance of two investments.

How to Compare the Risks of Different Investments

Enter *covariance*. This formula compares the differences in the annual returns of different investments.

$$cov\,xy = \frac{1}{N}\sum x_1 y_1 - \overline{xy}$$

Variance has a second, even worse, flaw, and you don't need a postgraduate degree in applied statistics to see it. Let's look again at the performance of the S&P 500 for the ten years ending December 31, 2006, shown in Figure 2.2. As before, you can see that the S&P 500 made money in some years and lost money in others. This dispersion created the variance we've been talking about. Standard deviation measured this variance for us, and we've learned that big deviations are bad.

But standard deviation tells us that *all* variances are equally bad. Are they, though?

Not at all. I doubt you'd be upset if your financial advisor tells you that your investment has earned 18% more than its average — which is what the S&P 500 did in 2003. But you might have freaked out when the S&P 500 lost 22% in 2002 — a return dramatically lower than its ten-year average.

Figure 2.2

Year	S&P 500
1997	33.4%
1998	28.6%
1999	21.0%
2000	−9.1%
2001	−11.9%
2002	−22.1%
2003	28.7%
2004	10.9%
2005	4.9%
2006	13.6%
Average Annual Return	**9.8%**

Yep, there's no doubt about it: Investors have no problem with *upside* variance. It's the *downside* variance that we dislike. Therefore, we need to look more closely at downside returns. How often do they occur? And how big are they? In other words, we need to examine (here it comes) *semivariance,* that half of variance which focuses on downside volatility.

And just to annoy you further, the brainiacs have created two formulas for semivariance, not just one. There's a formula for *below-mean* semivariance and another for *below-target* semivariance. The formulas are nearly identical, but the number geeks say there's a big difference between them.

Below-mean semivariance

$$SVm = \frac{1}{N} \sum_{T-1}^{N} Max[E - R_T, 0]^2 = \frac{1}{N} \sum_{T-1}^{N} Min[R_T - E, 0]^2$$

Below-target semivariance

$$SVt = \frac{1}{N} \sum_{T-1}^{N} Max[t - R_T, 0]^2 = \frac{1}{N} \sum_{T-1}^{N} Min[R_T - t, 0]^2$$

Think we're done? Don't be silly. If you're going to the trouble of creating covariance and semivariance, you're naturally going to create . . . semicovariance. I'm not kidding.

When you put everything to work that we've learned thus far, you're certain to become a much better, more successful investor. To help you, I've combined all the above formulas into one simple equation, found on the next page.

$$\text{🐦} = \sqrt{\dfrac{\dfrac{1}{\text{🐄}}\, R_2 D_2\, [\, t + \text{⊙}_q\,,\, ATM_{\circledR}\,]^{1{,}000{,}000^2}}{\text{🐐}\left(\text{🐈} + C\,\text{🐁} RUN\right)}}$$

Okay, now I'm kidding. Hey, I warned you to skip this chapter.

Statistical thinking will one day be as necessary for effective citizenship as the ability to read and write.

~H. G. Wells

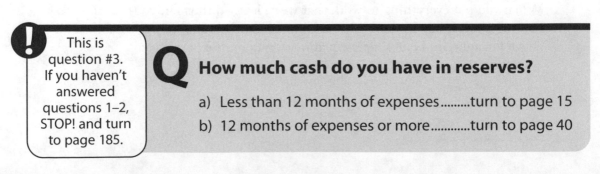

! This is question #3. If you haven't answered questions 1–2, STOP! and turn to page 185.

Q **How much cash do you have in reserves?**

a) Less than 12 months of expenses.........turn to page 15

b) 12 months of expenses or more............turn to page 40

The World Is Round — and Why That Matters to Your Investments

I am excited to reveal a startling fact:

> The world is round. You could sail a ship westward
> and return home without ever turning around.

Of course the world is round! you say. You marvel that there was such a time when people found this hard to believe.

But, as we all know, there was a time when people would have considered such a claim to be preposterous. In that light, let me offer you the following statement:

> You should be interested in risk as well as return.

Are you impressed with my brilliance? Envious of my epiphany? Or maybe you think I'm crazy?

Probably none of the above. Instead you're probably annoyed that I'm boring you with information you already know. *Of course I'm supposed to consider risk as well as return,* you say. *Everybody knows that!*

Well, yes, everybody knows that *now*. But nobody knew that sixty years ago. So let me introduce you to Harry Markowitz, the Ferdinand Magellan of the investment world. You see, Harry was the first person to say "You should be interested in risk as well as return."

He made the statement in 1952, as a graduate student at the University of Chicago. His master's thesis, "Portfolio Selection," suggested for the first time that it's not enough to be concerned with the investments we own. Harry said we also must be concerned with how our investments interrelate, for each investment affects the risk of the overall portfolio.

> You've got to feel bad for A. D. Ray. He published a similar paper, "Econometrica," three months after Markowitz published his thesis. Today nobody knows Ray's name. Just like nobody knows Bruce Robertson. He beat the world record in the 100-meter butterfly at the 1972 Olympics — and came in second. Mark Spitz beat him.
>
> Someone once said that the only thing worse than losing is coming in second.

Harry invented an entirely new approach to investment management. He didn't look at stocks as individual investments but as complete portfolios, and in the course of doing so, he invented the Efficient Frontier.[25]

Harry got little praise for his paper in 1952 (legend has it that he received a C). But today he is considered the Father of Modern Portfolio Theory, and his work earned him the Nobel Prize in Economic Sciences in 1990.

> People who don't understand that risk is as important as return often get disappointing results. They'll buy an investment because they've heard it grew by 15% per year over the past several years. They don't realize that the annual returns of such investments are volatile, so they are stunned when it loses 15% right after they bought it!

You see, it was Harry who introduced the concept of semivariance. But despite the advances his work offered in the field of investment analysis, Harry abandoned his work and returned to variance. Why? David Nawrocki of Villanova University explains in "A Brief History of Downside Risk Measures": "The semivariance optimization models using a semicovariance matrix require twice the number of data inputs than the variance model." So even though James Quirk and Rubin Saposnik (in 1962) and J. C. T. Mao (in 1970) confirmed that Markowitz was right — that semivariance is superior to variance as a risk measurement tool — he couldn't apply his research in the real world of stocks and bonds. As Nawrocki explains, "With the lack of cost-effective computer power and the fact that the variance model was already mathematically very complex, this was a significant consideration until the 1980s with the advent of the microcomputer."

In other words, Markowitz had designed an investment management tool that Wall Street wouldn't be able to use for decades — just as it would be hundreds of years before anyone would fly in

> *My ventures are not in one bottom trusted*
>
> *Nor to one place, nor is my whole estate*
>
> *Upon the fortune of this present year.*
>
> *Therefore, my merchandise makes me not sad.*
>
> ~William Shakespeare
> *The Merchant of Venice*, act I, scene 1
>
> "Clearly," Harry Markowitz once said, "Shakespeare not only knew about diversification but, at an intuitive level, understood covariance."

---

[25]Which I explained in *The Truth About Money*.

the helicopter that Leonardo da Vinci designed. Markowitz's work was inspirational nonetheless, and it led to a series of pioneering research that today forms the basis of professional investment management. In 1964 William Sharpe (who would share the Nobel Prize with Markowitz in 1990) created the Capital Asset Pricing Model, pronounced in shorthand as cap-m, which breaks investment performance into systematic and unsystematic risks.[26]

Sharpe also invented the Sharpe Ratio[27] which measures the risk-adjusted return of an investment. The formula is:

$$S(x) = (r_x - R_f) / StdDev(x)$$

Sharpe demonstrated that there's a big difference between the stock market and a market of stocks. While the overall stock market might generate a given return over a given time, an individual stock in that market might perform very differently. (You might think this is absurdly obvious, but Sharpe was the first to notice it.)

Essentially, the Capital Asset Pricing Model helps you determine if a given investment is worth the risk. It does this by separating the market's return (which Sharpe called *beta*) from the excess return expected from an individual security (called *alpha*).

The Capital Asset Pricing Model

$$R_{pt} - R_{ft} = a_p + \beta_p [R_{mt} - R_{ft}] + e_{pt}$$

| excess portfolio return | an average "abnormal" return | a market component | an error |

[26]Oops. Sorry for the jargon. *Systematic risk* refers to the overall risks of the stock market; *unsystematic risk* refers to the risks of investing in the stock of a specific company.
[27]Dr. Sharpe has noted that no one calls his formula by its proper name, the *Reward-to-Variability Ratio.* In a 1994 paper published in the *Journal of Portfolio Management,* he noted that his ratio has been called the Sharpe index (Radcliff, 1990, and Haugen, 1993), the Sharpe measure (Bodie, Kane, and Marcus, 1993; Elton and Gruber, 1991; and Reilly, 1989), the Sharpe ratio (Morningstar, 1993), and various other names. Hey, Bill, a rose is a rose.

Almost thirty years later, in 1992, Eugene Fama of the University of Chicago and Kenneth French, then at Yale University, expanded Sharpe's CAPM into what they call the Fama-French Three-Factor Model. While CAPM adjusts beta by only one factor (alpha), Fama-French adds two more by evaluating the company's size and whether its stock is considered *growth* or *value*. Today the Fama-French Three-Factor Model is widely regarded as the most advanced portfolio model in money management.[28]

The Fama-French Three-Factor Model has shown investors that, over long periods:

- Small stocks produce higher returns than large stocks.

- Value stocks produce higher returns than growth stocks.

- Poorly run companies are better investments than companies that are well run.

- Owning bonds with shorter maturities is more profitable than owning bonds with longer maturities.

All of these ideas were unheard of until the Three-Factor Model was introduced in 1992.

The Fama-French Three-Factor Model

$$R_{pt} - R_{ft} = a_p + b_p [R_{mt} - R_{ft}] + s_p SMB_t + h_p HML_t + e_{pt}$$

$R_{pt} - R_{ft}$ excess portfolio return	a_p an average "abnormal" return	$b_p [R_{mt} - R_{ft}]$ a market component	$s_p SMB_t$ a "size" component	$h_p HML_t$ a "price" component	e_{pt} an error

While Sharpe, Fama, and French were tinkering around with models to improve security selection within broadly based portfolios, Gary Brinson and his colleagues Randolph Hood and Gilbert Beebower were trying to figure out the root cause

---

[28]Some might challenge this statement, arguing that the latest step along the continuing evolution of portfolio management belongs to *lower partial moment*, developed in 1975. But LPM has yet to make its way out of academia.

of volatility. Their study, published in 1986, is considered the most important research since Markowitz's. In "Determinants of Portfolio Performance," the trio (known affectionately in financial circles as BHB) discovered that investment success isn't derived by picking the right stocks or bonds. Instead success is obtained by correctly mixing them together. Indeed, BHB's study shows that 93.6% of a portfolio's volatility — the variance that we've already studied — is determined by your *asset allocation*.

Figure 2.3

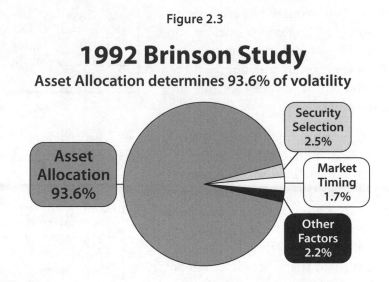

1992 Brinson Study
Asset Allocation determines 93.6% of volatility

If you're wondering what this means, consider this scenario: You have $1,000 to invest, so you decide to buy Berkshire Hathaway stock on Monday, January 3, 1977. The share price is $89. But you buy only one share, placing the rest of your money — $911 — into a passbook savings account that earns 1% per year. Your asset allocation is 9% stocks, 91% cash.

By December 31, 2006, your passbook account has grown to $1,216. Your single share of Berkshire is worth $109,990. Your total account is therefore worth $111,206.

Even though you've bought a stock that has gained 1,235% — an average annual return of 26.9%! — you're not very rich. That's because you didn't take much risk. If you had instead invested *all* your money into Berkshire shares — if your portfolio had been 100% in stocks and 0% in cash — you'd now have $1.3 million.

This is the crux of the BHB study: It shows that the overwhelming portion of portfolio volatility (and, by extrapolation, performance) is determined by how you allocate your assets among the various asset classes and market sectors — hence, asset allocation. By comparison, only 2.5% of your portfolio's volatility is determined by security selection (deciding which stock or bond to buy). Ditto for market timing: Only 1.7% of your results is determined by when you buy or sell the securities in your portfolio.

> The average investor would have 70% more money if he had used an effective asset allocation strategy over the past thirty years, according to a study by the mutual fund company AllianceBernstein. (Instead of having $589,000, for example, you'd have $1,001,300.)
>
> Yet, according to another study by the Hartford Financial Services Group, only 19% of those fifty-five or older are familiar with the concept of asset allocation.

Brinson, who now is regarded as the Father of Asset Allocation, published a second study in 1991, along with Beebower and Brian Singer, which confirmed the earlier findings. That was followed in 1999 by a study from Roger Ibbotson, a Yale finance professor and chairman of Ibbotson Associates, and Paul Kaplan, Ibbotson Associates chief economist, which verified that asset allocation not only explains more than 90% of the variation in a given portfolio's returns, on average, but 100% of the returns themselves.

> How unfortunate that, despite the fact that asset allocation is the key to investment success, few retail mutual fund companies provide their investors with any asset allocation tools. The market research firm Corporate Insight examined the offerings of eighteen of the largest retail mutual fund companies in America, and found that only four "provide valuable resources" for clients and prospective investors. Its review also found that the tools offered ranged from "complex" to "extremely limited" — neither of which is of much help to investors.
>
> So much for investors getting help from retail mutual fund companies. More on this later.

So let's put it all together:

1. Stocks are risky, and Pearson showed us how to measure that risk.

2. Markowitz explained that although stocks are risky, adding them to your portfolio can actually lower your portfolio's overall risk.

3. Sharpe showed that adding certain stocks to your portfolio is better than adding certain others, because some contribute more to your portfolio's total return than others.

4. Fama-French elaborated on Sharpe's work by showing that you should be adding entire *types* of stocks to your portfolio, not merely *certain* stocks.

5. Finally, Brinson verified all the above, showing that your overall investment success will be determined not just by the types of securities you place into your portfolio, but also by the combination of them.

Therefore, you want to own a highly diversified portfolio, one that holds many types of asset classes, many market sectors within each asset class, and many securities within each sector.

© United Feature Syndicate, Inc.

Fine, you say. You get it. You realize that this means you should own stocks *and* bonds *and* real estate *and* international securities *and* natural resources. But how many securities of each do you need to own?

This is the final question that we need to answer, and in so doing we will conclude our academic tour. So let's explore our final concept.

Concept #5: Terminal Wealth Dispersion

Let's say you want the high returns that stocks offer, but you don't want to lose all your money by accidentally investing in a company that will be the next Enron. So instead of buying one stock and hoping for the best, you buy two. Obviously, owning two stocks is safer than owning one.

By that logic, owning three is safer than owning two, right? Then four has to be safer than three, and five has — where does this end?

Benjamin Graham said it ends with fifteen. He said so in *The Intelligent Investor,* which he wrote in 1949.[29] Nearly twenty years later, in 1968, Graham's analysis was updated by research published in *The Journal of Finance,* which concluded that you need only ten stocks to be properly diversified.

If ten or fifteen stocks is all you need, why do I recommend (as you'll see later) that you own thousands of stocks? The answer is simple: Graham's book was written some sixty years ago, and he was talking about minimizing risk, not maximizing return. Based on today's research, we know to emphasize both.

You see, Graham said that if you own only one stock, 100% of your risk is in that stock, and if you add a second stock, you diversify (*disperse)* the risk. By the time you get to fifty stocks, you've dispersed the risk significantly. But Graham observed that a portfolio of fifty stocks isn't significantly safer than one holding twenty stocks. Therefore, Graham concluded, you might as well own just fifteen, because by the time you own that many, you've reduced the risk as much as you can. In other words, you cannot reduce risk any further. You've reached the end, the *terminus. Terminal wealth dispersion.* Get it?

---

[29]Graham deserves attention; he's the guy who taught Warren Buffett how to invest.

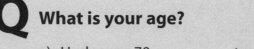

! This is question #4. If you haven't answered questions 1–3, STOP! and turn to page 185.

Q **What is your age?**

a) Under age 70 .... turn to page 135

b) 70 or older .... turn to page 253

Figure 2.4

Adding more stocks to your portfolio lowers your risk — but only to a point. This tells only half the story.

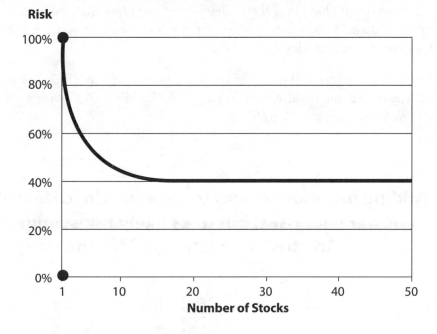

But — and this is a <u>big</u> but — Graham (and later, the *Journal of Finance)* was talking about lowering risk, not about maximizing returns. Sure, ten or fifteen stocks are enough to lower risk, but that's not the same as saying ten or fifteen stocks will generate high returns.

Here's what I mean: Say you want to invest in the stock market. You know you can optimally minimize your risk, *à la* Graham, by investing in fifteen stocks. So you pick fifteen from among the five hundred that comprise the S&P 500 Stock Index.

Congratulations! You've minimized your risk!

But how do you know that the fifteen stocks you picked will make more money than the other 485?

You see, by choosing only fifteen stocks out of five hundred, you're exposing yourself to alpha risk (the risk that a given stock might fall in value), and you're denying yourself the results of *beta* (the performance of the overall market).

Graham wasn't thinking in terms of alpha versus beta — because those concepts hadn't been invented yet. He was investing seventy-five years ago, in a world vastly different from ours. Since then, Sharpe has taught us that the market is broken into alpha and beta, and further research has shown that you can cut alpha risk. Graham never envisioned any of this.

In fact, new research shows that investing in twenty-five stocks cuts alpha risk by 80%, owning one hundred stocks cuts alpha by 90%, and owning four hundred stocks reduces alpha risk by 95%!

Figure 2.5

Adding lots more stocks to your portfolio doesn't further lower your risks, but does likely boost your return. And that's the other half of the story.

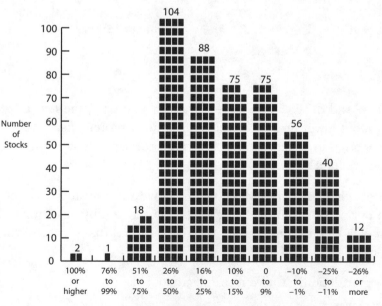

note: 29 stocks were merged or dropped from the index.

2006 Performance of the Stocks
Inside the S&P 500

Figure 2.5 shows how each of the five hundred stocks in the S&P 500 Stock Index performed in 2006. As you can see, a few stocks did extremely well, while most did OK, and a bunch performed very poorly. If you had picked only fifteen of these stocks, would your picks have landed on the left side of the chart, or might they have ended up on the right? Although the concept of terminal wealth dispersion argues that picking fifteen is enough to reduce the risk that you might go broke, it does not address the concern that you might end up with below-average returns. The only way to assure yourself of the market's returns is to invest in all five hundred stocks.[30]

If only you could buy a book that listed the one hundred best stocks to own in America. With that in hand, you could just buy the book, invest in those one hundred stocks, sit back, and enjoy the riches.

If only there was such a book.

Well, there is. Now in its seventh edition, *The 100 Best Stocks to Own in America* has sold three hundred thousand copies since first published. But has anyone actually made any money from it? The author has probably done pretty well, but I'm not sure anyone else has profited.

A study by professors at Florida International University and Seton Hall University, published in *Financial Services Review,* shows the results. The academicians built twenty-four hypothetical portfolios based on the first six editions of the book. Six portfolios were invested equally in each edition's top five picks. Another six invested equally in each edition's top ten picks. A third six comprised the top twenty picks, and the fourth set of six portfolios contained equal amounts of all one hundred stocks that appeared in each edition. These twenty-four portfolios were then compared to the S&P 500 Stock Index for the same time periods.

The results? Of the twenty-four portfolios, only five performed better than the S&P 500. And they were supposedly filled with only the "best" stocks!

What a dismal record. It's also further evidence of the folly of investing based on the hot tips that you find in books and magazines, see on TV or the Web, or hear on the radio.

---

[30]This example refers to the five hundred stocks of the S&P 500 Stock Index. An equally valid example could be used with the Wilshire 5000. In other words, do not take this example to necessarily mean that you should buy mutual funds that mimic the S&P 500 index. More on this in chapter 5.

And so, as we reach the end of our academic trek, you see why it's best to own thousands of securities. If you own just a few, the shenanigans of any one of them (say, Enron) could undermine your efforts to achieve financial success. Instead invest in thousands. Categorize them by asset class and market sector *à la* Fama-French and diversify across those asset classes and market sectors *à la* Brinson.

Out of the Lab and into the Marketplace

Eventually, inevitably, empirical research moves from the laboratory to practical application. Such is the case in the field of personal finance. Twenty years ago financial planners were largely unfamiliar with all this academic research. As recently as 2000, stocks and mutual funds were characterized colloquially rather than scientifically. For example, as Figure 2.6 shows, Lipper and Morningstar categorized mutual funds as *balanced* or *equity-income* or *growth-income*. In 2000 they and the rest of the industry began describing mutual funds the way Fama-French refer to them: as growth or value, and as large-cap, mid-cap or small-cap. By applying academia's empirical research, practitioners like me and my colleagues are now able to construct portfolios featuring sophisticated asset allocation models with much greater precision and control than ever before.

> **Why not simply pick the best mutual funds and stick with them?**
>
> Because "best" is fleeting. Every study that has reviewed mutual fund performance has reached the same conclusion: The best-performing funds of one time period are rarely the best-performing in future time periods.
>
> The most recent examination was conducted by Standard & Poor's. It found that of 269 large-cap stock funds, only 3 produced returns that placed them in the top quartile five years in a row (for the period ending July 2005). *None* of the 76 mid-cap funds succeeded, and only *1* of 124 small-cap funds achieved this feat.
>
> This is why you're much more likely to obtain the results you want by owning the entire market rather than trying to pick the winners from within the market.

! This is question #3. If you haven't answered questions 1–2, STOP! and turn to page 185.

Q **How much cash do you have in reserves?**

a) Less than 12 months of expenses......turn to page 226

b) 12 months of expenses or more...........turn to page 89

Figure 2.6

In the 1980s and 1990s, fund rating services used colloquial language to describe mutual fund objectives. By 2000, they adopted academic references.

Lipper Indexes

Monday, March 9, 1998

Equity Indexes	Prelim. Close	% Change Since		
		Prev.	Wk ago	Dec. 31
Capital Appreciation...	2015.03 −	0.50 +	0.28 +	8.00
Growth Fund...	6763.65 −	0.35 +	0.25 +	7.94
Small Cap Fund...	666.40 −	0.62 −	0.00 +	6.02
Growth & Income...	6485.63 −	0.15 +	0.70 +	7.41
Equity Income Fd...	3466.06 −	0.06 +	0.80 +	6.43
Science and Tech Fd...	542.28 +	2.21 −	3.51 +	8.36
International Fund...	665.53 +	0.62 −	0.58 +	9.79
Gold Fund...	83.62 +	0.91 −	0.78 +	2.60
Balanced Fund...	3865.53 +	0.01 +	0.46 +	5.07
Emerging Markets...	83.46 +	0.15 −	1.88 +	0.61
Bond Indexes	+			
Corp A-Rated Debt...	753.53 +	0.30 +	0.34 +	0.90
US Government...	284.68 +	0.24 +	0.32 +	1.00
GNMA...	309.80 +	0.24 +	0.41 +	1.40
High Current Yield...	784.13 +	0.09 −	0.16 +	2.69
Intmdt Inv Grade...	206.90 +	0.24 +	0.27 +	1.10
Short Inv Grade...	189.37 +	0.07 +	0.15 +	1.10
General Muni Debt...	542.77 +	0.12 −	0.19 +	0.37
High Yield Municipal...	264.57 +	0.08 −	0.15 +	0.75
Short Municipal...	116.21 +	0.03 −	0.01 +	0.73
Global Income...	202.55 +	0.34 −	0.12 +	1.43
International Income...	127.83 +	0.48 −	0.41 +	1.60

Indexes are based on the largest funds within the same investment objective and do not include multiple share classes of similar funds. The Yardsticks table, appearing with Friday's listings, includes all funds with the same objective.
Source: Lipper Analytical Services Inc. The Lipper Funds Inc. are not affiliated with the Lipper Analytical Services.

Ranges for investment companies with daily price data supplied by the National Association of Securities Dealers and performance and cost calculations by Lipper Analytical Services Inc. The NASD requires a mutual fund to have at least 1,000 shareholders or net assets of $25 million before being listed. NAV-Net Asset Value. Detailed explanatory notes appear elsewhere on this page.

Lipper Indexes

Monday, November 20, 2000

Equity Indexes	Prelim. Close	% Change Since		
		Prev.	Wk ago	Dec. 31
Large-Cap Growth...	4502.39 −	3.21 −	1.19 −	15.61
Large-Cap Core...	2580.32 −	2.10 −	0.35 −	6.15
Large-Cap Value...	9655.61 −	1.20 −	0.59 −	1.51
Multi-Cap Growth...	3702.06 −	3.95 −	2.44 −	9.31
Multi-Cap Core...	7435.83 −	1.70 −	0.43 −	2.51
Multi-Cap Value...	3434.63 −	1.29 −	0.69 +	4.00
Mid-Cap Growth...	836.92 −	4.07 −	3.26 −	13.55
Mid-Cap Core...	566.37 −	2.72 −	0.95 +	3.63
Mid-Cap Value...	690.53 −	1.79 −	0.42 +	3.92
Small-Cap Growth...	570.75 −	3.70 −	2.66 −	8.13
Small-Cap Core...	293.64 −	2.43 −	0.86 +	2.54
Small-Cap Value...	367.51 −	1.22 +	0.26 +	9.84
Equity Income Fd...	3882.21 −	1.04 −	0.76 +	2.47
Science and Tech Fd...	1247.68 −	5.34 −	3.93 −	20.75
Gold Fund...	52.92 −	0.26 −	0.22 −	28.75
International Fund...	782.39 −	1.52 −	1.01 −	16.86
Emerging Markets...	73.39 −	1.82 −	1.13 −	28.44
Balanced Fund...	4650.06 −	1.03 −	0.29 +	0.53
Bond Index	1.03			
Short Inv Grade...	217.03 +	+	0.14 −	5.83
Intmdt Inv Grade...	236.08 +	+	0.36 +	7.44
US Government...	322.43 +	+	0.47 +	8.51
GNMA...	354.80 +	+	0.29 +	8.09
Corp A-Rated Debt...	844.36 +	+	0.35 +	7.18
High Current Yield...	737.59 −		1.21 −	8.22
Global Income...	205.22 −		0.18 −	0.65
International Income...	130.80 −		0.67 −	3.96
Short Municipal...	128.84 +		0.07 +	4.00
General Muni Debt...	593.07 +		0.13 +	7.58
High Yield Municipal...	278.39 +		0.03 −	3.70

Indexes are based on the largest funds within the same investment objective and do not include multiple share classes of similar funds. The Yardsticks table, appearing with Friday's listings, includes all funds with the same objective.
Source: Lipper Analytical Services Inc. The Lipper Funds Inc. are not affiliated with the Lipper Analytical Services.

Ranges for investment companies with daily price data supplied by the National Association of Securities Dealers and performance and cost calculations by Lipper Analytical Services Inc. The NASD requires a mutual fund to have at least 1,000 shareholders or net assets of $25 million before being listed. NAV-Net Asset Value. Detailed explanatory notes appear elsewhere on this page.

Today academic research serves as the basis for how professional financial advisors construct portfolios for their clients — or, rather, how they *should* be doing it. If your advisor can't explain the difference between arithmetic and geometric means, and isn't familiar with standard deviation, variance and its derivatives, Modern Portfolio Theory and the Efficient Frontier; the Capital Asset Pricing Model, alpha and beta, the Fama-French Three-Factor Model; Asset Allocation and Terminal Wealth Dispersion, get yourself a new advisor. Pronto.[31]

---

[31]I mean, you don't have to understand the principles of internal combustion, but your auto mechanic sure does.

Speaking of financial advisors, does yours objectively collect and analyze information about your goals, income, assets, investments, and debts in order to identify the investments that best meet your needs, or is your advisor's primary job nothing more than selling financial products in order to earn commissions?

Certainly you'd prefer to hire an independent, objective advisor instead of a commission-hungry salesman. Guess what stockbrokers from coast to coast have been asserting in court?

In sworn testimony, stockbrokers from the biggest brokerage firms in the country say they are *not* financial advisors but merely commission-paid salespeople whose primary job is to sell financial products.

The stockbrokers' lawsuits are based on the Fair Labor Standards Act. Fact Sheet 17M, which pertains to FLSA and was issued by the U.S. Department of Labor, says stockbrokers *are* entitled to overtime pay if their "primary duty is selling financial products" while they *are not* entitled to overtime pay if their work includes "collecting and analyzing information regarding the customer's income, assets, investments, or debts; determining which financial products best meet the customer's needs and financial circumstances; advising the customer regarding the advantages and disadvantages of different financial products; and marketing, servicing, or promoting the employer's financial products."

Which type of advisor would you prefer to hire? Well, not only do you want a real advisor, you want an advisor who regards *himself* to be a real advisor. So it's interesting to see that some stockbrokers think of themselves as nothing more than salespeople.[32]

And the courts agree with them. In 2005, Merrill Lynch stockbrokers won a $37 million judgment. A couple of months later, stockbrokers at UBS Financial Services (formerly known as Paine Webber) won a similar lawsuit and collected $89 million. Smith Barney stockbrokers sued and won $98 million. In March 2006 Morgan Stanley stockbrokers received $42.5 million, while those at Wells Fargo Investments received $12.8 million. Similar lawsuits have been filed against Wachovia, A. G. Edwards, Bear Stearns, Ryan Beck, and others.

Although the brokers say they are just salespeople, the brokerage industry spent $8.5 billion in 2006, according to *Advertising Age*, bragging that its people offer advice. It gives brokers such lofty titles as financial advisor, financial planner, investment advisor, financial consultant, and vice president–investments. But the stockbrokers who work for these firms say — in court and under oath — that it ain't so. They say they have little or no control over the products they sell, that they sell certain products in order to win sales contests (in 2006 Merrill Lynch paid a $5 million fine for offering

---

[32]And successful salespeople at that. The average stockbroker earned an average of $125,112 in 2006, according to *Broker Dealer* magazine.

dinners, trips, and tickets to rock concerts as incentives), and that their firms' training is focused on sales techniques.

Further supporting the brokers' position is the U.S. Securities and Exchange Commission, which now requires all brokerage statements to display this message:

> *Your account is a brokerage account and not an advisory account. Our interests may not always be the same as yours. Please ask questions to make sure you understand your rights and our obligations to you, including the extent of our obligations to disclose conflicts of interest and to act in your best interests. We are paid both by you and sometimes by people who compensate us based on what you buy from us. Therefore, our profits and our salespersons' compensations may vary by product and over time.*

The SEC's position is that any advice you receive from a broker is "incidental" to the sale of an investment product and that investment advice is provided only by Registered Investment Advisors.[33] Such advisors are fiduciaries, and required by law to serve each client's best interests at all times. This is the highest legal standard. Brokers, by comparison, merely have a duty to "know your client" (meaning that brokers only need to know that a recommended investment is "suitable and appropriate." It does not have to be in the best interests of the client).

You can learn how to hire a Registered Investment Advisor by reading Part 13 of *The Truth About Money;* that information is also posted for you at RicEdelman.com.

As I've mentioned, the information in this chapter is merely a brief (and, some might argue, overly simplistic) review of the academic research. Want more? The Reference section contains a list of research papers on portfolio management that I consider noteworthy.

But no matter how much of the academic literature you read, you might not be convinced that diversification and asset allocation using mutual funds is the way to go. Surely, you might be thinking, there's got to be an easier way to obtain investment success.

So allow me to offer you alternative ways that you can pick investments. After all, I'm here to serve.

Let's start by picking specific investments. Obviously, you want to pick those that will make lots of money. But that research and analysis take lots of time that you

---

[33]Of which my firm is one.

don't have and require skills that you *know* you don't have. So all you need to do is hire a stock analyst to pick stocks for you. There are plenty from which to choose: 91,000 people hold the Chartered Financial Analyst designation, and 140,000 more are studying for it, according to the CFA Institute.

But these 176,000 people can't all pick the right stocks at the right times. Thus, most are destined to become *former* Chartered Financial Analysts. So said *Registered Rep.* magazine, which asked in December 2003 if stock pickers are about to experience the same fate as dodo birds. I made the same prediction four years earlier in my second book, *The New Rules of Money*.

Although their extinction is fast approaching, some insist on playing their game. Amazingly, people still subscribe to newsletters that offer "hot" stock tips; with each monthly issue, hapless readers buy and sell stocks. If you play this game, you'll be doing yourself far more harm than good; as I reported in *Discover the Wealth Within You*, researchers at the University of California, Davis, found that, over a six-year period, active traders underperformed the stock market by 10.3% per year — ten times worse than the average investor.

OK, so frequent buying and selling doesn't work. But how about buying and selling in sync with general market movements? This notion, called *trend analysis*, or *momentum investing*, is like saying it will rain tomorrow because it's been raining for the past week. To wit: In 1982 the Dow Jones Industrial Average was 1,046. By 1999 it had risen eleven-fold, to 11,497. Clearly, this meant that the Dow would continue zooming upward, right? So said *Dow 36,000*, published in 1999. Its co-authors probably wish they'd written *7,700* — because that's where the Dow went over the next three years.

At least the authors based their predictions on the stock market. Some trend followers actually predict stock movements by *ignoring* the stock market. Instead they track — are you ready for this? — pop music. According to that theory, as shown in Figure 2.7, the Beatles breakup in 1970 was clearly the sign of a market bottom.

! This is question #4. If you haven't answered questions 1–3, STOP! and turn to page 185.

Q **What is your age?**

a) Under age 70 .... turn to page 169
b) 70 or older .... turn to page 259

Figure 2.7

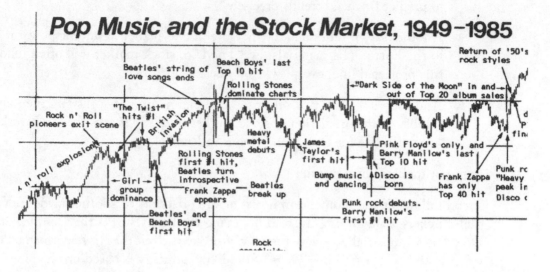

Pop Music and the Stock Market, 1949–1985

Others cite hemlines (they supposedly rise and fall in sync with the stock market), horror movies (the more that Hollywood releases, the worse the stock market), sports (stocks rise when an original NFC [National Football Conference] team wins the Super Bowl and crash whenever baseball's Oakland Athletics win the World Series), the Chinese calendar (the Year of the Pig, which occurs once every twelve years, is considered good for stocks and particularly small cap stocks), and even manned space launches (stocks rise upon launch and decline with reentry).

Perhaps the most fun place to seek trends is on the Internet, which requires no peer review. In other words, any loony can publish anything there.

- One site bills itself as "the world's first website to promote the fifty-six-year cycle of financial panics found in the U.S. and Western

> You can certainly hand over your hard-earned money to one of the thousands of market seers, newsletters, financial publications, and seminars, all aimed at helping you predict the stock market and individual stock prices. However, you stand to gain as much benefit doing that as you would by folding your money into paper boats and sailing them over Niagara Falls.
>
> ~ Gary Weiss, author of *Wall Street Versus America: The Rampant Greed and Dishonesty That Imperil Your Investments*

Europe." (Its fine print states, "The fifty-six-year panic cycle cannot be used to predict financial trends precisely.")

- Another says it relies on "the measure of two planet harmonic power relative to the Earth." (Its materials say, "The U.S. stock market will often follow this projected line, except when it doesn't.")

- And there's the site that refers to "artificial neuro networks and their applicability to the prediction of stock market trends." (It says these networks are "also effective for forecasting floods in Russia.")

I am not making this stuff up.

Trend following and momentum investing are offshoots of another favorite of get-rich-quickers: data mining. Instead of buying the thirty stocks that comprise the Dow Jones Industrial Average, they say, just buy the ten that have performed the worst in the past year. This "Dogs of the Dow" strategy is based on the premise that the worst stocks of one time period often become the best in subsequent periods.[34]

But wait! Don't stop there! Instead of buying all ten of the worst, skip the very worst and buy the next nine-worst. That's because additional mining has shown that the "very worst" usually fail to gain as much as the other nine.

No, wait! Other miners say that the top four of the bottom ten (?) actually do better than all of the bottom ten — and so it goes.

Dogs of the Dow . . . the Dow Five . . . the Dow Four . . . The Dow Dividends — perhaps the biggest supporter of these various Dow theories was the Motley Fool, which poured through reams of statistics in a desperate effort to find the Holy Grail of investing. In June 2005, after years of telling anyone who would listen that they knew the secrets to generating market-beating returns, the Fool finally admitted that, yes, its website is appropriately named:

> Our thinking and our expectations for all Dow-based
> strategies have changed. Please note that the returns

---

[34]Technically, the Dogs theory refers to "highest-yielding" stocks, not "worst-performing." But the result is pretty much the same: A high-yielding stock, by definition, features a high stock-to-dividend ratio. That ratio is high because the price is low, and the only way for the price to be low is for that stock to have performed worse than the other stocks. (This also explains why the theory is so stupid. Instead of increasing the stock price — which is what the Dogs followers hope will happen — the company could instead simply cut the dividend. It often happens, leaving investors in the, uh, doghouse.)

> [we quote] are based on calendar-year portfolios for the
> period 1974–1999. Additional research has shown that
> investors cannot expect such high returns from these
> strategies in the future.

Gee, I guess past performance doesn't predict future results after all.

It was nice to see the Motley Fool come clean. But it took them longer than everyone else. Six years earlier (March 1999), in an effort to put a stop to this, uh, foolishness, the *Financial Analyst Journal* wrote, "If one digs through enough data or trading rules, one is bound, just by chance, to find some that work." That was followed up by a study by Washburn University, published in 2001 in the *Journal of Personal Finance,* that evaluated two Dogs theories over a ten-year period and concluded, "The buy-and-hold strategy for either the Dow or the S&P 500 resulted in better returns than did the Dogs."

I am not suggesting that you ignore the media. Instead simply learn the difference between education and advice. When explaining issues and events, the media typically provide balanced, measured, complete explanations. But too often the stories morph from objective journalism into idiotic predictions — and that's when you need to be careful, because their predictions are no better than the clowns who are tracking Beatles tunes or hemlines.

Take Jim Cramer, the king of do-it-yourself investing. For decades Cramer has told investors that they can and should buy their own investments without the aid of a financial advisor. His nightly tirades on CNBC make my rants on the ABC Radio Networks sound like whispers in a library. Jim admonishes his viewers to get off their fannies and Buy! Buy! Buy! Sell! Sell! Sell!

Prior to his TV gig, Jim's website made the same claims: You-can-invest-on-your-own-and-beat-those-big-guys-at-their-own-game-if-you-just-listen-to-me-because-I'll-tell-you-what-to-buy.

Contrast that with the article he wrote in 2006 for *Registered Rep.*, a trade magazine for stockbrokers:

> *So we got it all wrong. We thought that the individual
> investor would storm the ramparts, manage the money him-
> self, and take over the world. I, in particular, as a founder
> of TheStreet.com, thought we could turn Wall Street into a
> Home Depot, where do-it-yourselfers could roam free, tak-*

ing care of their money and building up colossal nest eggs all by themselves. We ended up costing people fortunes with articles, newscasts, and advertising about how simple it was. The best of us were naive, and the worst of us were self-serving and shameful.

Yet Jim's nightly tirades on TV continue.[35]

Or consider Stan Hinden. For twenty-plus years, he wrote a personal finance column for the *Washington Post*. Week after week he told readers how to handle their finances. But ten years *after* he retired in 1996, he revealed the truth:

"Don't Do What I Did" was the headline of this astonishing *mea culpa*. In it Hinden wrote:

> *In my ideal life, I planned my retirement with great care. I saved regularly, invested wisely, and lived within my income. A savvy stock picker, I bought low, sold high, and made money. But in my real life, I had no plan for retirement. In my 30s and 40s . . . I saved hardly at all . . . As for stocks, I frequently lost money. It's embarrassing to admit all this because — as a financial writer at the* Washington Post *— I should have been well prepared for retirement. But I was always too busy to focus on what I needed to know and do. So while I did a couple of things right, I made several key mistakes.*

Hinden — called a "financial expert" in the article's subhead — went on to say, "I didn't think ahead." He admitted that he never tried "to consider how much money we'd need" in retirement. He also chastised himself for never consulting a financial planner or retirement expert. "I wish I had done so before I retired," he wrote, "because I needed an investment strategy that provided us with growth and income. I also needed to learn about Social Security, Medicare, Medigap insurance, pensions, long-term-care insurance, mandatory IRA withdrawals, and estate

---

[35]In an interview videotaped by TheStreet.com in December 2006, and which appeared on YouTube in March 2007, Cramer said that he manipulated stock prices in his earlier career as a trader. He said he spread rumors about stocks and felt his actions were safe because "the SEC never understands this." He added, "What's important when you are in hedge fund mode . . . is to not do anything remotely truthful because the truth is so against your view that it's important to create a new truth, to develop a fiction." Cramer has since recanted, saying he did not do any of these things when he ran a hedge fund, nor did he believe what he said. But investors are left to wonder if they can ever believe anything he says.

planning. Amazingly, all these subjects played a significant role in my retirement."

And then there's Suze Orman. In a 2007 interview with *The New York Times Magazine*, she revealed that she doesn't follow her own advice — she hasn't diversified her own investments (she's worth $32 million, she says), and she appears not to have done the proper estate planning to reduce estate taxes for herself and her partner, Kathy Travis.

So the next time you're tempted to buy an investment based on the predictions of an "expert," flip a coin instead.

Seriously. The folks at Bianca Research examined whether the so-called experts could accurately predict interest rate movements by reviewing their prognostications for every six-month period since 1982. Their conclusion: The experts were able to correctly predict future interest rates only 28% of the time.

I want to share with you a fascinating experience I once had.

During the 2000–2002 bear market, a journalist called me about a story she'd written for a well-known women's magazine. The writer had interviewed a financial planner for the story, but after it was written, the planner retracted his permission to be quoted. With the story already written, the reporter called to see if she could attribute the quotes to me.

I reviewed the piece but disagreed with the advice. So I offered new advice — the story was about investment strategy — and the reporter rewrote the story accordingly. After she submitted the revised story to her editors, she called back. The magazine's editor rejected the story because my advice did not match her own ideas. I was told that she was unhappy because my advice did not conform to the advice one typically reads in the personal finance press. Therefore, I was told, she changed my quotes to reflect what *she* wanted me to say, and the reporter wanted to know if that was OK with me.

No, it was not OK, I told her. Now understanding why the first financial planner had backed away from the story, I did the same thing, explaining that if the editor didn't like my advice, they shouldn't change it; instead they simply should not print it. The writer agreed, and admitted that she was frustrated by the situation. She took my objections to her editor, assuring me the story would reflect my actual advice.

A week later she faxed me a new version. It still attributed to me advice that was the opposite of what I actually advise consumers. "My editor fancies herself an investment whiz," the reporter told me. "She's panicking about the market and thinks everyone else is too. I'm disgusted with the situation."

I insisted that they remove my name from the piece, which the reporter assured me she would do. In the end, the magazine's article contained unattributed advice that was in fact written by the magazine's editor, a person with no financial background who was consumed by financial panic.

Think about this anecdote the next time you read a financial article in a general-interest magazine. Whose advice are you really reading?

That's even worse than you think: Since interest rates can do only one of three things (rise, fall, or remain constant), random guesses should be correct 33% of the time. But the experts couldn't perform even that well. Indeed, making investment decisions because of what "experts" say is worse than relying on chance.

> If it makes sense to ignore the hot tips offered by media mavens, it certainly makes sense to ignore the *ads* you see in the media. A 2007 study by Ohio State University found that mutual funds that spend a lot of money on advertising attract more assets than other funds, but they generate lower returns — mostly because of the higher costs incurred as a result of all their ad spending. "Mutual fund investors who pay attention to ads could end up with less money available for retirement," said Henrik Cronqvist, the study's author.

Fortunately, there are lots of outstanding publications and writers in the personal finance field. My favorite is *USA Today*. Virtually every day's edition features thoughtful, helpful news and information that are of significant value to your personal finances. Sandra Block, *USA Today's* long-time writer, is my favorite personal finance columnist.

Also, Jason Zweig and Jean Chatzky of *Money* magazine are terrific. Thoughtful, insightful writers both, they stand in stark contrast to the rest of the publication — which you should otherwise completely ignore.

Gretchen Morgenson, formerly of *Forbes*, now with the *New York Times*, is my favorite investigative journalist in the business sector. Her sharp, biting stories force CEOs to pay attention. You should too. *Newsweek's* Allan Sloan is every bit her equal.

Mark Hulbert publishes the *Hulbert Financial Digest* and writes a column for the *New York Times*. His mutual fund and investment manager research is probably the best there is.

From the business press, you can't live without *The Wall Street Journal*. Read it every day, and don't fret that you won't understand it. You will; the writing is that good. And give yourself weekly, biweekly, and monthly doses of *BusinessWeek*, *Forbes*, and *Fortune*, respectively. And, if you have the time, Alan Ableson (*Barron's*) and Stanley Bing (*Fortune)* are the funniest (and I mean laugh-out-loud funny) writers in finance.

Two interesting reads come from *Washington Post* columnists Michelle Singletary and Martha Hamilton. From the school of "I don't always know what I'm doing either, but I'm really trying," they let readers join them as they search for effective solutions to everyday personal finance problems. They humanize personal finance, making it real for the rest of us.

I cite all these folks not because we always agree (my good friend Michelle and I fight all the time — sometimes on stage together) but because they are professional, objective writers who don't let their personal biases interfere with their mission of providing their readers with valuable information. They don't pretend to be experts, pundits, or prognosticators. They won't tell you what the market is going to do next or who will win the upcoming election. Instead they'll tell you how the world of Wall Street works and how you can make it work for you. With these writers, you'll always know where they stand and why, and you can be confident that they are interested in your best interests.[36]

Unfortunately, people continue to believe in "experts" — especially when the "experts" use facts and figures to support their assertions.

Enter Calendar Rules. If you look closely at the historical performance of the stock market, you can (supposedly) find patterns — and you can apply these patterns to predict future stock prices. Hey, Edmund Halley did it to predict when a comet would reappear, so it ought to work for the stock market, right?

---

[36]I've surely left off some deserving names; please consider that an error and not necessarily a commentary.

This is question #3. If you haven't answered questions 1–2, STOP! and turn to page 185.

Q How much cash do you have in reserves?

a) Less than 12 months of expenses.........turn to page 95

b) 12 months of expenses or more...........turn to page 31

Wrong, but the folks who pore through the data (called data miners) think it does. For example, they note that the stock market has risen an average of 34.6% in the fifth year of every decade since 1926. Therefore, they conclude, the stock market will earn huge returns in *every* decade's fifth year.[37]

Several books on Calendar Rules have been published. They agree that you should never sell stocks on Monday, because stock prices are lowest on Monday and highest on Friday. But if that's true, will Monday's prices be higher than the previous Friday's? If so, maybe we should not sell on Friday, either, but instead wait until the following Monday. But then we'd have to wait until the coming Friday, at which point we'd have to wait until Monday again, and . . . .

Although many of these assertions are wacky, some of the writers have bona fide credentials. For example, two researchers at Georgia Tech College of Management — one a professor emeritus, the other an assistant professor of finance — say that stock prices tend to rise substantially in the two years prior to a presidential election. Of course, that's 50% of the entire time, but let's not nitpick.

Can you really invest successfully by paying attention to the calendar? In a word, no. In eighty-four words, consider the analysis conducted by Halbert White, professor of economics at the University of California, San Diego:

> We had a universe of 300 calendar rules and 9,000 calendar trading rules — things like buy and hold the stock for a particular day of the week of a particular month, or sell short on Tuesdays. Using one hundred years of daily data on the Dow Jones Industrial Average and about 25 years of daily data on the S&P 500 Stock Index, we found the best calendar rule . . . [falls] well within the range of what you would expect chance to be.

Agreed the *Journal of Economics* in 2001, "Even supposedly strongly empirical phenomena may not stand up to closer scrutiny."

I don't know about you, but I'll stick to diversification and asset allocation, *thankyouverymuch.*

---

[37]Before you think 2015 will be a great year, think again: The fifth year of a decade is year 2xx4, not 2xx5.

But does all this mean we've figured it all out? Do we now know everything we need to know in order to achieve optimal investment results?

Not by a long shot. No academician or Wall Street professional would claim that we've found the Holy Grail of investing. Despite our accumulated knowledge to date, our search for the ideal investment strategy continues.

One thing is clear: There will be no *Eureka!* moment, no sudden blast of brilliance that reveals the secret that has thus far eluded us. There will be no revolution in the field of investment management. Instead we are participating in an evolutionary process, fueled and furthered by meticulous research conducted by serious-minded people.

Even the leaders of the field realize that their past work requires expansion, elaboration and, sometimes, revision. In 2005 William Sharpe announced that The Capital Asset Pricing Model, which won him the Nobel Prize, needed to be revamped. Sharpe said he'd found a better way to determine how portfolios are constructed and how securities are priced. Considering that CAPM serves as the basis for virtually every finance curriculum in the country (and probably the world), this is no small statement.

> *October. This is one of the particularly dangerous months to invest in stocks. Other dangerous months are July, January, September, April, November, May, March, June, December, August, and February.*
>
> ~ Mark Twain

Sharpe refers to his new work, *Investors and Markets: Portfolio Choices, Asset Prices and Investment Advice*, published in 2006 by Princeton University Press as "beyond mean-variance" — words that by now are at least familiar to you if not fully understandable. Sharpe says his former approach was too complex compared to his new methodology. He hasn't yet applied his new model to asset allocation; if it works, investment managers are likely to change how they manage money, just as the introduction of CAPM in 1964 caused a major shift in traditional money management methods.

Sharpe believes he needs to abandon CAPM because it has too many flaws. For example, the model fails to consider extraordinary economic events such as market bubbles, depression, hyperinflation, or terrorist attacks. It also ignores taxes, transaction costs, and illiquidity. Such weaknesses were tolerated forty years ago, just as top speeds of twenty-five miles per hour were acceptable for the earliest cars, but today's sophisticated markets require new, equally sophisticated models. Harry Markowitz, the Father of Modern Portfolio Theory, says he's convinced that Dr. Sharpe's new work will prove effective; additional research will help determine the answer. In the meantime, CAPM remains in vogue, but its days seem to be numbered.

William Sharpe isn't the only one to think that we haven't figured it all out. No less than Benjamin Graham, the greatest investor who ever lived, later believed that the investment strategies he'd developed, and which he and David Dodd revealed in their landmark book *Security Analysis* in 1940, were wrong. In a 1976 interview published by the *Financial Analyst Journal*, Graham said:

> I am no longer an advocate of elaborate techniques of security analysis in order to find superior value opportunities. This was a rewarding activity, say, 40 years ago, when our textbook was first published; but the situation has changed a great deal since then. In the old days any well-trained security analyst could do a good professional job of selecting undervalued issues through detailed studies; but in the light of the enormous amount of research now being carried on, I doubt whether in most cases such extensive efforts will generate sufficiently superior selections to justify their cost. To that very limited extent I'm on the side of the "efficient market" school of thought now generally accepted by the professors.

! This is question #2. If you haven't answered question #1, STOP! and turn to page 185.

Q Will you be adding money to this account on a regular basis?

a) Yes ....turn to page 99

b) No ....turn to page 28

Yes, we've gotten pretty good at investment management, but we haven't figured it all out quite yet. This is why you must regard the field of investment management as one immersed in a continuing evolutionary process, and you must be willing to alter your strategies as new research emerges. Don't fall in love with your current methods. Instead remain willing to discard them in favor of newer methods as they are developed, verified, and applied by the greatest minds in the field.

For now, that research clearly shows that the most successful investment strategy consists of a long-term focus using extensive diversification and periodic rebalancing, paying equal attention to risk and return.

This chapter has shown you how proper investment management is conducted, thanks to academic study and research. In the next chapter, you'll learn why mutual funds offer you the best way to exploit that research. Afterward you'll discover what's gone wrong in the retail mutual fund industry and how you can fix the problem to secure yourself on the path toward financial security.

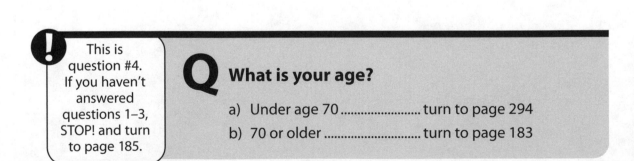

This is question #4. If you haven't answered questions 1–3, STOP! and turn to page 185.

Q **What is your age?**

a) Under age 70 .... turn to page 294

b) 70 or older .... turn to page 183

Chapter 3
Why You Should Use Mutual Funds

By now you understand that the best way to manage your investments is via a long-term approach using extensive diversification and periodic rebalancing. Now let's see why the best way to implement this strategy is by investing in mutual funds. That means you need to understand how mutual funds work. To do that, you should know how they evolved.

The story begins in 1792,[38] when Alexander Hamilton launched a plan to keep our young nation from disintegrating. As the first secretary of the treasury, Hamilton proposed that the federal government assume all the debts that the states incurred in fighting the Revolutionary War.

The states and Congress agreed, but this left Hamilton with a dilemma: The federal government didn't have the money to pay those debts. To raise the cash, Hamilton sold bonds backed by the fledgling U.S. government — in effect launching the first *initial public offering*, or IPO, in the nation's history. In the course of doing so, he essentially invented the public financial markets.[39] Rules for trading these bonds, as well as the handful of stocks then available, were formalized later that year by twenty-four stockbrokers who met under a buttonwood tree in Lower Manhattan. The site, along Wall Street, established what later would be called the New York Stock Exchange.

---

[38]Don't worry, this won't take long.

[39]Hamilton's actions also inadvertently triggered the first instance of widespread securities fraud. The states had sold bonds to finance the Revolutionary War; many who bought them were the troops in General George Washington's army. After the war, with states deeply in debt, many veterans feared that the bonds were worthless, and few knew that Hamilton planned to replace the state bonds with new federal paper. So when those who knew of his plan offered to buy state bonds for pennies on the dollar, most bondholders took the offer — giving the insiders huge profits when Hamilton later redeemed the bonds for full face value. By creating an opportunity for insiders to make huge profits at the expense of Revolutionary War widows and veterans, the first public offering in our nation's history also created the first case of insider trading.

And that was that. For the next two hundred years, the world of investing changed very little; stocks and bonds were pretty much the only regulated investment vehicles available to consumers. (Indeed, trading continued on the streets of Lower Manhattan long after the Buttonwood Agreement was signed, and brokers became known as curb traders; it wasn't until 1836 that the NYSE forced everybody indoors.)

The Curb Market, Midsummer in New York City, 1909

Stocks and bonds both have risk, of course; you pay your money, and you take your chances, as they say. But risk can be reduced with information: Had holders of Revolutionary War bonds known that Hamilton was planning to swap them at full value (see Footnote 39), they would not have sold them for pennies on the dollar.

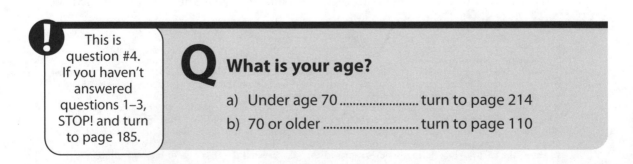

! This is question #4. If you haven't answered questions 1–3, STOP! and turn to page 185.

Q **What is your age?**

a) Under age 70 .... turn to page 214
b) 70 or older .... turn to page 110

Knowledge is not merely power, it's also the key to wealth. That's why critics complain about the lack of disclosure in the world of finance. The first of many efforts to improve corporate disclosure occurred in 1853, when the U.S. government required corporations to disclose their distributions of shares and capital. Other improvements would follow:

1866   Rules adopted for the issuance of new public offerings.

1869   Corporate shares must be registered.

1895   Companies must issue annual reports.

1899   Companies must issue regular financial statements.

1911   States began enacting "blue-sky laws" requiring state registration of securities.

1926   Equal voting rights established for shareholders.

1933   The Securities Act created. Often regarded as the "truth in securities" law, it requires that securities being offered for public sale disclose financial and other significant information. The law also prohibits deceit, misrepresentations, and other fraud in the sale of securities.

1934   The Securities Exchange Act is passed. It creates the Securities and Exchange Commission, granting it broad authority — including disciplinary powers — over all aspects of the securities industry.

1940   The Investment Advisers Act is approved, requiring that those who receive compensation for advising others about securities investments must register with the SEC and conform to regulations designed to protect investors.

How did the prime rate gets its name?

No, its moniker does not derive from the fact that the prime rate is the "best" interest rate; banks' best customers routinely pay less than prime.

In 1802 a broker named Nathaniel Prime began publishing a list of bonds so that investors could check prices and interest rates. Prime's list became known as Prime's Rates and — well, you know the rest.

1956   The New York Stock Exchange urges companies to place outsiders on their boards of directors.

1959   The New York Stock Exchange discourages insider transactions.

1970   Congress creates the Securities Investor Protection Corporation to restore funds to investors whose assets are held by brokerage firms that are bankrupt or financially troubled. (SIPC does not combat fraud.)

1973   The New York Stock Exchange issues a white paper on corporate disclosure.

2000   The SEC issues Regulation Fair Disclosure to prevent public companies from disclosing information to market analysts and important shareholders without simultaneously informing the public.

2002   The Sarbanes-Oxley Act is created in response to the debacles at Enron, WorldCom, and other companies. SOX is designed to enhance corporate responsibility and financial disclosures while combating corporate and accounting fraud. President George W. Bush calls SOX "the most far-reaching reforms of American business practices since the time of Franklin Delano Roosevelt."

It's hard to believe that consumers were willing to buy stocks when they didn't know how many shares were being issued, when they weren't permitted to vote at annual meetings, when companies released no financial information, when fraud was legal, and when companies were permitted (as recently as 1999) to disclose important information to Wall Street insiders and favored shareholders before informing everyone else. Thanks to government reforms over the past two centuries, the system provides a higher level of fairness than ever before.

> But is everything perfect? Far from it. In its annual report to Congress in 2005, the SEC said, "There remains room for improvement in the transparency of financial reporting." And in December 2006, the SEC voted to propose a rule that would prohibit fraud by investment advisors who deal with hedge funds. The SEC didn't actually make hedge fund fraud a crime, mind you. It merely *proposed* to do so. It will decide later whether or not to actually make fraud a crime.

But let's face it: Transparency concerns do not keep most people away from the stock market. No, people stay away for a much more fundamental reason: They simply can't afford it.

It takes money to buy a stock, and owning just one is risky. You can reduce your risk by owning lots of stocks, but that's impossible if you have a limited amount of money.

Fortunately, there's a simple, elegant solution: You simply pool your money with some friends, and the total is used to buy a variety of stocks. As a result, you and your friends own more stocks than any of you would have been able to afford on your own.

Congratulations! You've just invented a mutual fund; you each have a *mutual* interest in a *fund* containing stocks. Thanks to this concept, you no longer need a huge amount of money; these days you can join a fund with as little as $25.[40] You get the same level of professional management that big investors get, with the likelihood of substantially better returns and greater safety, thanks to the wonders of diversification.

Less Filling *and* Tastes Great: The Incredible Power of Mutual Funds

Investors are a notoriously demanding bunch. They want high returns *and* low risks. And amazingly, mutual funds deliver.

Consider the study reported in the March 2007 issue of *Financial Planning* magazine. Based on Morningstar data over the past one-, three-, five-, and ten-year periods (as of December 31, 2006), researchers at the University of Missouri-Columbia showed that, on average, 35.3% of all U.S. stocks managed to lose money, compared to only 3.5% of U.S. stock mutual funds. <u>In other words, by investing in a stock instead of a mutual fund, you were ten times more likely to lose money.</u>

---

[40]Admittedly, this removes status as a reason for owning mutual funds. I mean, you can't brag to your friends, "Hey, guess what! I just bought a *mutual fund*!" You'd have better luck with a jar of Grey Poupon.

Furthermore, the data show, the median return of all U.S. stocks for these time periods was 8.2%, compared to 9.9% for U.S. stock mutual funds. <u>In other words, by investing in the typical stock instead of the typical stock fund, you made 21% less money.</u>

Since you're a long-term investor, look closest at the 10-year data. Comparing the frequency of negative returns to the number of securities that existed for the entire 10 years (as shown in Figure 3.1), you can see that 1,134 individual stocks lost money compared to just six stock mutual funds.

What's even more astonishing is that this abysmal performance by individual stocks was not an aberration. In *Discover the Wealth Within You*, I showed you data for the 10-year period of 1990–1999. Those results, which *didn't* include the 2000–2002 bear market, were the same: 22% of stocks lost money in that decade, compared to 0.4% of stock funds, and the median gain for stocks was 9%, compared to 15% for stock funds.

There is no question that, over long periods, diversification offers you higher returns and lower risks, and there is no question that you can achieve diversification more effectively through mutual funds than any other way.

Figure 3.1

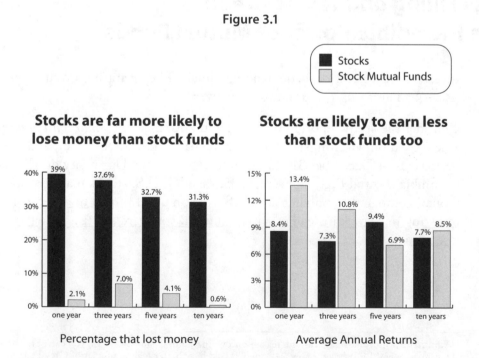

All data as of December 31, 2006

Scotch, Golf, and . . . Mutual Funds

Scotland, of course, is famous for inventing scotch whisky and golf. But would you have guessed that it also invented the mutual fund?

Indeed, the first mutual fund was opened for business in 1815 by Scottish sea merchants who wanted to protect the families of the men lost at sea. Today the Scottish Widows Fund is one of Europe's largest financial institutions, managing £99 billion ($191 billion) in assets.

**Corporate Logo of the
Scottish Widows Fund**

SCOTTISH WIDOWS
preparation is everything

Corporate logo/photo courtesy of Scottish Widows.

(Maybe it's just me, but I would not have guessed that Scottish widows look like this.)

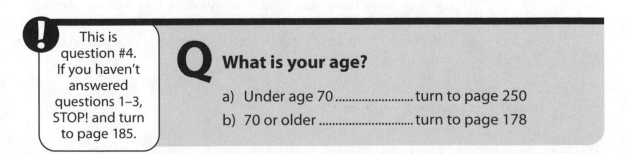

This is question #4. If you haven't answered questions 1–3, STOP! and turn to page 185.

Q **What is your age?**

a) Under age 70 .... turn to page 250

b) 70 or older .... turn to page 178

The first pooled fund in the United States was established by Harvard University in 1893 for its faculty and staff. Then, in 1924, the first true mutual fund (as we know it today) was established.

But there were no regulations governing these investments. As a result, investors couldn't be sure they were receiving their fair share, nor did sponsors disclose what they were collecting in fees. To solve the problem, Congress created the Investment Company Act of 1940. This landmark legislation legitimized mutual funds and standardized their operations.

Thus, a mutual fund is an "investment company" (one of several types covered by the law) — a company whose purpose is to invest in other companies.

And that's all there is. Stock and bond trading was regulated shortly after our nation was born, and investment companies (mutual funds) became official in 1940. These remain your investment choices today.

That's all there is? Stocks, bonds, and investment companies?

Yep, that's it.

But what about options, warrants, and commodity and currency futures?

Those are all variations of stocks, also known as equities. Say you invest in some shares of a bank's stock. By doing so, you become an owner of the bank. The more shares you buy, the bigger your share of ownership. With options, warrants, and futures, you obtain the right to buy (or sell) stock at some predetermined date and price.

What, then, are bank accounts, certificates of deposit, money markets, junk bonds, government securities, collateralized mortgage obligations, fixed annuities, and so on?

They are all variations of bonds. When you invest in these securities, you are acting as a lender; you hope the borrower pays you interest and returns your money to you at some predetermined date. Say you invest in a bank CD. You are loaning your money to the bank — you are not becoming an owner of the institution. In exchange for your loan, the bank pays you interest and promises to return your capital in the future.

Thus, stockholders care about the company's profitability; debtholders care only that the company remains in business.

Oh yeah? Well, what about real estate investment trusts (REITs), unit investment trusts (UITs), closed-end funds, variable annuities, and hedge funds?

All of them are investment companies, regulated by the '40 Act just like mutual funds. (Except for that last one: Hedge funds are exempt from '40 Act registration and are thus largely unregulated. Congress is debating legislation to fix this.)

The only investments not covered above are such assets as real estate, artwork, rare coins and stamps, and other collectibles. None of these is a registered security, and all are equities.

And what about investing in insurance?

Well, we haven't gotten to chapter 13 yet. Before we get there, there's much more to cover. Put on your seat belt, because the next chapter reveals the horrifying behavior of the retail mutual fund industry. Then you'll discover how to fight back and win — how to restore sanity to your investments and avoid the high risks, excessive fees, and lower returns of the retail fund world so that you obtain the financial success you want for yourself and your family. Much later, we'll talk about insurance as an investment.

! This is question #2. If you haven't answered question #1, STOP! and turn to page 185.

Q **Will you be adding money to this account on a regular basis?**

a) Yes .... turn to page 115
b) No .... turn to page 268

Chapter 4
The Demise of the Retail Mutual Fund Industry

I've explained why we love mutual funds, and why we've used them in our financial planning practice for more than twenty years. Unfortunately, the retail mutual fund industry no longer operates the way it once did. That's why, wherever possible, we have sold all our retail mutual funds and why you should too.

When I started investing in mutual funds in the 1980s, the industry's top concern was serving shareholders. Today, though, the industry is more concerned with making profits for itself than serving its shareholders. This comes at the expense of people like you and me who have invested our life's savings in mutual funds. As a result, owners of retail mutual funds today often earn lower returns, incur higher risks, and pay more in fees and taxes than we should.

Indeed, here are an astonishing twenty-five business practices that are common in today's retail mutual fund industry:

1. Frequent Manager Changes

Half of retail mutual fund managers have been on the job for only three years, according to Lipper Analytical Services, and 20% have less than two years of experience. Only 8% have been managing their funds for ten years or more.

This high rate of change in management creates havoc for your investments. According to the *Wall Street Journal*, new managers replace an average of 95% of a fund's investments, in many cases changing the basic nature of their funds — all without shareholder knowledge or consent. (For an example, read about **Style Drift** on page 97.)

> ~~When a tree falls in th~~ When a fund manager leaves, does anyone notice?
>
> Usually not, at least not right away. That's because funds are required to report such changes only in the prospectus — a document that is printed only once a year, and which most investors never bother to read. Thus, it might take you months to learn that your manager has left, and you might not ever realize it. Yet that manager is responsible for your fund's performance. Replacing him is as significant as replacing the driver of a race car.

2. Manager Moonlighting

What's worse than having a manager quit your fund? Having one stay while working somewhere else. According to Morningstar, 450 fund managers (including some at Vanguard, Pioneer, Nationwide, and Ameriprise Financial) were also running hedge funds in 2006. That's a 206% increase since 2002. At this rate, the majority of retail mutual fund managers will be in the hedge fund business in less than five years.

The trend has regulators and consumer advocates worried. They note that hedge funds reap as much as 5% in fees *plus* 44% of the profits, according to *Money Management Executive,* while mutual funds earn only a 1% fee. This could cause managers to work harder for their rich hedge fund clients than their ordinary retail mutual fund shareholders.

Worse, they could manipulate their activities to boost the hedge fund's return at the expense of the retail mutual fund. For example, if a manager holds the same stock in both portfolios, he could sell the hedge fund's position first if he fears that doing so might cause the stock price to decline. That way, the retail mutual fund gets stuck with the lower price. Or he might engage in "cherry picking" (similar to **Fund Seeding**, page 108) — the practice of buying a stock and decid-

The managers of mutual funds have enjoyed virtually free rein to place their interests ahead of the interests of the owners of their funds.

~John Bogle

ing *later* whether to allocate the shares to the hedge fund or the retail mutual fund — depending on how profitable the trade turns out to be. In another example, the manager might sell the shares in one portfolio and buy them in another, to the benefit of the hedge fund, where the fund's take is twenty times larger.

Susan Wyderko, former director of the SEC's Office of Investor Education and Assistance, told Congress in 2006 that moonlighting "presents significant conflicts of interest that could lead the advisor to favor the hedge fund over other clients."

She appears to be right: When hedge funds and retail mutual funds were managed by the same person, the hedge funds earned 1.2% more per year, according to a ten-year study by the Mason School of Business at the College of William and Mary and the University of Pennsylvania's Wharton School of Business.

Further evidence that hedge funds are out-muscling mutual funds comes from Greenwich Associates, which found that the average hedge fund pays $33 million a year in brokerage commissions, compared to $16 million for mutual funds. Hedge funds generate additional business for brokerage firms too, including prime brokerage, securities loans, and complex trades. As a result, says an analysis published by Bloomberg, brokerage firms instruct their analysts to brush aside mutual fund managers so they can spend more time with hedge fund managers, who are deemed to be more lucrative clients. Consequently, retail mutual funds can't get the information they need to make good investment decisions.

3. High Turnover

Forty years ago, according to the Investment Company Institute, the average holding period for securities held inside retail mutual funds was five years. That was indeed long-term investing — exactly what we want from our investments. But today the average holding period is less than a year, according to Morningstar.

This is question #4. If you haven't answered questions 1–3, STOP! and turn to page 185.

Q What is your age?

a) Under age 70 .... turn to page 239

b) 70 or older .... turn to page 288

Figure 4.1

Mutual funds used to hold stocks for more than five years before selling them. The typical holding period is now less than six months.

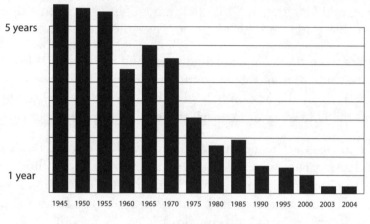

Stock Holding Periods

Figure 4.2

Mutual funds used to sell less than 20% of their holdings each year. Now they flip the entire portfolio more than once a year.

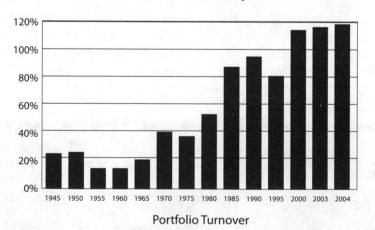

Portfolio Turnover

This excessive trading, called *turnover*, occurs because retail mutual fund managers are trying to capture short-term gains. That's risky, because such profits are elusive. It's expensive too, because the high turnover generates substantial trading costs. And when the retail mutual fund does manage to capture a short-term profit, you and I are forced to pay very high taxes. In fact, we may pay as much as three times more in taxes on these short-term profits than if trading were kept to a minimum. Higher risks, higher fees, and higher taxes. It's a bad combination. And it gets worse, due to…

> *The burden [of fund fees] may cause American equity investors, overall, to earn only 80% or so of what they would earn if [the fund managers] just sat still.*
>
> ~Warren Buffett

4. Style Drift and Bracket Creep

When a manager sells a stock, he replaces it — but often with an entirely different *kind* of stock. If you bought a retail mutual fund because it owned growth stocks, you might be upset to discover that the fund replaced its growth stocks with value stocks (a phenomenon known as style drift) or replaced its mid-cap stocks with large-cap stocks (bracket creep).

In the past, retail mutual funds enjoyed low turnover, and that meant high consistency in a fund's holdings. But with all the constant buying and selling by today's retail mutual fund managers, it's impossible to keep up with all the changes! As a result, you no longer know what your portfolio holds.

How common is this problem? Studies by Morningstar, the University of Missouri, and Northwestern University all show that more than half of all retail mutual funds drift annually from their investment objective. For example, in February 2006, according to Morningstar, more than one hundred retail U.S. stock funds had placed 20% or more of their assets into foreign securities.

> One of the most egregious examples of style drift is Fidelity Magellan, one of the largest retail stock mutual funds in the country (more than five million people own Magellan). In May 1996 its manager, Jeffrey Vinik, decided to place 30% of the fund's assets into bonds, betting that interest rates would decline. He guessed wrong, the fund took a huge loss, and Vinik was replaced by Robert Stansky.

How could the manager of a *stock* fund place 30% of the fund's assets into *bonds*? Amazingly, SEC rules at the time permitted retail mutual funds to invest up to 35% of the assets *without regard* to the fund's objectives. So even though Vinik was managing a stock fund, he was permitted to invest a third of the assets elsewhere — without informing shareholders and without obtaining their consent.

The SEC now says that 80% of a retail mutual fund's assets must conform to the fund's objective (as stated in the prospectus). But this still lets fund managers do as they please with 20% of the assets entrusted to them.

And many retail mutual fund companies have rewritten their prospectuses to give their managers virtually unlimited flexibility to invest as they wish. For example, when Harry Lange took over Magellan in November 2005, he abandoned former manager Stansky's tack of mimicking the S&P 500 Stock Index[41] and drastically altered Magellan's composition. Lange has referred to his strategy — and I'm quoting here — as a "go anywhere fund."[42]

Shareholders probably wish that Lange "went somewhere else." In 2006, his first full year at Magellan's helm, the fund gained 7.2%, compared to 15.8% for the S&P 500. And Magellan's investors are paying dearly for that poor performance. According to a study by the State University of New York, 91% of Magellan's U.S. stock holdings mimic the S&P 500 (a reference to **Closet Indexing** — more on this soon), while only 9% of the stock picks are based on Lange's acumen. But Magellan charges its investors 0.70% per year, while Fidelity's Spartan S&P 500 Index Fund charges only 0.18% per year.

If 91% mimics the index, then 91% of its fee should be assessed at the rate of its index fund's fee. That means 91% should be charged 0.18%, and 9% should be charged 0.70%. That means Magellan's fee should be 0.23%, or two-thirds less than it really charges investors. Stated another way, Magellan's investors are paying 5.87% per year for the portion of the fund that Lange is actually managing — meaning Lange must earn nearly 6% per year for his investors to break even. Is that a bet you'd want to make?

Fidelity Magellan is closed to new investors. But that doesn't explain why existing investors still own it.

---

[41]See **Closet Indexing** on page 101.
[42]And go anywhere it has. As of July 2006, nearly 30% of Magellan's assets were placed in foreign stocks.

5. Excessive Cash or Margin

Another reason your retail mutual fund might not perform as you might expect is because it hasn't invested all the money you've given it. If you invest $100,000 in a stock fund, you expect to own $100,000 worth of stocks, right? But in 2002, according to Carpenter Analytical Services, the average retail mutual fund manager invested only 85% of the money that investors provided; the other 15% was kept in cash. The typical investor is not aware of this.

Worse, Carpenter's analysis shows, by 2006 the typical retail mutual fund had not only eliminated that cash position, but it went out and *borrowed* money to boost its total investments to $121,000 for every $100,000 invested.

This is called *buying on margin*, and it allows a fund to take out loans and invest the borrowed money. The fund — or, rather, its investors — must pay interest on this loan. The manager is betting that the fund will earn enough money to cover this cost, but if he's wrong — if prices decline — the fund's investors will not only lose money on their investments, they'll lose even *more* money as they're forced to pay the interest on the loan.

These practices dramatically increase a fund's volatility: When money is held in cash, its results are truncated, and when

> Watch out for the retail mutual fund industry's latest gimmick: 130/30 funds. For every $100 that investors contribute, these funds buy $100 in stocks. Then they "short" $30 worth of stocks — meaning they sell stocks they don't actually own — and use the proceeds to buy more stocks.
>
> This is an extremely risky strategy. By selling stocks you don't own, you're gambling that the prices will fall (so you can buy them back at lower prices); losses are therefore potentially unlimited. You also incur interest expenses, which you're forced to pay whether your strategy succeeds or fails. If that's not bad enough, the *Wall Street Journal* says most retail mutual fund managers don't have experience shorting stocks.

! This is question #3. If you haven't answered questions 1–2, STOP! and turn to page 185.

Q How much cash do you have in reserves?

a) Less than 12 months of expenses......turn to page 103

b) 12 months of expenses or more...........turn to page 62

money is borrowed, its profits and losses are exaggerated. In each case, investors are hard pressed to understand what's going on or why.

Margin is but one way that retail mutual fund managers can *leverage* their portfolios (meaning, invest more money than investors provide them). Many retail mutual fund prospectuses permit managers to invest in derivatives, options and futures contracts, and other speculative ways that are really nothing more than big bets. These strategies increase investor costs and risks and are undertaken without investor knowledge.

6. Window Dressing

You want to buy a fund that owns stocks that have performed well. So what does a retail mutual fund manager do if his fund doesn't own top-performing stocks? He simply buys them after the fact! That way, you'll see those stocks listed when you review the semiannual or annual report. Clever, huh?

Conveniently for the managers, the reports don't disclose when the fund bought its stocks or the prices it paid, so casual readers have no way of knowing that *Window Dressing* has occurred. According to a study by Northwestern University, 15% of all retail mutual funds engage in this practice, resulting in high turnover, high expenses, and poor performance.

7. Misleading Fund Names

More than half of all retail mutual funds — 54% — are misclassified, according to a study by Yale University, published in the *Journal of Economics and Business*. A "growth" fund might own value stocks, while a "large-cap" fund may own small- and mid-cap stocks. As a result, investors don't own what they think they own much of the time.

8. Cosmetic Name Changes

Since 2000, hundreds of retail mutual funds have changed their names. Purdue University discovered that when funds change their names to reflect whatever is in vogue, the new names attract disproportionately large amounts of new money from investors — 28% more than normal. The Purdue scholars found that this is true even for funds that experience no other changes, such as in the fund's management, investments, or methods.

Thus, while the new name boosts the fund's assets (and profits for the fund company), there are no benefits for you. As the study concluded, "Investors are irrationally influenced by cosmetic changes."

9. Closet Indexing

One in three retail mutual funds that claim to be "actively managed" actually contain portfolios that largely mimic the S&P 500 Stock Index or some other common benchmark, according to a 2006 study by Yale University professors, but such closet indexers charge fees that are up to ten times more than what investors would pay for an index fund.

Managers mimic indexes to avoid the risk that their stock picks might perform far worse than the index by which they're measured. If that were to happen, investors would leave, and the manager would be fired. To prevent this, the manager simply imitates the S&P 500. This way, his results will be similar, and he doesn't have to worry that he might lose his job.

According to the February 2007 issue of *Investment Advisor* magazine, the average stock mutual fund mimics a stock index to such a degree that the real cost for managing the "active" portion of the portfolio is 5.2% per year.

"If you want active management," says a researcher quoted in *Financial Planning* magazine, "make sure you get what you pay for. There are many funds in the closet, charging fees for very little active management."

10. Funds That Close and Reopen

There's a truism that New Yorkers never visit the Statue of Liberty. After all, why should they? It will always be there. But if you were to suddenly announce that Lady Liberty is closing, people would stand in line for hours to see her before it was too late.

The same phenomenon occurs with retail mutual funds: People throw money at funds that announce they are closing. The new assets generate additional profits for the retail mutual fund companies, but the new assets do not boost performance or lower fees, so investors receive no benefit.

In fact, they might incur significant harm. Morningstar examined all retail mutual funds that closed from 1980 through 1996. It found that in the three years prior to closing, each fund's performance was among the top 20% of all funds. But in the three years after closing, the fund's average performance fell to the bottom 62nd percentile.

And then guess what happens a couple of years after a retail mutual fund has closed? Yep, the company reopens it. The press release generates another wave of new money, from investors who treat the news as they do when a once-famous rock group comes out of retirement to sell tickets to its reunion tour at exorbitant prices. Such marketing gimmicks serve only the retail mutual fund company, not its investors.

It's bad when investors throw money at funds that are closing strictly for marketing reasons. But is it OK to invest if the fund is closing for legitimate reasons?

No.

The most legitimate reason for closing a fund is its size: Some funds simply get too big for the manager to be able to handle effectively. To stop the inflows, the company announces that the fund will close. Unfortunately, the announcement causes new investors to rush in — and the new money makes the problem even worse. (Consider a person jumping into an elevator just after the elevator operator says, "I'm about to close the door because there are already too many people inside!")

According to Morningstar and Lipper, this is exactly what happens. Examining eight retail mutual funds that closed, they found that in the twelve months prior to closing, the average gain was 46.9%; in the twelve months afterward, the average gain was a paltry 1.8%.

> If a retail mutual fund closes because it's too big, does closing the fund solve the problem?
>
> Unfortunately, no. When a fund closes, that merely means it won't open new accounts. But existing shareholders are free to add money — and they often do. Also, many funds are used by 401(k) plans, whose participants add to their holdings with every paycheck. Finally, the fund will grow in size as its assets appreciate in value. Being in a fund that was closed because it was too big is like being trapped in an elevator filled with pregnant passengers who are all about to give birth. If you think size was a problem before, just wait.

11. Fund Bloating

The above suggests that some funds legitimately close because they are too big, but that doing so doesn't solve the problem. So does this mean that the funds are better off staying open?

Nope, that doesn't work, either. Consider that the average large-cap stock fund has $18 billion in assets, according to Morningstar. What, then, might you think about the Growth Fund of America, which was worth $147 billion as of December 31, 2006?

> The Growth Fund of America has nearly doubled in size since 2003; it's so big that in 2006 Morningstar called for its sponsor, American Funds, to close it, arguing that the fund practically mirrors the S&P 500 (see **Closet Indexing** on page 101). But American Funds has said it will not close the fund. As a result, GFA continues to open new accounts and collect new assets.

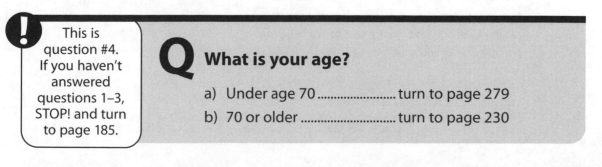

This is question #4. If you haven't answered questions 1–3, STOP! and turn to page 185.

Q **What is your age?**

a) Under age 70 .... turn to page 279

b) 70 or older .... turn to page 230

American Funds's position is understandable. The company makes money managing assets, so the more it manages, the more money it makes. It has become the largest retail mutual fund family in the country, with $765 billion in stock funds as of December 31, 2006, compared to $684 billion for Vanguard and $663 billion for Fidelity.[43] So why close?

No wonder a 2006 analysis published online by MSNMoney called American "a bad investment idea." I'm not sure I go that far, but the situation is worth pondering.

In the world of retail mutual funds, big isn't better: In a 2004 study, Morningstar ranked all funds according to size and found that the biggest 30% of funds had lower returns than the smallest 30%.

Too often, success breeds failure. Consider that all funds start small. If they perform well, they grow in size (if a fund with $10 million generates a 20% gain, it will now be worth $12 million). The good track record attracts new investors. Soon the fund is awash in new cash.

Eventually (sooner for small-cap funds and later for large-cap funds), the retail mutual fund manager finds that he can't replicate his prior success. Say you're a fund manager, and you decide you like a certain stock. If your fund holds $10 million, and you want to place 3% of your assets in a given stock, you'll invest $300,000. A trade of that size won't get noticed. But if your fund holds $100 billion, you need to invest $300 million — a trade that will literally rock

Want a glimpse of the thinking that guides American Funds? Here are excerpts of a speech by Paul Haaga Jr., vice chairman of Capital Research and Management (the firm that operates American Funds), at the annual conference of the National Investment Company Service Association in 2007:

"We all need critics, but it is only useful when we do not blindly accept what they say."

"Not everyone always wants to beat the S&P 500 Stock Index."

"Why is self-interest a conflict of interest?"

Referring to regulatory issues: "We need to remember that there will be occasional police riots."

This is the type of organization with which you want to invest your life's savings?

---

[43]Vanguard and Fidelity each has more in total assets under management, but that's because they have as much as twenty times more in money market funds, according to Financial Research Corporation. If you look only at assets in stock funds, American is the biggest family.

Wall Street. An order of that size would take weeks to fill and could require you to file with the SEC. Worse, your order will cause the stock's price to skyrocket — giving smaller funds (you used to be one of them, remember) an opportunity to capitalize on the situation. The same problem will occur when you try to sell a large position: Dumping lots of shares onto the Street at one time will cause the price to sink.

It gets even worse when you realize that most funds won't buy more than 10% of a company's outstanding shares. Say that a fund has $50 billion, and its manager likes the stock of a company that has a $100 billion market cap. He'll purchase $100 million worth of shares in that company — which sounds like a big purchase. But it's only 0.2% of the fund's assets, meaning the manager still has to invest the other 99.8% of his fund's assets. Exactly how many "great ideas" can this guy possibly have? Odds are, he'll end up buying stocks that are on his B list or even his C list, simply because he has so much money to spend.

This is why performance wanes as funds grow in size. Big funds tend to buy bigger stocks than they did when they were smaller. Smaller companies have fewer shares outstanding, lower prices, and smaller *float* (fewer shares trade daily) — making it hard to buy in large quantities.

It has happened to every big fund.[44] Big is bulky and cumbersome; small is agile and quick.

12. Cloning

If a retail mutual fund closes, the fund company can't accept new accounts. To solve that problem, it borrows an idea from Hollywood and releases a sequel. The XYZ Fund II, it tells you, is just as good as the original XYZ Fund. What isn't touted is the fact that the clone's objective — and even its manager — may be different from the original, meaning the clone will not perform like the original. That concern is irrelevant to the retail mutual fund industry; what matters is that the ploy attracts new money from investors.

---

[44]The most famous example is Fidelity Magellan. It held a mere $22 million in assets in 1977. After it set records, it grew to $100 billion by 1999 and has been mediocre ever since.

13. Survivorship Bias

Retail mutual fund companies are happy to tell you how they've done overall. If they offer one hundred funds, they'll tell you the average return of all their funds — ostensibly to demonstrate to consumers that, overall, they are good at managing money. (After all, if only one fund did well while ninety-nine fared poorly, you'd shy away.)

Unfortunately, the statistics refer only to their funds that currently exist! So if one of the company's funds has been performing poorly for several years, the firm simply terminates the fund or merges it with another. Thus, the offending fund's statistics are wiped away, as though it never existed. This misleads investors into believing that a fund company's overall performance is better than it really is.

This explains why in 1995, Lipper Analytical Services said that the average annual return for retail stock mutual funds in 1986 was 13.4%. Today, though, Lipper says the average return for 1986 was 14.7%. Why the difference? In 1995, 568 retail stock funds had 1986 performance data; but by 2005, only 434 of those funds were still in existence. The other 134 funds had disappeared — 24% of the total! Obviously, those 134 had lower-than-average performance records. Thus, the current record only reflects the results of the funds that still exist.

When a retail mutual fund terminates, it triggers tax liabilities that *you* must pay. Even worse is when a fund is merged into another: You find yourself owning shares of a fund you might not want. In both cases — termination and merger — you get no advance warning and have no say in the matter; the termination or merger occurs whether you like it or not.

Q Will you want to receive income from your account immediately?

This is question #5. If you haven't answered questions 1–4, STOP! and turn to page 185.

a) Yes......**ERROR!** In Question #2, you said you'd make additional deposits, but here in Question #5 you say you want immediate withdrawals. Start over on page 192 — and change one of your answers.

b) No.......**Congratulations!** You've completed Part 1 of the Edelman Guide to Portfolio Selection. **Your Letter Score is B.** Return to page 193 and continue to Part 2.

These strategies didn't exist in the 1980s, but they are rampant today. According to the Center for Research in Security Prices, the CFA Institute, and Morningstar, 5,519 mutual funds were terminated or merged in the first five years of this decade. In the same period of the 1980s, terminations occurred in fewer than 400 funds.

Figure 4-3

Decade	Number of dying funds
1980s	78
1990s	462
2000s	1,045

Failure Rates of Stock Funds

Note: Figures for the 2000s represent the first four years.

14. The Incubation Strategy (Creation Bias)

This is one of the retail mutual fund industry's most devious ploys. Here's how it works: Create a whole bunch of mutual funds. Wait three years. Then evaluate the results of each fund.

The results for each fund will be either good or bad. If a fund's performance was bad, close it before anybody hears about it. But if a fund posts good results, send the data to Morningstar, which will award a five-star rating (Morningstar won't rate funds that are less than three years old.)

Investors love to buy top-rated funds![45] If you incubate enough funds, you can expect at least one of them to post a track record good enough to win Morningstar's blessing — and that will let you collect lots of deposits from new investors who will be happy to invest in the hot new fund. This explains why so many small, young funds

---

[45]In 2006, 60% of all fund purchases went into 4-star and 5-star funds, according to Morningstar.

have 4- and 5-star ratings, and why you rarely see three-year-old funds with just one star. The industry manipulates the process to its advantage.

15. Fund Seeding

When a company issues stock, it offers a limited number of shares. A given retail mutual fund company buys as many shares as it can, and when it does, it doesn't say which of its individual funds is doing the buying.

Later, if the IPO proves to be successful, the fund company disproportionately allocates the shares to its newer, smaller funds. Result: The IPO artificially boosts the return of these funds, supporting the **Incubation Strategy** (see prior page). The investors who buy seeded funds are in for a rude surprise when the fund proves to be incapable of repeating its earlier "success."

16. Confusing Share Classes

Retail mutual funds are now available with a dizzying array of pricing models. In many cases, a single fund might offer a half dozen share classes, and the only difference among them is the cost. If you select the wrong share class, you could pay more than necessary.

It wasn't always this way. In the 1980s there were only two kinds of retail mutual fund shares: load and no-load. Load funds levied a sales charge, or commission, when you bought shares; no-loads didn't. Naturally, investors didn't like to pay loads. But instead of eliminating them, the industry made the loads less obvious.

Its first tactic was to create a *reverse load* fund, where you paid the load when you sold your shares instead of when you bought them. To distinguish these shares from the original load funds, the reverse-load funds were called Class B shares.

Talk about opening Pandora's Box. Today fund investors must choose among Class A, B, C, D, F, I, J, K, M, N, R, S, T, X, Y, and Z shares. Depending on the share class you purchase, you might incur a load when you buy, when you sell, or annually. The load might disappear after a time, or it might remain forever. In some cases, you might enjoy a lower load but incur higher annual expenses, or vice versa.

And in some instances, you might buy one share class only to have your shares automatically converted to another share class in the future!

Which share class is right for you? The answer depends on the amount you initially invest, the amount you plan to invest in the future, when you plan to make those additional investments, how long you plan to leave the money invested, how much you might withdraw in a single year, and how much other members of your family are also investing (both now and in the future).

You obviously want to choose the least expensive share class for your situation. But if your situation develops differently from how you expected, you could find yourself in the wrong share class, paying much more than necessary. I've met a lot of people who are in this predicament.

17. Hidden Fees

You know that all mutual funds charge fees, right? I mean, none of them works for free, right?

I ask because I've occasionally found myself arguing with people over this question. They adamantly claim that they do not pay any fees for their retail mutual funds because they own no-load funds. But as explained above, *load* means "sales charge"; by buying no-load funds, you avoid sales charges.

However, avoiding loads does not mean that you avoid fees. All mutual funds charge a fee. Actually, they charge two. The first is the *Annual Expense Ratio*. This pays for the fund's recurring operating costs, from the fund manager's salary to the toll-free phone number investors call to talk to customer service representatives. The average expense ratio of retail mutual funds is 1.33% per year, according to Morningstar, although many are more than 2%. The highest in the industry is a staggering 15%!

Although the expense ratio is expressed as an annual figure, it's actually debited on a daily basis. But you never notice it, because the charge does not appear on your monthly statement. (It's hidden.) To find it, you must look in the fund's prospectus. There the expense ratio is expressed as a percentage. (The fund further hides the amount you're paying by showing the figure as a percentage instead of dollars.)

Many investors — and, astonishingly, even many investment advisors — think the annual expense ratio covers all of the fund's expenses. But it doesn't. The expense ratio covers only the perennial costs: salaries, marketing, overhead, and the like. There are many variable costs for operating a fund, and these are excluded from the expense ratio. Indeed, a study by Wake Forest University, the University of Florida, and the Zero Alpha Group found that 44% of mutual fund fees are *not* disclosed in the prospectus.

The biggest of these omitted costs is trading expenses. Whenever the retail mutual fund manager buys or sells a security, he pays brokerage commissions (just like you would if you bought or sold a stock or bond). Considering that retail mutual funds trade millions of shares representing billions of dollars, their trading costs are huge — and the more the fund trades, the more it spends on brokerage commissions. According to Greenwich Associates, the average retail mutual fund spends $16 million in trading costs per year.

You own mutual funds in your retirement plan — and those fees deserve scrutiny too.

The U.S. Government Accountability Office says participants in 401(k) plans may be losing thousands of dollars due to excessive fees levied by the retail mutual funds and insurance companies that commonly serve as plan sponsors. The GAO wants the Labor Department to require plan sponsors to submit a regular summary of all expenses paid by plan participants — something they currently are not required to do.

The 401(k) business practices, said the GAO's report, "may not be in the best interests of investors."

But to find them, you must look in the fund's Statement of Additional Information, an arcane document that's even bigger, denser, and harder to read than the prospectus — and which fund companies, stockbrokers, and brokerage firms are not required to give you. To get a copy, you must ask for it; something few investors do, since few have ever heard of the document.

These additional costs represent an average of 1.25% in annual expenses. When you add that to the expenses listed in the prospectus, you find that the average retail mutual fund charges its investors 2.58% per year, according to Morningstar. Compare that to 1945, when the average fund charged only 0.76% per year.

! This is the end of Part 1. If you haven't answered questions 1–4, STOP! and turn to page 185.

Congratulations! You've finished Part 1 of the Edelman Guide to Portfolio Selection.

Your Letter Score is D.

Remember this Letter Score and return to page 193.

Instead of showing the fee you pay in dollars right on your statement, you must look for the fee in the prospectus. Then you must convert the percentage into real numbers. And because almost half of the fund's expenses are not included in the prospectus, you must also turn to the Statement of Additional Information. There you must compute the expenses, determine the ratio of expenses to fund assets, and convert this figure into dollars based on the amount you have invested. In this way, you are able to determine how much you are paying to own your mutual fund.

> So be careful if an advisor tells you his fee is only 1%. He might be quoting his firm's advisory fee rather than the retail mutual fund's expenses, which you must also pay. When you are interviewing potential advisors, make sure they tell you the *total* costs you'll pay to work with them.

The retail mutual fund industry will tell you that it provides full disclosure about its fees. No, they say, nothing is hidden at all.

The fund industry is so good at hiding fees that even MBA students can't figure it out. As part of a test of mutual fund disclosure practices, MBA students at Harvard University, the University of Pennsylvania, and Yale University were given a list of retail mutual funds. Every fund on the list was an S&P 500 Stock Index fund. Researchers asked the students just two questions:

1. What is the most important factor in selecting the best fund from this list?

The correct answer is "the fee" — and every MBA student got it right.[46]

2. Which fund is best?

Obviously, the correct answer is "the cheapest fund." After all, every fund on the list owns identical investments. The students had already agreed that the only difference was cost, so they went about determining which fund was cheapest. Yet, to the astonishment of the faculty, even after being given prospectuses on each fund so they could evaluate the costs, only 20% of the MBA students picked the cheapest one. Eighty percent were incapable of correctly reading the prospectus to determine the correct answer.

And these were MBA students at prestigious universities! What hope is there for ordinary investors?

---

[47]Since all the funds were S&P 500 index funds, their risk and performance were the same. Therefore, the only difference is the fee they charge — making that criterion the most important when choosing among them.

18. Stale Pricing

What is each share of your mutual fund worth? If you're like most investors, you think funds determine the value of the share once per day, right? They multiply the number of shares of each stock they own by each stock's price, and add all that together to produce the total assets. Then they divide that figure by the number of shares outstanding in the mutual fund to produce the Net Asset Value, or share price, of the fund. Right?

Well, theoretically, yes, that's how they're *supposed* to do it. But a 2006 study by Harvard University and Analysis Group confirmed that it is standard practice for retail mutual funds to calculate their NAVs by applying that day's closing prices to the investments they held the day *before*. The methodology is known as *T+1 accounting*.

In other words, Thursday's newspaper shows mutual fund prices that reflect Wednesday's closing values for shares the fund owned on Tuesday. Got that?[47]

T+1 accounting, a relic from days when funds had to calculate prices manually, can be wildly inaccurate. The study cited a fund that reported a 0.7% loss on a day when the fund actually lost 4.7%. In another example, a fund said it earned 3.7% when, in fact, it had gained 5.3%.

There's no reason for funds to continue using T+1 accounting, but they refuse to switch to real-time pricing because of the cost of doing so. But the study makes it clear that the benefits to shareholders far outweigh the expenses. At the very least, say the researchers, funds should be required to disclose how they calculate their daily NAV.

---

[47]In case you don't: The price reported on Thursday fails to take into account all the shares that the fund manager bought or sold on Wednesday.

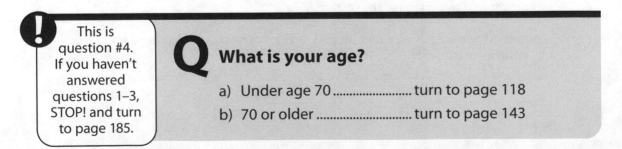

This is question #4. If you haven't answered questions 1–3, STOP! and turn to page 185.

Q **What is your age?**

a) Under age 70 .... turn to page 118

b) 70 or older .... turn to page 143

19. Rising Costs

In 1989 the retail mutual fund industry was managing $500 billion; today its assets are $10 trillion, a twenty-fold increase. This should allow funds to spread the operational costs over a greater asset base, reducing the cost for each shareholder. But instead of reducing expenses, retail mutual fund expense ratios are twice what they were in 1945 (1.33% versus 0.75%).

Indeed, *BusinessWeek* reported in 2004 that many well-known retail mutual funds increased their fees even though they dramatically increased their assets under management. So much for economies of scale.

20. No Discounts for Larger Investors

Whether or not a fund features a load, all mutual funds charge fees. But they don't reduce their large annual fees for investors who invest lots of money! It's true: No matter how much money you invest, you pay the same rate as everyone else. This makes no sense! After all, it doesn't cost a fund company ten times more to process your deposit merely because you add a zero to the check.

Charging all investors the same fee allows fund companies to overcharge consumers who invest more than others. Fund companies should provide economies of scale to save investors money; they don't because doing so would reduce their profits.

And their own profit seems to be all they care about. The few fund companies that are publicly held have all been incredibly profitable. In fact, the number one stock of the past twenty-five years is Franklin Resources, which has posted a 30% average annual return since 1981. A $10,000 investment in Franklin stock would have been worth $6.4 million by December 31, 2006, according to *USA Today*. That's more than you'd have made from Microsoft (23% annual return), or even Warren Buffett's company, Berkshire Hathaway (25% return).

Indeed, you would have fared much better had you invested in Franklin Resources than in its retail stock mutual funds. Whereas Franklin's own share price gained an average of 27.1% per year in the five years ending December 31, 2006, its retail stock funds gained only 7.8% per year, according to Morningstar. Ditto for other publicy traded mutual fund companies, as shown in Figure 4.4

Figure 4.4

The stock prices of mutual funds companies have performed much better than their stock funds

Fund Family	5-Year average of its own share price	Average results of the family's stock funds
Blackrock	30.8%	7.9%
Franklin Resources	27.1%	7.8%
Legg Mason	24.3%	6.6%
T. Rowe Price	22.3%	8.2%

Average Annual Return for the 5-year period ending December 31, 2006.

The conclusion of all this is clear: Too many retail mutual fund companies are now primarily concerned with their own profits instead of the well-being of the people who invest in their funds. As a result of their self-interest:

- They've demoted you from the rank of stock *owner* to that of mere stock *trader*.

- They've put you into investments that are different from what you wanted.

- They're foiling your efforts to follow a long-term buy-and-hold approach.

- They're charging you more for your investments than you should be paying.

- They're forcing you to incur higher and more frequent taxes than necessary.

In short, the retail mutual fund industry's schemes constitute a huge obstacle to your efforts to create wealth.

It would be bad enough if their business practices were the end of the story. But they're not. Unfortunately, *unforgivably*, the previous tactics are just the beginning. Going from distasteful to outright illegal are the following business practices:

21. Illegal Market Timing

Regulators have discovered that dozens of retail mutual fund companies have allowed some investors to shift massive amounts of money in and out of their funds, despite the fact that the practice is prohibited. Market timing increases

---

Investors have paid a staggering price for the excessive costs and excessive marketing focus of the mutual fund industry.

~John Bogle

Want proof that the retail mutual fund industry offers no economy of scale? Consider this: Franklin Templeton funds reported that its assets under management for the quarter ending December 31, 2006, rose 19%. Since Franklin earns a fee managing those assets, you'd assume that its revenue rose similarly. And you'd be right: Franklin reported that revenues were up 21%. And you'd also assume that Franklin's profits would rise by the same amount, right? But here you'd be wrong, for Franklin's quarterly profits rose 34%, amounting to $427 million.

Yes, Franklin Templeton funds earned nearly a half billion dollars in three months. If Franklin had merely tied profits to its asset growth, it still would have earned $264 million, and its fund investors would be saving $163 million *every three months*.

So much for offering investors economies of scale.

! This is question #3. If you haven't answered questions 1–2, STOP! and turn to page 185.

Q How much cash do you have in reserves?

a) Less than 12 months of expenses........turn to page 70

b) 12 months of expenses or more.........turn to page 281

the volatility in the fund's share price and boosts the costs of operating the fund — costs that the other fund investors (you and I) have to pay.

22. Late Trading

Many retail mutual funds have allowed stockbrokers to illegally place trades after the markets close at 4:00 P.M. — essentially betting on a race after it's been run. This has enabled a few crooks to capture millions of dollars in illicit profits at the expense of ordinary investors like you and me.

23. Personal Trading by Portfolio Managers

In perhaps the most egregious examples of fraud and abuse, some retail mutual fund managers were found to have sold stocks in their personal brokerage accounts while buying those same stocks for the mutual funds they've managed. In other words, they're buying a stock for you while they're personally selling it — scoring big profits for themselves in the meantime. This conflict of interest represents the ultimate betrayal.

24. Steering Business

Retail mutual funds are the biggest customers of Wall Street brokerage firms. Regulators have found that some funds steered their trading business to certain brokerage firms in exchange for under-the-table payments.

25. Shelf-Space Payments

More than 58% of investors obtain their retail mutual funds from stockbrokers, according to the Investment Company Institute, but brokers can only sell funds that have been "approved" by their brokerage firms. Regulators have discovered that

Think we'll ever get these scandalous corporate practices behind us? Apparently not. Fifty-six percent of business grad students admit to cheating in the past academic year, according to a study published in *Academy of Management Learning & Education*.

Just wait for these budding MBAs to enter the corporate world.

retail mutual fund companies have paid tens of millions of dollars (called "shelf-space payments")to get on the "approved lists" of the nation's brokerage firms — fees that have not been shared with (or even disclosed to) the brokers or their clients.

For example, in his book *Wall Street Versus America: The Rampant Greed and Dishonesty That Imperil Your Investments,* former *BusinessWeek* investigative reporter Gary Weiss shows that 99.2% of all the mutual fund sales by Smith Barney in 2003 consisted of retail mutual funds that paid extra for the privilege. Smith Barney, with more than thirteen thousand stockbrokers, is the nation's largest brokerage firm.

Think these activities are isolated incidents? Think again. Since October 2003, $5 billion in fines have been assessed against virtually every big-name mutual fund company and brokerage firm in the nation. In response, the SEC has introduced regulations that it says will cost the industry more than $1.1 billion to implement, involving 231 million new pages of disclosure documents requiring 200,000 labor hours to produce and mail — all in an effort to snuff out the scandalous practices. (Guess who pays for that?)

The retail mutual fund scandal began in October 2003 with charges by regulators of improper activity at Putnam Investments. The charges ultimately included the following:

- Some Putnam fund managers were selling stocks in their own accounts while buying the same stocks in the funds they managed,

- Some Putnam employees permitted late trading and market timing in Putnam's funds,

- Putnam was allegedly paying tens of millions of dollars in secret payments to the nation's biggest brokerage firms so that their brokers would push Putnam funds to their clients,

- Putnam's executives knew about much of this, in some cases authorized it and in no case stopped any of it.

I immediately realized that, as awful as all these revelations were, this couldn't be just about Putnam. I suspected that similar kinds of activities might be discovered or alleged to be occurring at other retail mutual fund companies and brokerage firms too. So I began to track the stories. The Mutual Fund Scandal Timeline that follows shows the almost daily announcements and disclosures by federal and state regulators and, sometimes, the companies themselves.

You'll be astonished and probably infuriated by the magnitude of the scandal. Some of the items are so shocking that you'll find yourself laughing — albeit in a sick, twisted sort of way. Reading the timeline will likely convince you that you should not trust your life savings to these people and that you must choose another way. Later in the book, I'll show you that way.

! This is the end of Part 1. If you haven't answered questions 1–4, STOP! and turn to page 185.

Congratulations! You've finished Part 1 of the Edelman Guide to Portfolio Selection.

Your Letter Score is D.

Remember this Letter Score and return to page 193.

THE MUTUAL FUND SCANDAL TIMELINE

The entries in the following timeline are derived from public accounts, such as press releases and news stories. Allegations of misconduct — whether by regulatory or government entities, plaintiffs in civil actions or any other person or entity — do not necessarily indicate that a firm or individual engaged in or was found culpable of the activity alleged, or that charges were ultimately pursued. In some instances, actions may still be pending. In addition, the reader should bear in mind that settlements are typically entered into by firms and individuals without any admission of wrongdoing.

THE THREE KEY ABUSES

KEY ABUSE #1: MARKET TIMING

Mutual funds are designed to be held for years, even decades. Market timing occurs when shares are sold within days or weeks of purchase in an effort to capture short-term price anomalies. The activity creates three problems for mutual funds and their investors: First, trading increases expenses. Second, it reduces returns, because fund managers are forced to maintain larger-than-normal cash positions to accommodate the timers' withdrawal requests. Third, the practice increases volatility. Timers are immune to these problems because they own the shares for such a short period. Thus, it's the fund's ordinary shareholders who suffer the consequences. For this reason, fund prospectuses generally prohibit market timing.

KEY ABUSE #2: LATE TRADING

Mutual funds are priced once per day, after the markets close at 4:00 P.M. It takes a few hours for funds to compute their net asset values, which are based on the number of shares of each security they hold and the closing price of each of those securities. Trades placed after 4:00 P.M. are supposed to be executed on the next trading day. Late trading occurs when such trades are recorded as having occurred prior to the day's close — in essence, enabling investors to "predict" results that have already occurred. It not only gives participants illicit gains, it reduces the returns of the fund's ordinary shareholders.

KEY ABUSE #3: REVENUE SHARING

Mutual fund companies earn fees from managing assets; the more assets they manage, the more fees they collect. Revenue sharing (also known as shelf-space payments) occurs when fund companies secretly pay brokerage firms and financial advisors to get them to sell their products to clients. Clients believe they are receiving recommendations designed for their benefit when, in fact, the firms and their brokers are simply trying to garner extra commissions and other incentives, such as trips to luxury resorts, jewelry, tickets to concerts and sporting events, and other enticements.

2003

10/29/2003 Massachusetts and federal regulators announce plans to file civil complaints against **Putnam Investments**, the nation's fourth largest mutual fund company, alleging that the firm failed to prevent repeated short-term trading by employees and some customers.

11/4/2003 **Putnam** CEO Larry Lasser resigns.

12/02/2003 SEC and New York attorney general say they will recommend enforcement actions against **Invesco Funds** for market-timing violations.

12/8/2003 SEC to recommend enforcement action against **MFS Funds** for market-timing violations.

12/17/2003 Employees at the **Federal Reserve** caught market timing in the Fed's retirement plan account; Fed officials ask them to stop.

12/17/2003 **Putnam Investments** discharges nine employees for improper trading.

12/18/2003 **Alliance Funds** to pay New York $250 million to settle market-timing charges.

12/23/2003 **Principal Financial Group** says some staff improperly traded in their personal accounts.

2004

1/14/2004 Former vice chairman of **Fred Alger Management** sentenced to one to three years in prison for tampering with evidence.

1/20/2004 **MFS** appears to have known about market timing in its funds but was slow to curtail it.

1/23/2004 New York subpoenas **Conseco, Lincoln**, and **Hartford** in connection with variable annuity sales practices.

1/23/2004 **MFS** named in $100 million late-trading scam.

1/30/2004	**Vanguard** employee tells regulators that the firm is unable to service shareholder accounts efficiently.
2/3/2004	New York arrests former executive of **Canadian Imperial Bank of Commerce** for allegedly stealing $1 million from mutual funds in a late-trading scheme.
2/5/2004	Massachusetts regulators say **Franklin Templeton** funds has fraudulently harmed long-term investors by allowing a Las Vegas broker to market-time the funds.
2/5/2004	**CIBC's** world markets head David Kassie quits.
2/6/2004	**MFS** to pay $225 million and cut its fees by $125 million to settle federal and state late-trading charges; two MFS executives suspended.
2/10/2004	**Franklin Templeton** says it expects SEC to file charges against it and two executives for market timing. Investors file lawsuit against the firm.
2/11/2004	Congress proposes legislation that would require mutual funds to disclose hidden fees.
2/12/2004	Fifteen firms settle with SEC and NASD, agreeing to pay a total of $21.5 million to settle charges they did not provide investors with discounts when buying mutual funds.
2/18/2004	New Jersey regulators sue four entities related to **PIMCO** funds, saying they defrauded investors by allowing a hedge fund to trade improperly.
2/18/2004	**MFS** says it is under SEC investigation related to directed-brokerage and revenue-sharing arrangements with brokerage firms.
2/19/2004	CalPERS, largest pension fund in U.S., puts **Franklin Templeton** on probation amid SEC probe.
2/19/2004	North Carolina blasts mutual fund industry for paying association dues with investors' money.
2/20/2004	**State Street** to pay $1.5 million to settle NASD market-timing charges.
2/24/2004	SEC says three **FleetBoston** mutual funds, including one designed for kids, allowed market timing.

2/25/2004	**Fidelity** tells Massachusetts regulators that 12(b)(1) fees are "fair."
2/26/2004	Senate bill on mutual funds calls for disclosure of actual costs paid by shareholders.
2/26/2004	**FleetBoston** puts eight executives on leave for market timing.
2/26/2004	In an effort to stifle market timing, SEC might make 2% redemption fees mandatory for shares redeemed within five days of purchase.
2/27/2004	West Virginia subpoenas mutual fund trading records of **Strong Funds** and **Morgan Stanley.**
2/27/2004	**AXA Financial** to pay NASD fine to settle charges that clients paid fees to transfer money between funds; transfers were supposed to be free.
3/3/2004	**Putnam** says two executives have left the firm following discovery of "operational errors."
3/3/2004	**RS Investments** says it expects fraud charges pertaining to market-timing allegations.
3/7/2004	SEC probes **MetLife** for market timing in its mutual funds and variable annuities.
3/16/2004	**Bank of America** and **FleetBoston** to pay $675 million fine settling mutual-fund trading allegations.
3/19/2004	NASD investigates six securities firms for misconduct in sales of 529 college savings plans.
3/23/2004	**Putnam** says three top execs knew of managers' improper mutual fund trades.

! This is question #5. If you haven't answered questions 1–4, STOP! and turn to page 185.

Q Will you want to receive income from your account immediately?

a) Yes ....Your letter score is L.
b) No ....Your letter score is J.

Congratulations! You're finished with Part 1 of the Edelman Guide to Portfolio Selection. Remember your Letter Score and return to page 193.

3/25/2004	New York attorney general blasts mutual fund boards for poor oversight.
3/25/2004	Consumer Federation of America pressures Congress to reform mutual fund industry.
3/25/2004	SEC says portfolio manager pay at **Putnam** is "lavish."
3/29/2004	Two more **Putnam** fund managers resign.
3/29/2004	New York may force **Janus** funds CEO to resign.
3/30/2004	President of **Federated** funds quits amid late-trading allegations.
3/31/2004	**RS Investments** near settlement with New York about market timing.
3/31/2004	**Edward D. Jones & Co**. says SEC might file charges of revenue-sharing violations.
3/31/2004	**MFS** to pay $50 million fine to settle SEC action for not disclosing directed-brokerage agreements.
4/2/2004	Massachusetts looking into whether **Putnam** issued rebates to favored 401(k) plans.
4/3/2004	Federal judges hold hearing on one hundred private lawsuits against six mutual fund companies that allowed wealthy clients to market-time and late-trade.
4/5/2004	SEC may ask court to make **Putnam** pay $830 million in fines.
4/7/2004	SEC examining **Morgan Stanley** for potential market timing in mutual funds; two Morgan Stanley executives fired.
4/8/2004	**Janus** announces it paid lofty bonuses to senior executives.
4/8/2004	**Scudder** funds admits problems in the way it calculated fund expenses.
4/9/2004	**Putnam** admits employees cheated in retirement plans.
4/9/2004	**Putnam** to pay $110 million to settle federal and state allegations of improper market timing in its mutual funds.

America's mutual fund industry has lost its way.
~John Bogle

4/13/2004	**David Lerner Associates** to pay $100,000 to settle NASD charges that it conducted illegal mutual fund sales contests.
4/21/2004	**Janus** funds chief executive quits amid mutual fund probe.
4/22/2004	Department of Labor launches mutual fund investigation to see if market timing and sales practices have harmed workers investing in retirement plans.
4/27/2004	NASD issues rules requiring brokers to make sure investors understand variable annuities.
4/28/2004	**Janus** to pay $100 million in fines and restitution to investors and to reduce fees $125 million to settle charges that it allowed abusive trading in its mutual funds.
5/6/2004	**Jefferson National Life Insurance Co.,** a former unit of Conseco, says it may be charged by regulators for improper fund trading within its annuities.
5/7/2004	SEC files fraud charges against **PIMCO** funds for market timing.
5/7/2004	Canadian insurance giant ends relationship with **Putnam** because of timing scandal.
5/10/2004	**Janus** talking with SEC about its relationships with brokers.
5/10/2004	New York subpoenas **Putnam** over 401(k) fee rebates.
5/11/2004	**Prudential** probed regarding sales practices of mutual funds and variable annuities.
5/12/2004	Ontario Securities Commission reviews Canadian mutual funds, looking for trading abuses and undisclosed market timing.
5/12/2004	Federal regulators ask if banks pressure their mutual fund units to buy the banks' IPOs.
5/12/2004	**Seligman Funds** says it reimbursed investors $3.7 million for losses incurred by market timing.
5/12/2004	NASD forms task force to make mutual fund costs and distribution agreements more transparent to investors.

5/14/2004	SEC says 12(b)(1) fees benefit mutual fund companies, not shareholders.
5/14/2004	SEC says unit of **MetLife** may be charged for letting investors market-time annuities.
5/17/2004	SEC identifies weak broker-dealer practices regarding sales suitability, disclosure, supervision, training, and records maintenance for variable annuities.
5/19/2004	**Franklin Templeton** funds anticipates settlement with SEC for allowing investors to time its funds.
5/20/2004	**Strong Funds** and founder Richard Strong to pay a total of $140 million to settle fraud charges concerning undisclosed mutual fund trading.
5/20/2004	NASD fines **American Express** $300,000 over revenue-sharing agreements with mutual funds.
5/20/2004	NASD fines three securities firms and one broker a total of $503,000 to settle charges of faulty record keeping and inadequate variable annuity sales procedures and marketing materials.
5/26/2004	SEC enhances disclosure of mutual fund discounts.
5/26/2004	**Putnam, Janus** lose a total of $3.9 billion in assets in April as investors pull money out.
5/27/2004	SEC investigates trading practices and procedures at **Wellington**, subadvisor to Vanguard Funds.
5/28/2004	SEC warns of enforcement actions against **Empire Financial** for market timing and late trading.
6/2/2004	**Davenport** to pay NASD $738,000 to settle charges that variable annuity shareholders were harmed by the firm's market timing and late trading of mutual fund shares.
6/7/2004	U.S. requests information from **AIM** funds.
6/10/2004	Schwab CEO David Pottruck says he expects fund scandal to grow.

6/11/2004	Former **Putnam** CEO Larry Lasser to receive $78 million as he severs ties with firm.
6/14/2004	New York investigates conflict of interest over fees insurers pay brokers to sell their products.
6/16/2004	Regulators shift focus to sales practices of variable annuities.
6/17/2004	SEC puts **Bear Stearns** on notice of possible civil charges for improper mutual fund trading.
6/19/2004	Three senior executives at **Invesco** depart over market-timing scandal at firm.
6/22/2004	**Pilgrim Funds** to pay $100 million to settle SEC charges it allowed select clients to engage in market timing.
6/22/2004	**Smith Barney** and **Salomon** sued; investors say they offered rewards to brokers who pushed their funds.
6/24/2004	Five brokerage firms to pay $625,000 to NASD to settle charges relating to lax trading guidelines.
6/25/2004	**Empire Financial** CEO resigns amid SEC probe of mutual fund trading practices.
6/30/2004	**Bank One** to pay $90 million for its role in mutual fund scandal.
7/2/2004	**Goldman Sachs** to pay $2 million to settle SEC charges relating to making illegal offers of securities.
7/2/2004	SEC questions **MainStay Fund**'s "guarantee" that shareholders will be made whole in 10 years if their investments fall below original value.
7/7/2004	SEC asks **Putnam** and **T. Rowe Price** about their revenue-sharing arrangements with 401(k) administrators.
7/9/2004	SEC announces plan to expand number of individuals facing fraud charges for abusive trades at **Invesco**.
7/12/2004	**Fremont Investment Advisors** may face SEC action for market timing.

7/15/2004	SEC says five former **Prudential Securities** brokers used false identities to trade $1.3 billion in market-timing scheme.
7/19/2004	Three **Invesco** execs leave amid allegations they let investors market-time.
7/21/2004	Investors file class action suit against **Salomon Brothers** and **Smith Barney** for allegedly breaching fiduciary duties by steering them to more expensive funds.
8/3/2004	**Franklin Templeton** funds to pay $50 million for market timing.
8/3/2004	**Fidelity Brokerage Services** to pay $2 million to settle SEC and NYSE charges of document alteration and destruction.
8/6/2004	**Piper Jaffray** says it faces action for directed-brokerage arrangements.
8/9/2004	**Conseco** and **Jefferson National** to pay $20 million to settle charges they permitted market timing of funds through their variable annuities.
8/9/2004	Morningstar suspects **Evergreen** manager of market timing.
8/10/2004	SEC probes **Federated Investments** for money laundering.
8/10/2004	**Olympic Cascade** to settle market-timing issues with NASD.
8/13/2004	**Evergreen Investments**, part of Wachovia, says two of its funds are being investigated in the mutual fund scandal.
8/13/2004	SEC says **Van Eck** funds may be next target in mutual fund probe.
8/18/2004	**Janus** funds to pay $100 million to settle SEC fraud charges for undisclosed market-timing agreements.

Q **Will you want to receive income from your account immediately?**

This is question #5. If you haven't answered questions 1–4, STOP! and turn to page 185.

a) Yes......**ERROR!** In Question #2, you said you'd make additional deposits, but here in Question #5 you say you want immediate withdrawals. Start over on page 192 — and change one of your answers.

b) No.......**Congratulations!** You've completed Part 1 of the Edelman Guide to Portfolio Selection. **Your Letter Score is H.** Return to page 193 and continue to Part 2.

8/19/2004	NASD prohibits Seattle firm from opening mutual fund accounts for thirty days, citing improper market-timing trades. Firm also to pay $300,000 in fines.
8/24/2004	Ex-**CIBC** rep sentenced to year in jail for committing $20 million mutual fund fraud.
8/25/2004	SEC files civil fraud charges against **JB Oxford Holdings, National Clearing Corporation,** and three officers for facilitating late trading and market timing.
8/26/2004	SEC files fraud action against **Van Wagoner Funds** and Garrett Van Wagoner, including $800,000 penalty and certain restrictions on industry activities by Van Wagoner.
8/27/2004	**Putnam** investors withdraw $83 billion in one year.
8/30/2004	SEC in settlement talks with **AMVESCAP** for market timing.
8/31/2004	**Franklin Templeton** funds says it expects charges by California for revenue-sharing payments to brokerage firms.
9/1/2004	Three former employees of **Invesco Funds** settle charges related to market-timing abuses.
9/3/2004	Vanguard accuses **Fidelity** of misleading investors about fee roll-backs.
9/7/2004	New York promises to bring more mutual fund abuse cases.
9/8/2004	**AMVESCAP**, parent of fund companies Invesco and AIM, to pay $450 million to settle charges of improper trading activity.
9/9/2004	Internal **ING Funds** review says improper trades are "isolated."
9/9/2004	Former CEO of **Invesco Funds** to pay $500,000 to settle lawsuits over improper mutual fund trading; agrees to two-year ban from working in industry.
9/10/2004	AMVESCAP kills **Invesco** brand name for U.S. retail investors.
9/13/2004	**PIMCO** funds to pay $50 million to settle SEC charges.

9/14/2004	SEC claims **Charles Schwab & Co.** allowed certain customers to late trade in mutual funds.
9/15/2004	**PIMCO** to pay $11.6 million to settle SEC charges it failed to disclose directed-brokerage and shelf-space payments at brokerage firms.
9/16/2004	**Bridgeway Capital Management** and its president to pay a total of $5 million to settle SEC charges of illegal performance fees.
9/17/2004	California says 12(b)(1) fees can undermine fund performance.
9/20/2004	**Franklin Templeton** to pay $5 million to settle Massachusetts charges that it failed to admit wrongdoing in an SEC filing referring to its market-timing settlement with the state.
9/21/2004	**TD Waterhouse** to pay $2 million to settle SEC charges of undisclosed cash payments to three investment advisers to encourage them to place client assets at the firm.
9/21/2004	**Franklin Templeton** funds to pay $5 million fine to settle charges of collaborating with market timer.
9/22/2004	Ontario Securities Commission warns four mutual fund managers of potential enforcement proceedings for market timing.
9/28/2004	**Wachovia** says it may face SEC enforcement action against retail brokerage unit for mutual fund trading activity.
9/29/2004	SEC probes fund managers for using personal assets to make improper investments.

NON SEQUITUR WILEY

NON SEQUITUR © 2002 Wiley Miller. Dist. By UNIVERSAL PRESS SYNDICATE. Reprinted with permission. All rights reserved.

9/30/2004	SEC files fraud charges against **Raymond James Financial Services** in connection with scheme by former broker.
9/30/2004	Civil lawsuit alleges **J. P. Morgan, Lehman Brothers** improperly traded funds, hurting investors.
10/1/2004	Tainted by fund scandal, **Pilgrim Baxter** changes name to Liberty Ridge Capital.
10/5/2004	**RS Investment Management** to pay $25 million to settle SEC market-timing charges.
10/6/2004	**AIM's** chief investment officer takes leave of absence over his role in market-timing investigations.
10/7/2004	NASD fines **Sentinel Funds** $700,000 for not stopping market timing in its funds.
10/8/2004	**Invesco**'s former CEO to pay $500,000 fine to settle charges related to market-timing abuses.
10/8/2004	Study says scandal will force mutual fund companies to hire thousands of more lawyers.
10/8/2004	SEC examines **Putnam**, **Gartmore**, and **WWW Internet Fund** for alleged mistakes in performance-based fee calculations.
10/8/2004	**Invesco**, **AIM** pay a total of $375 million to settle SEC market-timing allegations.
10/11/2004	SEC subpoenas **Gabelli** mutual funds related to investigation of possible improper trading.
10/12/2004	**Sentinel** to pay $700,000 fine to settle NASD charges it failed to stop market timing in its funds.
10/13/2004	Brokerage firm **A. G. Edwards** says Justice Department examining possible improper fund trades; two brokers fired for market timing in mutual funds, NASD bars one from the industry for a year.
10/13/2004	**Bear Stearns** reviewing its employee emails in market timing probe.
0/15/2004	**A. G. Edwards** says it expects revenue to decline due to ban on directed brokerage.

10/19/2004	SEC investigating **FMI Mutual Funds** for possible improper fund trading practices.
10/19/2004	SEC probes **Bear Stearns** for its municipal bond offerings.
10/20/2004	Regulators vow to become even stricter, threatening to take firms to trial.
10/21/2004	SEC censures **KPMG** and partners for improper professional conduct in Gemstar audit.
10/22/2004	**Strong Funds** to slash workforce by 12%.
10/23/2004	SEC considers charges against former **Citigroup** executive over financial relationship with transfer agent.
10/25/2004	SEC suspects kickbacks to retirement consultants.
10/26/2004	**Citigroup Global Capital Markets** to pay $250,000 to settle NASD charges of distributing inappropriate hedge fund sales literature.
10/26/2004	Massachusetts charges **Franklin Templeton** with fraud for not admitting wrongdoing in mutual fund case.
11/2/2004	NASD mulls enforcement action against **ING** for frequent trading at **Pilgrim Funds**.
11/5/2004	**Fremont Funds** to pay SEC $4 million to settle market-timing and late-trading charges.
11/5/2004	New York, SEC subpoena **OppenheimerFunds** in their investigations of improper mutual fund trading.
11/9/2004	**Legg Mason** to pay $1 million to settle SEC changes of improper mutual fund trades.

! This is the end of Part 1. If you haven't answered questions 1–4, STOP! and turn to page 185.

Congratulations! You've finished Part 1 of the Edelman Guide to Portfolio Selection.

Your Letter Score is G.

Remember this Letter Score and return to page 193.

11/10/2004   **Janus** funds investors pull $900 million during October.

11/10/2004   **Marsh & McLennan Companies,** Putnam parent, to cut three thousand jobs.

11/15/2004   **American Funds** investigated by California Attorney General about shelf-space payments.

11/15/2004   **Putnam** funds to lay off one hundred.

11/15/2004   Study says mutual fund investors pay $17.3 billion in costs not reported in prospectuses.

11/18/2004   **Pilgrim Baxter**'s Harold Baxter and Gary Pilgrim to pay a combined $160 million to settle fraud charges concerning undisclosed market timing.

11/18/2004   **Franklin Templeton** to pay $18 million to settle California charges it paid kickbacks to brokers.

11/24/2004   SEC may target funds for failing to provide proper information to their boards.

11/24/2004   Two managers of **Harvard**'s endowment fund have combined paychecks totalling$50 million.

11/30/2004   **AIG** to pay $126 million to settle fraud charges regarding offer and sale of an earnings management product.

12/1/2004   NASD bars former **AmSouth** broker for life for not disclosing risks to clients; sales assistant charged with forgery.

12/2/2004   NASD fines twenty-nine firms a total of $9.2 million for failing to disclose information about brokers.

12/14/2004   Two companies that sell **Franklin Templeton** funds to pay $20 million to settle charges regarding shelf-space payments.

12/15/2004   SEC says no end in sight for fund industry probes.

12/15/2004   **Franklin Templeton** funds under Canadian microscope.

12/16/2004   NASD and SEC question gifts exchanged between brokerage firms and fund managers.

12/17/2004	**First Command** to pay $12 million to settle SEC and NASD charges involving misleading sales practices to members of the military.
12/17/2004	**Fidelity** disciplines fourteen traders; two others depart amid gift probe.
12/20/2004	Seven Canadian financial firms to pay total of $163 million to settle market-timing charges.
12/20/2004	Head trader at **Fidelity** fined amid gift probe.
12/21/2004	SEC examiner probed for bribery attempt.
12/21/2004	**Edward D. Jones & Co**. to pay $75 million to settle late-trading, revenue-sharing charges.
12/22/2004	**H&R Block** to pay $825,000 to settle charges it helped a hedge fund engage in abusive mutual fund trading practices.
12/28/2004	**Edward D. Jones & Co**. says its top exec will step down.
12/28/2004	Industry survey says 12(b)(1) fees, annuities targets of reform.
12/29/2004	More funds cutting fees, scrapping Class B shares because of fund scandal.
12/29/2004	**Putnam** funds delivers some of the worst performances of the year; investors yank $26.8 billion.
12/29/2004	**Edward D. Jones & Co**. lampooned in financial press for having bragged in ads about its good conduct.
12/30/2004	**J. P. Morgan Chase** suspected of role in late trading.

2005

1/3/2005	NASD says it collected $102 million in fines in 2004, filed 1,360 enforcement actions and barred or suspended 830 people.
1/7/2005	**Morgan Stanley** accused of taking kickbacks on variable annuity sales.

1/10/2005	Former **CBS MarketWatch** columnist to pay $540,000 to settle SEC fraud charges of illegal trading scheme.
1/10/2005	**Southwest Securities** to pay $10 million to settle SEC and NYSE charges related to fraudulent market timing and late trading.
1/11/2005	Canadian firms said to have permitted market timing in fifty-four funds.
1/12/2005	Two former reps with Boca Raton brokerage settle market-timing and late-trading charges.
1/13/2005	NASD fines **Banc One** $400,000 to settle late-trading charges.
1/14/2005	Brokerage firm **Edward D. Jones & Co**. admits that seven mutual fund companies (**Goldman Sachs, American, Federated, Hartford, Lord Abbett, Putnam** and **Van Kampen**) paid it a total of $82.4 million in the first eleven months of 2004 so its brokers would recommend these funds instead of others.
1/20/2005	Mutual fund investors file lawsuits against more than forty mutual fund companies; firms allegedly failed to collect money owed to shareholders.
1/20/2005	Massachusetts subpoenas **Morgan Stanley** and others in investigation of whether they received payments to have their brokers push variable annuities.
1/21/2005	Two more traders leave **Fidelity Investments** amid investigation over lavish gifts and entertainment paid by brokers vying for Fidelity's trading business.

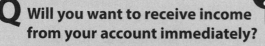

Q **Will you want to receive income from your account immediately?**

This is question #5. If you haven't answered questions 1–4, STOP! and turn to page 185.

a) Yes......**ERROR!** In Question #2, you said you'd make additional deposits, but here in Question #5 you say you want immediate withdrawals. Start over on page 192 — and change one of your answers.

b) No.......**Congratulations!** You've completed Part 1 of the Edelman Guide to Portfolio Selection. **Your Letter Score is K.** Return to page 193 and continue to Part 2.

1/24/2005	**Pax World Funds**, which pioneered the concept of "socially responsible investing," admits that market timing occurred in its mutual funds.
1/24/2005	New research shows revenue-sharing boosted fund revenues as much as tenfold.
1/25/2005	**Strong Funds** name to be dropped after Wells Fargo buys firm.
1/31/2005	**Linsco/Private Ledger** and **Morgan Stanley** sued over fee-sharing agreements that allegedly caused customers to pay higher premiums in certain variable annuities.
2/1/2005	**Charles Schwab & Co**. accused of elder abuse in its sale of variable annuities.
2/4/2005	**Putnam** whistleblower who broke the fund scandal gets job with securities regulator.
2/7/2005	SEC requires mutual fund companies to disclose portfolio managers' compensation and to indicate managers' investments in the funds they oversee.
2/9/2005	**Columbia Mutual Funds** to pay $140 million to settle SEC fraud charges of undisclosed market timing.
2/9/2005	**Bank of America** to pay SEC $515 million and reduce fees by $160 million to settle market-timing charges.
2/16/2005	NASD says **American Funds Distributors** paid $100 million to fifty brokerage firms that sold its funds.
2/16/2005	**Bear Stearns** to pay $250 million to settle SEC investigation of mutual fund market timing and late trading.
2/16/2005	**Brean Murray** to pay $150,000 to settle SEC charges for improper trading of mutual funds.
2/17/2005	NASD accuses **American Funds** of paying kickbacks to brokerage firms that aggressively sold its funds.
2/17/2005	**A. G. Edwards** admits illegal fund trading was rampant.

2/18/2005	Massachusetts subpoenas fifteen banks and broker/dealers regarding variable annuity sales to seniors.
2/22/2005	SEC settles with brokerage firm **Brean Murray**; **Bear Stearns** said to have helped firm engage in late trading.
2/22/2005	**Quick & Reilly**, now part of Bank of America, to pay fine of $570,000 relating to NASD directed-brokerage charges.
2/22/2005	**Piper Jaffray** to pay $275,000 to settle NASD directed-brokerage charges.
2/23/2005	**Edward D. Jones & Co**. and **American Funds** found guilty of kickbacks.
2/24/2005	SEC considers charges against a **Bear Stearns** executive and three former brokers over improper mutual fund trades.
3/1/2005	**Franklin Templeton** funds settles market-timing charges in Canada.
3/2/2005	NASD may levy market-timing charges against **Diversified Investment Advisors**.
3/2/2005	**Bank of New York** says SEC is investigating marketing and distribution costs at its BNY **Hamilton Funds** mutual fund subsidiary.
3/3/2005	Illinois asks **Bear Stearns** for documents regarding market timing in funds.
3/4/2005	SEC investigates **Nuveen** funds for $2.8 million in performance-fee overcharges.
3/4/2005	**Putnam** says it will pay $153.5 million to shareholders harmed by the firm's market-timing activities.
3/8/2005	**Merrill Lynch** to pay $13.5 million to states and NYSE to settle charges it failed to supervise brokers who engaged in market timing in its mutual funds.
3/11/2005	Regulators investigate **Putnam** over conflicts of interest arising from its multiple roles as investment adviser, retirement plan servicer, and employer.

3/15/2005	**Janus** funds closes California office and cuts entire institutional money management team, including cofounder and chief executive officer Bill Schaff.
3/16/2005	NASD says **Jefferson Pilot** failed to prevent market timing and excessive trading in its variable universal life (VUL) insurance policies.
3/17/2005	SEC investigates conflicts of interest and rebating practices of 401(k) plan administrators.
3/21/2005	**Alliance Funds** has settlement discussions with NASD over sales practices and directed brokerage.
3/21/2005	New Jersey regulators ban three former **Merrill Lynch** brokers for helping a hedge fund make tens of thousands of market-timing trades.
3/23/2005	NASD looking at sales contests, says more disclosure likely needed.
3/23/2005	**Citigroup Global Markets** to pay $20 million to settle SEC charges that it failed to tell customers of revenue-sharing program.
3/23/2005	SEC fines **Putnam** funds for revenue-sharing arrangements.
3/24/2005	Brokerage firm **Capital Analysts** to pay $450,000 to settle SEC revenue-sharing charges.
3/24/2005	**American Express Financial Advisors** fined $13 million for not disclosing revenue sharing with funds.
3/25/2005	**Fidelity** trader investigated for giving his mom's account preferential treatment.
4/5/2005	NASD proposes that brokerage firm **Edward D. Jones & Co**. pay $1.7 million fine and reimburse customers to settle possible charges of mutual fund sales abuses.
4/5/2005	**Putnam** says its new chief executive earned $13.7 million in 2004.
4/6/2005	Former CEO of **AIM** funds to pay $175,000 fine to settle SEC allegations of fraudulent trading.

4/12/2005	SEC institutes administrative and cease-and-desist proceedings against twenty former NYSE specialists on charges of securities fraud and other improper trading practices.
4/13/2005	SEC investigates two **Bear Stearns** executives for improper mutual fund trading.
4/14/2005	Class action lawsuit alleges **A. G. Edwards** brokerage firm took millions of dollars in secret kickbacks to promote certain mutual funds.
4/19/2005	**American Express Financial Advisors** says New Hampshire lacks jurisdiction, can't press fraud charges against its brokers.
4/20/2005	**BISYS Group** says SEC is investigating its relationship with certain mutual funds.
4/21/2005	**Fiserv** securities to pay $15 million to settle charges it failed to supervise employees engaged in market timing and late trading.
4/27/2005	**Raymond James** to pay $888,000 to settle NASD charges that it failed to honor customer suitability standards.
4/29/2005	Brokerage firm **Waddell & Reed** to pay up to $16 million to settle charges that it profited by inappropriately switching the variable annuities of more than five thousand customers.
5/6/2005	Federal regulators investigating gift bartering practices at **Fidelity**.
5/9/2005	Two **Putnam** portfolio managers lose their jobs.
5/10/2005	**Bank One** sued by West Virginia over allegations of trading abuses.

© Scott Adams/Dist. by United Feature Syndicate, Inc.

5/11/2005	NASD proposes payment by **Paulson Investment Company** of $866,000 to settle charges of market-timing.
5/20/2005	**SunTrust Securities** to pay $200,000 to settle claim it overcharged mutual fund investors.
5/25/2005	**Waddell & Reed** chief steps down and takes on consulting role with firm after variable-annuity sales scandal.
5/31/2005	**Citigroup** to pay $208 million to settle SEC charges that it fraudulently created an affiliated transfer agent to serve its **Smith Barney** family of mutual funds at steeply discounted rates, then kept the discount instead of passing the savings to investors of its funds.
6/1/2005	SEC says most pension consultants provide products and services to pension plan advisory clients and money managers and mutual funds, creating conflicts of interest.
6/23/2005	**Bear Sterns** says SEC may take action over improper trading of mutual funds.
6/23/2005	**MassMutual** claims its former CEO engaged in unauthorized trading, made false statements, interfered with an investigation, and destroyed documents. The firm also claims the CEO's son passed confidential trading tips at **OppenheimerFunds**, a MassMutual subsidiary.
6/30/2005	SEC bans **Fiserv** manager from the industry for three years for alleged market timing in mutual funds.
7/1/2005	**American Express Financial Advisors (now Ameriprise Financial)** to pay New Jersey $5 million to settle charges it failed to supervise its financial advisors. An Amex advisor had stolen $400,000 from twenty-two clients; Amex had failed to detect the fraud.
7/6/2005	The man who launched the mutual fund scandal is suing Massachusetts for denying him a reward under the state's whistle-blower law.
7/8/2005	A **Trautman Wasserman** broker faces four years in prison and an SEC civil suit for executing tens of thousands of illegal late trades in mutual funds, creating false records to hide the trading, and deceptively evading restrictions on market timing in those funds.

7/12/2005	**Fidelity** reassigns one of the most powerful traders on Wall Street for failing to supervise employees who accepted lavish gifts from firms seeking business.
7/12/2005	**Bear Stearns** may pay $200 million to settle SEC probe of alleged late-trading activities in mutual funds.
7/13/2005	**Ameriprise** to pay New Hampshire $7.4 million to settle charges its brokers received additional compensation for pushing clients into American Express mutual funds from January 1999 to March 2003.
8/2/2005	**Skifter Ajro**, a former Prudential Securities broker, is accused of helping other Pru brokers process $1.3 billion in mutual fund market-timing trades, generating hundreds of thousands of dollars in commissions.
8/4/2005	**Utah's 529 college savings plan** will reimburse investors for losses incurred when a top executive stole $500,000 from the plan. When the fraud was uncovered, Utah officials falsely told SEC that consumers had not been harmed.
8/8/2005	SEC again tells **Fidelity Investments** it is likely to face charges for accepting improper compensation in the form of gifts and lavish entertainment.
8/8/2005	**Alliance Capital** announces it is being investigated by the New York Stock Exchange for improper short-sale stock transactions.
8/10/2005	NASD to file charges against **Oppenheimer's** chairman and chief executive officer because the firm did not provide consumers with discounts when buying its mutual funds.
8/10/2005	Former **Prudential Securities** broker **Skifter Ajro** pleads guilty to four counts of fraud for market timing in mutual funds.
8/11/2005	**Jefferies & Company** says a former trader allegedly spent $1.5 million on hotel rooms, private jets, and a dwarf to win business with Fidelity Investments.
8/11/2005	**Putnam Investments** says it is again in talks with SEC, this time because Putnam has not fully complied with regulations on performance fees.

8/11/2005	SEC considers fraud charge against **Fidelity Investments** because its traders received gifts from brokers trying to win business.
8/11/2005	**Hantz Financial Services** to pay $675,000 to settle NASD charges it accepted millions of dollars from brokerage firms in exchange for pushing their products. Hantz's CEO also is fined $25,000, censured, and suspended from acting in supervisory capacity for thirty days.
8/15/2005	The former CEO of **MassMutual Financial Group**, fired for misconduct, is being investigated by the SEC. MassMutual is the parent of **OppenheimerFunds**.
8/15/2005	SEC says four brokers, one each formerly of **Citigroup** and **Lehman Brothers**, and two formerly with **Merrill Lynch**, took secret cash payments to help a day trader cheat investors.
8/18/2005	**Merrill Lynch** to pay NYSE $10 million to settle charges it failed to deliver mutual fund prospectuses to clients in at least sixty-four thousand transactions.
8/18/2005	NASD says brokers may be pushing clients to invest in high-risk hedge funds to win sales contests.
8/23/2005	The Department of Labor is investigating kickbacks in the 401(k) industry, saying mutual funds are employing questionable revenue-sharing practices in the retirement business.
8/23/2005	**HSBC Securities** to pay Canadian regulators approximately $1 million to settle charges it engaged in market timing.
8/24/2005	SEC OKs **Morgan Stanley** plan to reimburse clients injured by inappropriate sales of class B shares by its brokers. Most clients will receive $7.50; those who invested $1 million will receive $800.
8/29/2005	The chairman of Canada's mutual fund trade group, the **Investment Funds Institute of Canada,** resigns after police say $70 million — nearly half of what five thousand people had invested — is missing from his firm, **Norbourg Asset Management**. Just days earlier, IFIC issued a press release saying, "Canadians Trust Mutual Funds for the Long Term."
8/30/2005	The former CEO and the former president of **Security Trust Company** plead guilty to criminal market-timing and late-trading

charges, but neither goes to prison. Instead they pay $50,000 fines. "No one thought [market timing in mutual funds] was criminal at the time," one of their lawyers says.

9/2/2005	SEC is investigating the **Investment Company Institute** after the ICI president says it represents the mutual fund industry, not fund investors — despite the fact that investors pay ICI's $29.5 million annual budget.
9/7/2005	SEC brings enforcement action against **Bank of America**'s securities division over trading and research-related matters.
9/14/2005	SEC orders **Putnam** to distribute $40 million to wronged shareholders. But Putnam says it cannot identify the shareholders, so SEC is allowing Putnam to put the money back into funds where the scandals occurred — thus benefiting current shareholders instead of those who were financially injured. Putnam also resumes earning management fees on those assets.
9/16/2005	**Raymond James** to pay $6.9 million to settle SEC charges it failed to properly supervise a rogue broker.
9/21/2005	Another former broker with **Prudential Securities** who earned $1 million in commissions faces up to twenty years in jail after pleading guilty to four counts of fraud for illicit market timing.
9/23/2005	**Legg Mason Wood Walker** to pay $1 million to settle SEC charges it fraudulently late-traded 18,000 mutual fund orders.
9/29/2005	Brokerage firm **Edward D. Jones & Co**. to pay $300,000 to settle charges it failed to disclose municipal bond yields on confirmations to clients in more than 86,000 transactions.

! This is the end of Part 1. If you haven't answered questions 1–4, STOP! and turn to page 185.

Congratulations! You've finished Part 1 of the Edelman Guide to Portfolio Selection.

Your Letter Score is D.

Remember this Letter Score and return to page 193.

9/29/2005   New York says improper trading at **Seligman** funds brought more harm to investors than Seligman earlier admitted. The firm had admitted to four market-timing arrangements and paid a $2 million fine; New York now says the firm had at least a dozen arrangements that cost investors at least $80 million.

10/3/2005   **Janney Montgomery Scott** to pay $2.2 million to settle NASD charges it permitted 1,600 improper market-timing trades

10/3/2005   **ING Financial Services** to pay $1.5 million to settle NASD charges of excessive mutual fund trading. An ING broker to pay $25,000 and is issued supervisory suspension for thirty days. ING also settles with SEC for reselling $202 million worth of company securities without registering them.

10/3/2005   **First Allied Securities** to pay more than $700,000 to settle NASD charges it helped three hedge funds market-time mutual funds.

10/4/2005   A **Bank of Hawaii** executive is fired for allegedly earning profits of $110,000 from illicit mutual fund market timing.

10/10/2005   Eight broker-dealers pay $7.75 million to settle NASD charges that their brokers urged clients to buy **Lord Abbett Funds** in exchange for kickbacks. **Invest Financial** to pay $1.52 million; **Commonwealth Financial Network**, $1.4 million; **National Planning Corporation**, $1.308 million; **Mutual Service Corporation**, $1.3 million; **Lincoln Financial Advisors Corp.**, $950,000; **SII Investments**, $658,500; and **Investment Centers of America**, $363,500. Lord Abbett to pay $255,000 to settle charges.

10/11/2005   The Ontario Securities Commission charges the former president of **Portus Alternative Asset Management** with destruction of documents, lying to regulators, trading in mutual funds without a license, and distributing mutual funds without a prospectus. Charges also filed against three associates.

10/12/2005   The chief compliance officer and the chief legal counsel of **Manulife Securities** resign over fraud allegations against Portus Alternative Asset Management. Manulife's president and chief executive, and manager of investment research quit previously.

10/12/2005   A former broker at **Banc of America Securities** to pay a $200,000 penalty and is banned from the securities industry for five years to settle charges that he helped a customer engage in late trading of mutual funds.

10/13/2005   SEC and NYSE say they will take action against **A. G. Edwards** because the firm allowed clients to market-time mutual funds.

10/21/2005   **Evergreen Funds** faces NASD action for inappropriately rewarding financial advisers for selling Evergreen products. Evergreen's CEO says it was "a fairly common industry practice."

10/26/2005   **Ameriprise Financial** to pay NASD $1.25 million to settle charges of improper sales practices related to 529 college savings plans.

10/28/2005   **Putnam's** CEO says new regulations may harm investors by flooding them with information. Charles E. Haldeman tells an industry conference that disclosures have become so long and detailed that they draw attention away from more pressing investor concerns.

10/31/2005   SEC is looking into whether traders at **Fidelity Investments** asked brokerage firms to place false trades to boost traders' compensation and erase unprofitable trades from their books.

11/3/2005   The owner of **Millennium Partners** is trying to settle market-timing charges with New York and SEC. Regulators say the firm market timed and late-traded $1 billion worth of mutual funds.

11/9/2005   SEC OKs **Morgan Stanley** payment of $50 million to mutual fund investors who bought its funds between January 2000 and November 2003. Investors were not told that the firm's brokers received higher compensation for selling certain funds.

11/10/2005   Old Mutual is renaming its eighteen **PBHG** funds in wake of negative connotations associated with mutual fund scandal.

11/17/2005   A California court says the state lacks the jurisdiction to sue **American Funds.** The state wanted to sue American Funds, alleging that it did not tell investors that it paid $426 million to brokerage firms over five years so that its brokers would push American's funds.

11/21/2005   A California appeals court allows California to proceed with a lawsuit against **Edward D. Jones & Co**. The state alleges the firm did not disclose payments it received from mutual fund companies to sell their products. This ruling contrasts with a ruling in the case against American Funds.

11/21/2005   A federal court in California fines a former executive for **National Clearing Corporation** $50,000 for helping institutional clients engage in more than twelve thousand late trades in at least seventy-four mutual funds. The scheme earned NCC more than $1 million in profits; the institutional clients reaped more than $8 million in illegal revenue.

11/22/2005   Massachusetts files another lawsuit against **Massachusetts Mutual Life Insurance Company,** charging the firm with disregarding repeated demands to produce documentation regarding wrongdoing in the company's mutual fund and insurance divisions.

11/29/2005   Three affiliates of **Federated** funds to pay $72 million, settling regulatory charges that they harmed long-term mutual fund shareholders by allowing market timing and late trading.

12/2/2005   **Millennium Partners** and several top executives to pay more than $180 million to settle SEC charges of market timing in mutual funds.

12/2/2005   **Ameriprise Financial** to pay $57.3 million to settle SEC and NASD directed-brokerage, market-timing, and revenue-sharing allegations. SEC says Ameriprise "ignored its responsibility to treat all fund shareholders fairly and honestly."

JEFF MacNELLY'S SHOE   CHRIS CASSATT & GARY BROOKINS

12/5/2005   A business owner alleges in a lawsuit that **Fidelity Investments** and **ADP** tried to hide the costs of their SIMPLE retirement plans and didn't disclose a revenue-sharing agreement between them.

12/8/2005   A Canadian class action lawsuit alleges that investor losses exceed the $150 million paid by **IG Investment Management, CI Mutual Funds, Franklin Templeton Funds** and AGF funds to settle charges that they allowed market timing to occur in their funds.

12/13/2005   **Chase Investment Services** to pay $290,000 to settle NASD charges it allowed a hedge fund to market-time nineteen mutual funds, including **American Funds, Vanguard**, and **TIAA-CREF**.

12/16/2005   **Bear Stearns** offers to pay $250 million to settle SEC and NYSE charges of mutual fund late trading.

12/19/2005   A class action lawsuit is filed claiming investors did not know that **Wells Fargo** investment advisors pushed certain funds in order to earn bonuses.

12/20/2005   NASD fines **Merrill Lynch, Wells Fargo Investments**, and **Linsco/ Private Ledger** a total of $19.4 million for violations related to the sales of mutual fund shares involving 29,000 households and 140,000 transactions.

12/21/2005   A former **Prudential Securities** broker to pay $50,000 to settle SEC charges he executed thousands of trades worth more than $300 million, costing mutual fund companies and investors $400,000.

12/23/2005   **Alger Funds** says SEC is investigating fund market timing and late trading at the firm.

12/23/2005   SEC files a civil suit against two hedge fund traders for placing three thousand late trades in more than four hundred mutual funds, allegedly costing long-term mutual fund shareholders $49 million.

12/28/2005   SEC is scrutinizing the amount mutual funds pay affiliates, to verify that funds are making proper disclosures to their boards, and that the boards are approving the deals.

2006

1/4/2006	SEC charges six former officers of a trust company owned by **Putnam** for defrauding a client and some **Putnam** funds of $4 million.
1/9/2006	NASD says **Oppenheimer** and its CEO intentionally submitted flawed data pertaining to discounts that clients were to receive when purchasing mutual funds. Oppenheimer also to pay NASD $250,000 to settle charges that it failed to report 230 cases of problems with its brokers, including terminations, broker misconduct, customer complaints, and regulatory actions.
1/10/2006	**Security Brokerage** and its former owner to pay total of $153 million to settle SEC charges of late trading and market timing in **Alliance Capital** and **MFS** mutual funds.
1/13/2006	**UBS Financial Services** to pay $54 million to settle NYSE, New Jersey, and Connecticut market-timing charges involving at least seven UBS branch offices. Regulators say UBS received more than one thousand complaints from mutual fund companies about deceptive trading practices, but UBS but did not stop the activity until the end of 2001.
1/18/2006	**Canary Capital Partners** and its former managing principal to pay New Jersey a total of $10 million to settle charges of market timing and late trading in mutual funds and sub-accounts in variable annuities. The former principal is also barred from acting as broker/dealer or investment advisor for twelve years.
1/20/2006	**JB Oxford Holdings** to pay $2.1 million to settle SEC charges of late trading and market timing in mutual funds.
1/24/2006	NASD will take disciplinary action against brokerage firm **A. G. Edwards** over allegations that it took kickbacks from mutual fund companies in exchange for marketing their products to retail customers.
1/31/2006	**Deutsche Bank Asset Management** announces plan to pay more than $127 million to settle SEC market-timing charges in its Scudder funds.

2/9/2006	**Sanford C. Bernstein**, a subsidiary of **Alliance Capital Management**, to pay $350,000, and one of its analysts to pay $200,000 NASD fine for personally selling stocks he was telling clients to buy.
2/10/2006	SEC fines **Morgan Keegan** $558,807 to settle charges that it allowed late trading by a hedge fund.
2/10/2006	**Bear Stearns** to pay $1.5 million to settle NYSE charges that it violated rules pertaining to index arbitrage trading.
3/10/2006	Justice Department says it will pursue a civil lawsuit against famed mutual fund manager Mario Gabelli, alleging he created bogus minority-owned and small-business companies to qualify for millions of dollars' worth of discounted FCC licenses for cell phones and other communications devices, only to turn around and sell those licenses for a $206 million profit.
3/15/2006	**Merrill Lynch** to pay $5 million to settle NASD charges that it held impermissible sales contests and engaged in unsuitable mutual fund switches at its call centers between 2001 and 2004. NASD says Merrill agents misrepresented information about mutual funds or omitted facts as they vied for prizes offered by the firm, including dinners and tickets to rock concerts and sporting events. NASD also says Merrill prohibited its reps from recommending any investment other than Merrill's mutual funds.
3/15/2006	California court allows California lawsuit to go forward against brokerage firm **Edward D. Jones & Co**. Lawsuit alleges it accepted $300 million in shelf-space payments from seven mutual fund companies between 2000 and 2004.
3/20/2006	New York subpoenas **AXA Equitable Life Insurance Company**, a division of AXA Financial, on suspicions of market timing in its variable annuities and other insurance products.
3/21/2006	**Boston Capital Securities** to pay $1.2 million to settle NASD charges of improper financial disclosure and compensation, as the firm continued to sell limited partnerships despite an NASD deficiency notice.
3/24/2006	Criminal charges are filed against the former president of **Monarch International Holdings** for allegedly taking money from investors for a nonexistent mutual fund.

| 3/25/2006 | SEC charges two former **Merrill Lynch** brokers, a broker formerly with **Lehman Brothers** and four former day traders and managers from broker-dealer **A. B. Watley** with fraudulently using confidential information to trade ahead of other customers on more than four hundred occasions, garnering millions of dollars in illicit profits. |

| 3/28/2006 | *The Wall Street Journal* says that executives at **Dreyfus Funds** gave written permission to a hedge fund to engage in market timing in its mutual funds. |

| 4/5/2006 | AIG unit **American General** to pay more than $1.1 million to settle NASD charges that it accepted payments to promote twelve mutual fund families. |

| 4/6/2006 | NASD files complaint against **A. B. Watley Direct** for facilitating late trading and improper market timing of mutual funds on behalf of hedge fund clients. |

| 5/10/2006 | **Morgan Stanley** to pay $15 million to settle SEC charges that it failed to produce tens of thousands of emails during an SEC investigation. |

| 5/10/2006 | **The Hartford** to pay $20 million to settle charges that it provided kickbacks to brokers from 1998 to 2004 without disclosing the payments to customers, who invested $800 million in Hartford's products. Internal emails showed that Hartford executives paid the kickbacks to entice the brokers to sell its products despite their knowing that the products were not competitive. |

NON SEQUITUR WILEY

THE UNFORTUNATE TIMING FOR CHARLES ELTON O'BRIEN TO GET PERSONALIZED LICENSE PLATES...

CEO

6/5/2006   A California court dismisses a fraud case against **Edward D. Jones & Co.,** saying the state lacks jurisdiction. The state had claimed that the firm did not tell clients it was paying stockbrokers to get them to sell certain products.

6/9/2006   New Hampshire sees wrongdoing in the state retirement plan. It accuses **ING** of accepting undisclosed fees from mutual funds and failed to reimburse employees whose accounts were depleted by market timing.

6/13/2006   **Fred Alger Management** to pay $40 million and will reduce fees by $1 million a year for five years to settle New York and SEC mutual fund market-timing and late-trading charges.

6/13/2006   The former chairman of a **PIMCO** affiliate to pay $200,000 to settle SEC market-timing charges that he permitted a hedge fund to execute $4 billion worth of trades in PIMCO funds.

6/14/2006   A New York union settles with the state over allegations it accepted annual shelf-space payments of $3 million from **ING** without telling its members. ING allegedly paid the union to endorse its products; the union told members to attend sales presentations that were disguised as financial planning seminars, and redirected member inquiries to ING marketing personnel, who did not reveal their identities. The union will disclose future payments and reimburse the state $100,000 for the cost of the investigation.

6/15/2006   New Hampshire says **ING** allowed market timing in its funds as early as 2001.

6/28/2006   **Morgan Stanley Dean Witter** to pay $10 million to settle SEC charges that it failed to prevent insider trading,

6/30/2006   A jury says **PIMCO**'s former chairman defrauded the firm's mutual fund investors by approving undisclosed market timing.

7/13/2006   Former fund manager Mario Gabelli and his partners agree to pay $130 million to settle Justice Department allegations of fraud in connection with FCC bandwidth auctions.

7/24/2006   **Waddell & Reed** to pay $50 million and to reduce fees by $5 million a year for five years and to pay Kansas $2 million for investor education to settle charges that it permitted market timing in its mutual funds between 1995 and 2003.

7/31/2006   SEC says three former **Janus** mutual fund executives — including a portfolio manager — allowed or facilitated market timing at the firm.

8/7/2006   **A. G. Edwards** to pay $900,000 to settle NYSE charges of excessive fees.

8/7/2006   A former **Fiserv** senior VP in charge of mutual fund trading to pay $628,020 to settle SEC charges that he engaged in 855 instances of late trading in mutual funds for his own account.

8/10/2006   Four ING broker/dealers (**Financial Network Investment Corporation, ING Financial Partners, PrimeVest Financial Services, and Multi-Financial Securities**) to pay NASD a total of more than $7 million to settle charges that they accepted $25.7 million in brokerage commissions from ten mutual fund companies. The fund companies were said to have made the payments so that the firm's stockbrokers would sell more of their products to their clients.

8/11/2006   **Citigroup Global Markets** to pay $1.1 million to settle NASD charges that it failed to prevent more than one hundred of its brokers from filing false documents regarding mutual fund sales charges assessed to clients. NASD says Citigroup was sanctioned for similar misconduct in 1997.

8/28/2006   **Prudential Securities** to pay $600 million to settle market-timing charges by various regulators. NASD alleges that some Pru brokers misrepresented identities in order to execute more than $116 billion in market timing trades in 1,600 customer accounts, and that the trading continued even after Prudential received more than 1,000

! This is question #2. If you haven't answered question #1, STOP! and turn to page 185.

Q **Will you be adding money to this account on a regular basis?**

a) Yes ....turn to page 66
b) No ....turn to page 36

letters and emails from more than 50 mutual fund companies asking it to stop the trading.

8/30/2006   **American Funds** to pay $5 million NASD fine relating to charges that the firm gave more than $98 million between 2001 and 2003 to fifty brokerage firms that were top sellers of its products. In exchange, the firms encouraged their brokers to sell American's funds to their clients.

9/1/2006   **Edward D. Jones & Co**. tentatively settles nine class action lawsuits by agreeing to pay its customers $127 million plus legal fees over three years. The lawsuits complained that the firm secretly accepted fees from **American, Federated, Goldman Sachs, Hartford, Lord Abbett, Putnam**, and **Van Kampen** in exchange for promoting those funds to its customers..

9/5/2006   SEC says five mutual fund companies charged $7.4 million in excessive fees from April 1997 through December 2004. **Dreyfus** will repay $3.2 million; **Putnam,** $1.6 million; **Numeric,** $1 million; **Kensington,** $790,962; and **Gartmore,** $653,882.

9/6/2006   A broker says he was wrongfully terminated for facilitating market timing by **Bear Stearns** and files a $30 million arbitration claim against the firm. He says the firm "facilitated and supported" the activity but fired him when was investigated by regulators.

9/18/2006   New York says a broker with **Trautman Wasserman** engaged in late trading in mutual funds from late 2000 to September 2003.

9/19/2006   Civil lawsuit accuses seven major corporations — **Bechtel Group, Caterpillar, Exelon, General Dynamics, International Paper, Lockheed Martin,** and **United Technologies** — of allowing mutual fund firms to charge millions of dollars in excessive 401(k) fees through hidden revenue-sharing agreements. The fund companies allegedly charged higher fees and shared the extra money with the 401(k) administrators without letting employees participating in the plans know about the deals.

9/19/2006   MetLife subsidiaries **MetLife Securities, New England Securities,** and **Walnut Street Securities** to pay $5 million to settle NASD charges that they allowed late trading of mutual funds, provided inaccurate and misleading information to NASD, and failed to produce emails in a timely fashion. The companies told NASD they were not aware of any late-trading transactions, but NASD later found that the companies knew of eight hundred such trades.

9/25/2006 — A federal judge bans the former controller of **Smith Barney World Funds** from the financial industry. He had previously been ordered to repay $14,528, and had been sentenced to one year of supervised release for embezzling $47,529 from the funds under his control.

9/27/2006 — Mutual fund administrator **BISYS Funds Services** to pay $21.4 million to settle SEC allegations that it helped two dozen mutual fund firms defraud fund investors. SEC says BISYS entered into undisclosed side agreements to enable the funds to improperly use investors' assets to pay for marketing expenses.

9/27/2006 — New York seeks $80 million from **J. W. Seligman** and its president, Brian Zino, to settle charges of market timing in mutual funds. The firm had said its activities were limited and had cost investors only $2 million, but the state alleges additional market-timing agreements and that Seligman's senior managers were aware of the activity and its harmful effect on investors.

9/27/2006 — **Dunham & Associates Investment Counsel** to pay $150,000, and its CEO to pay $50,000, to settle SEC charges that they collected $350 million from 1,700 investors and placed the money into thirteen unregistered mutual funds.

9/29/2006 — SEC bars the former president of **Cornerstone Equity Advisors** from the securities industry for allegedly assisting with the misappropriation of $126,741 from the company's mutual funds.

RHYMES WITH ORANGE HILARY PRICE

© HILARY B. PRICE. KING FEATURES SYNDICATE

10/2/2006	**Deutsche Asset Management**, parent of **Scudder funds**, to pay $19.3 million to settle SEC charges that Scudder engaged in directed-brokerage and revenue-sharing arrangements. Scudder allegedly paid broker-dealers $17 million so their brokers would sell Scudder funds to customers. Scudder funds previously paid $134 million to settle SEC charges relating to market-timing.
10/4/2006	SEC accuses a former **Wall Street Access** broker with allowing a hedge fund to engage in late trading and market timing in mutual funds two thousand times. SEC says the broker earned $630,000 from the activity.
10/4/2006	**Oppenheimer** to pay $800,000 relating to NASD charges that it failed to timely and accurately report 6,100 municipal securities transactions.
10/12/2006	A former trader with **Millennium Partners** is charged with violating the terms of his ban from the industry, which was instituted after he was charged with late trading. SEC says the trader has been running an offshore fund that places trades through New York. SEC is penalizing him $570,000 for the earlier charges.
10/16/2006	**Citizens Bank's** broker-dealer subsidiary, **CCO Investment Services**, to pay $850,000 relating to NASD charges that it did not properly supervise sales of 529 college savings plans and annuities to insure that the products were suitable for investors.
10/25/2006	The chairman and CEO of **James River Capital** to pay $2.25 million to settle NASD charges of market-timing mutual funds through annuities. The fine includes a sixty-day suspension from the industry.
10/27/2006	**ING** to pay $30 million to New York and $2.75 million to New Hampshire to settle charges that it paid a teachers' union to steer business its way.
10/27/2006	The former chairman of **PIMCO** equity mutual funds to pay $572,000 to settle SEC charges that he allowed market timing in his firm's funds. SEC bans him from serving as an officer or a director of a mutual fund company for one year.
10/27/2006	SEC is investigating twenty-seven mutual fund companies, mostly operated by banks, to see if they accepted millions of dollars in kickbacks from fund administrators as a reward for granting shareholder

services contracts. Investigation follows an agreement by **BISYS** to pay $21.4 million to settle SEC charges that it paid $230 million in kickbacks between July 1999 and June 2004.

10/31/2006   **JPMorgan Chase** says its **One Group Funds** unit is among the twenty-seven fund companies SEC is investigating for accepting kickbacks from fund administrators.

11/6/2006   **Chase** to pay $500,000 NASD fine and will reimburse customers $288,500 to settle charges that it failed to properly supervise the sales of 529 college saving plans from January 2002 through August 2004. During this period, Chase's 529 plan sales exceeded $134 million.

11/6/2006   **MetLife** to pay $500,000 NASD fine and will reimburse customers $376,000 to settle charges it failed to properly supervise the sales of 529 college saving plans from January 2002 through March 2005. During this period, MetLife's 529 plan sales exceeded $150 million.

11/8/2006   **Three subsidiaries of the Hartford** pay $55 million to settle SEC charges that they misrepresented and failed to disclose that they used shareholder assets to pay for marketing expenses of Hartford mutual funds and annuities.

11/9/2006   **HighMark Funds**, operated by the **Union Bank of California,** says it is among twenty-seven fund companies SEC is investigating for accepting kickbacks from fund administrators.

11/15/2006   **1st Global Capital Corp**. to pay $100,000 to settle SEC charges that it allowed its brokers to make unsuitable recommendations in the sale of 529 college savings plans between 2001 and 2004.

11/16/2006   SEC is examining whether **Allegiant Asset Management** accepted kickbacks from the company that administers its funds, using the money for marketing expenses.

11/16/2006   The Government Accountability Office says some 401(k) business practices "may not be in the best interest of investors." GAO is criticizing poor fee disclosures, inappropriate use of expensive share classes, high administrative fees, and "pay to play" deals that cause consultants to recommend funds that pay them the most instead of funds that are best for employers and their workers. Most 401(k) plans are operated by mutual fund companies.

11/17/2006	New York sues two hedge funds and their principals for fraudulently timing mutual funds.

11/20/2006   An arbitration panel says **Prudential**, which fired a stockbroker over market-timing allegations, must pay the broker $3.8 million bonus that the firm had withheld. The broker is still being sued by SEC, which says he and three others engaged in market timing that cost twenty-five mutual funds a total of about $2.5 billion.

11/30/2006   A **Principal Financial Group** employee is charged with stealing money from the firm's mutual funds since 1997. The company didn't discover the thefts — totaling $167,000 — until recently.

12/4/2006   **Jefferies & Company** to pay $9.7 million in fines — $4.2 million to SEC and $5.5 million to NASD — to settle charges that it lavished $1.6 million in gifts, extravagant travel and entertainment, and other gratuities to win mutual fund trading business from Fidelity Investments. The firm's director of equities is fined $50,000 and suspended for three months, while the firm's former senior vice president and equity sales trader to pay $468,000 and is permanently barred from the industry. Fidelity traders received expensive golf trips, including private jet travel, lodging at resorts, fine wine and merchandise, plus tickets to the Super Bowl, Broadway shows, and concerts. The firm also helped pay for an elaborate bachelor party in Miami.

12/6/2006   A class action lawsuit alleges that **Franklin Templeton** funds paid kickbacks to broker-dealers for nearly five years so the firms would tell their customers to buy Franklin Templeton funds, without disclosing the practice to the fund's investors.

12/8/2006   Regulators say they are investigating **Fidelity** because its traders received $1.6 million in gifts from **Jefferies & Company**, which wanted additional trading business from the mutual fund giant.

Q **Will you want to receive income from your account immediately?**

This is question #5. If you haven't answered questions 1–4, STOP! and turn to page 185.

a) Yes......**ERROR!** In Question #2, you said you'd make additional deposits, but here in Question #5 you say you want immediate withdrawals. Start over on page 192 — and change one of your answers.

b) No.......**Congratulations!** You've completed Part 1 of the Edelman Guide to Portfolio Selection. **Your Letter Score is H.** Return to page 193 and continue to Part 2.

Fidelity admits it paid $4 million in trading commissions to Jefferies in the year before its traders received the gifts and $30 million in the year after the gifts were received. Fidelity says there were "legitimate reasons" for the increase and that "there is no proof" that investors were financially harmed.

12/12/2006   **Prudential Securities Insurance** to pay $19 million to settle allegations by New York that it engaged in deceptive and anti-competitive pricing in the sale of group insurance.

12/13/2006   Four brokerage firms refund $43.8 million to investors to settle charges that they collected fees for moving money between mutual funds when the transactions were supposed to be free. **Morgan Stanley Dean Witter** will refund $10.4 million to investors; **Edward D. Jones & Co.**, $25 million; **RBC Dain Rauscher**, $6.8 million; and **Royal Alliance Associates**, $1.6 million. The firms, collectively, were also fined $850,000.

12/13/2006   New York sues **UBS Financial Services**, saying the firm placed some clients into investment programs that cost as much as $23,000 per trade.

12/19/2006   NASD charges **Morgan Stanley Dean Witter** with routinely failing to provide emails to regulators and to claimants suing the firm, and with falsely claiming that millions of emails were lost when its email servers were destroyed along with the World Trade Center on September 11, 2001. In fact, says NASD, millions of emails were quickly restored using back-up tapes.

12/21/2006   **Fidelity Investments** says it will pay $42 million plus interest to its mutual funds to redress acceptance of gifts by Fidelity traders and portfolio.

12/27/2006   **Deutsche Bank** to pay $208 million to New York and $17 million to SEC to settle charges that it permitted market timing in its mutual funds and that its broker-dealer allowed clients to late trade funds.

12/28/2006   A NASD arbitration panel fines **Ameriprise** subsidiary **Securities America** a total of $9.3 million in connection with charges that the company and one of its stockbrokers steered three retired airline pilots into high-fee mutual funds.

12/31/2006   **Allstate** to pay $18 million to settle New York charges that a subsidiary failed to tell 6,500 customers of risks involved when replacing insurance policies.

2007

1/2/2007   **MetLife** to pay $19 million to settle New York charges that it paid brokers to steer business to it.

1/3/2007   **Evergreen Investments,** the mutual fund subsidiary of Wachovia, to pay $4.2 million to settle NASD charges that it gave **Wachovia Securities** $25.7 million in commissions generated from trades in Evergreen's funds.

1/3/2007   Massachusetts subpoenas **UBS** and other investment banks in investigation of whether banks charge low rent to hedge funds in exchange for trading and prime brokerage business.

1/10/2007   Lawrence Lasser, **Putnam**'s former CEO, to pay $75,000 to settle SEC charges that he authorized the company to make undisclosed shelf-space payments to eighty brokerage firms from 2000 to 2003. Putnam has paid $40 million in fines related to the practice and gave Lasser $78 million when he left the firm. "We are holding him accountable for his conduct," an SEC spokesman says.

1/11/2007   Illinois regulators accuse **A. G. Edwards** of facilitating market timing between January 2001 and October 2003.

1/12/2007   **ING** is sued for allegedly boosting fees and accepting kickbacks from mutual fund companies in its retirement plans.

1/16/2007   Three brokers under investigation by the New York Stock Exchange are accused of helping hedge fund clients improperly trade mutual funds. **Merrill Lynch** already paid $13.5 million, and **UBS** paid $49.5 million for failing to stop the trading.

1/17/2007   A former trader at **Millennium Partners**, who pled guilty to improper trading after cooperating with a New York investigation of the mutual fund industry, was sentenced to five years' probation and three hundred hours of community service for engaging in late trading of mutual funds. His firm previously paid SEC $180 million to settle charges against it.

1/17/2007	NASD is expected to fine dozens of brokerages for failing to award discounts to mutual fund investors in 2001 and 2002. Fifteen firms paid $21.5 million in 2004 for such violations, which NASD says are still occurring.
1/18/2007	**Fred Alger Management** and **Fred Alger & Co**. to pay a total of $40 million to settle SEC charges that it allowed market timing and late trading in Alger funds from at least 2000 through October 2003.
1/19/2007	**Kelmoore Investments** to pay $100,000 to settle SEC charges that it told clients it was charging them 1% of assets under management when, in fact, fees between 1999 and 2005 were actually as high as 3.63%.
2/1/2007	SEC is pursuing former **CIBC** brokers for allegedly assisting hedge funds market-time mutual funds between 1999 and at least 2003. A former CIBC executive has agreed to pay $100,000 to settle charges of failing to supervise the brokers.
2/1/2007	**Putnam** is sold to a Canadian firm, Power Financial Corp. Its chairman says the firm plans no significant changes in Putnam's business.
2/5/2007	A California appeals court says the attorney general can sue **American Funds** for fraud stemming from allegations that the fund company did not inform investors that it was paying kickbacks to brokerage firms to entice brokers to recommend the funds to their clients. A lower court had ruled that the state lacked jurisdiction to file suit.
2/5/2007	**Merrill Lynch** to pay $40 million to settle three class action lawsuits filed by four hundred thousand mutual fund investors who say the firm issued misleading investment information.
2/5/2007	Four Fidelity broker-dealers, including **Fidelity Brokerage Services**, **Fidelity Institutional Asset Management**, and **National Financial Services**, to pay NASD a total of $3.75 million to settle charges that they improperly registered 1,100 individuals, failed to assign supervisors, failed to retain the email of 1,900 employees, and other electronic recordkeeping failures.
3/2/2007	SEC's top mutual fund regulator says mutual fund fraud investigations will continue.

3/20/2007	Utah accuses **First Western** and two of its brokers of securities fraud, saying the brokers invested $20 million in client money in Class B shares to earn higher commissions while attempting to make the clients believe they were invested in less expensive Class A shares.
3/21/2007	Justice Department files first-ever criminal case against a hedge fund for market timing. **Beacon Rock Capital** is accused of defrauding mutual funds of $2.4 million through twenty-six thousand trades.
3/21/2007	The **Veras Investment Partners** hedge fund agrees to return $38 million to 810 mutual funds to settle SEC accusations of market timing.
3/22/2007	The **Jefferies** broker who was banned from the brokerage and mutual fund industries for life for lavishing gifts on **Fidelity** traders in an effort to win business from them is opening a hedge fund.
3/26/2007	**Fidelity** negotiating with the SEC over possible fines because its traders accepted lavish gifts. The SEC says shareholders were harmed; Fidelity disagrees but has already reimbursed it mutual funds $42 million following an internal investigation into the matter.
3/27/2007	A New York federal district court upholds a $14 million defamation award against **Merrill Lynch** issued in an arbitration case brought by three of its former brokers who were fired for allegedly timing mutual funds. Merrill Lynch sought to have the award vacated. The judge says Merrill's policy to prevent market timing was "vague and unworkable."
3/28/2007	**Janus** files documents with SEC showing that it paid its CEO $10.6 million in 2006.
3/28/2007	Mutual funds charge investors $11 billion annually in 12(b)1 fees. Funds are supposed to use the money for advertising expenses, but SEC says only 2% goes to that purpose; the rest is used to pay commissions to stock brokers and financial advisors.
3/30/2007	NASD orders **AllianceBernstein** to pay broker, fired for alleged role in market-timing scandal, $3.1 million.
4/2/2007	Kansas denies former **Waddell & Reed** CEO's claim that he lived in Texas and thus did not owe a Kansas tax. IRS still seeking $22 million in taxes and penalties, claiming he took improper deductions.

4/11/2007   SEC says manager of an **ING** mutual fund failed to disclose 3,500 personal trades in the fund he managed. SEC says trading generated $410,000 in profits.

4/17/2007   **Edward Jones & Co.** offers $127.5 million to settle class-action lawsuits that it accepted bribes from mutual fund companies so its brokers would push certain funds to its clients.

5/2/2007   **A. G. Edwards** to pay $3.9 million to settle SEC charges of failing to supervise brokers who engaged in mutual fund market timing.

5/7/2007   **Zurich Capital** to pay $16.8 million to settle SEC charges it helped hedge funds market time mutual funds.

5/8/2007   NASD fines two **Fidelity** broker-dealers $400,000 for distributing misleading investment sales literature to military personnel.

5/16/2007   **PIMCO**'s former CEO pays $75,000 to settle SEC charges of directed brokerage violations.

5/18/2007   The SEC, struggling to figure out how to return $3.4 billion in fines collected from the mutual fund industry over the past four years, tells Congress it plans to establish an office to focus solely on this issue, suggesting it will still be years before injured investors receive restitution.

The Scandal Continues!

Learn the latest revelations about the Mutual Fund Scandal by visiting theliesaboutmoney.com. The site — which continues Ric's Mutual Fund Scandal Timeline with entries that occurred after this book went to press — is available only with the password provided below. You'll learn about new claims, lawsuits, fines and other penalties involving the business practices of Citigroup, Wachovia, John Hancock, Fidelity, Edward Jones, NYLIFE, Securities America, Northwestern Mutual, Allianz, Bank of America, Morgan Stanley, The Hartford, Smith Barney and others.

Go to: http://**www.theliesaboutmoney.com**

Enter this password: tellmemore

Since the mutual fund scandal started making headlines in 2003, nearly every retail mutual fund company has been ensnared; investigators from the NASD, SEC, New York Stock Exchange, and several state attorneys generals, most notably those in New York and Massachusetts, continue to uncover mischief and wrong-doing in the retail mutual fund world. A substantial portion of the fines paid is supposed to be returned to the investors who were harmed by the scandal.

But regulators are still trying to figure out how to do that. The SEC and other regulators have hired consultants, academics — and even the financial firms themselves — to help answer the question: How do we determine who gets the money?

Many of the victims who owned the funds while the crimes were occurring have since sold their shares. Fund companies have their addresses, but many have moved. And many shareholders purchased their funds through employer retirement accounts; in those cases, the funds only have the names of the companies, not the individual employees. Some of those employers have since gone out of business, merged with other firms, or moved their retirement plans to other fund companies. And some of the employees at those firms have since left, with no forwarding address. For all these reasons, finding harmed investors is a challenge.

The problem isn't resolved even when the fund company knows who you are and where to find you. The next challenge is to determine the amount you lost. In most cases, the objectionable activities occurred over many years — during which time you may have added or withdrawn money from the mutual funds in question. Exactly how many shares did you own when an instance of late trading or market timing occurred, and how much of a loss in share price did each instance generate?

As if all this isn't enough, the IRS says it may consider any settlement to be taxable income. This issue gets really complicated for refunds paid into retirement accounts and IRAs.

Thus, the entire restitution process is going to be very expensive — and, of course, the expenses will likely be deducted from the money paid to investors. One analyst involved in the effort has predicted that 90% of the refunds will amount to less than ten dollars.

Because of the difficulty in identifying victims and determining the extent of their losses, several mutual fund companies have suggested that regulators simply deposit the refunds back into the funds where the problems occurred. They argue that many victims are still shareholders, so they'll automatically benefit. As for the fact that newer shareholders who weren't hurt by the scandal also will benefit, the funds say that the amount received by the victims won't be reduced, thanks to the cost savings of their solution. In essence, they say, some shareholders will simply enjoy a windfall profit.

What these fund companies haven't said is that their plan produces a windfall for them too. Indeed, they'd become beneficiaries of their own wrongdoing! Consider: A company pays a fine to redress a past impropriety. They use the profits gained from such impropriety to pay the fine. Then they suggest placing the fine back into the funds they manage, so they can resume generating profits — by collecting fees — on the money invested!

Ain't America great?!

A Different Point of View?

It's interesting to consider the scandal from the point of view of stockbrokers and financial advisors. Consider the following cover stories from the industry trade publication, *Registered Rep*. The magazine calls itself "The Source for Investment Professionals." Its headlines make you wonder: Are some brokers and advisors more upset over the disruption to their business than the scandal itself?

July 2004	"Witch Hunt! Regulators Have Turned Up the Heat on Everyone — CEOs, Compliance Officers, Directors, and Branch Managers — and Now They're Gunning for You"
October 2004	"From Top Dog to Compliance Monkey: The Rise and Fall of the Branch Manager"
December 2004	"Sink or Sell? Rising Compliance Costs Are Swamping Small Broker/Dealers"
April 2005	"Mutual Distrust: New Fund-marketing Disclosure Rules Complicate Relations with Clients — and Generate Piles of Paperwork. How Will Reps Cope?"
January 2005	"A New Ballgame: With Regulators Watching, Fund Wholesalers Are Changing Their M.O. Goodbye Free Lunch, Sports Tickets, Drinks?"
February 2006	"Our Interests May *Not* Always Be the Same As Yours. You Can Be a Rep and Offer Financial-planning Advice. But It Just Got a Lot Harder"
May 2007	"SCREWED: After Eight Years, Registered Reps May No Longer Be Able to Position Themselves as 'Advisors.'"
June 2007	"They're Watching You: The Rules for What Reps Can Say in Written Communications to Clients Have Gotten Overly *restrictive*. The Games Some Reps Play to Get Around the *all-seeing* Compliance Department."

Turn Your Outrage Into Action

I'm sure you share my outrage over the retail mutual fund industry's behavior. But is that enough of a reason to sell your investments in the funds owned by these fund companies?

Most people would say yes. But some might take a different view. Cynics might say that corporate scandals are nothing new, that there's nothing we can do to stop such scandals, and that any investment we might pick is likely to land us in the same mess as the one we're already in. Essentially, these people say, righteous indignation is one thing, but as long as the funds keep producing profits, they're willing to tolerate the scandals.

Well, the profits *aren't* there. Retail mutual funds are simply no longer able to consistently generate above-average returns. This sad fact is demonstrated by Standard & Poor's Mutual Fund Persistence Scorecard, which shows that, for the five years ending December 31, 2006, only 1 stock fund in 13 was able to generate returns good enough to score in the top 50% of all funds all five years. By being unable to offer consistently good performance, funds can't justify their expenses — especially after they've been caught with their hands in the cookie jar.

No wonder that the highly regarded David Swensen, chief investment officer of Yale University's $15 billion endowment fund, wrote in *Unconventional Success: A Fundamental Approach to Personal Investment* that there is "overwhelming evidence that proves the failure of the mutual fund industry."

Mr. Swensen is right. The industry's ethical breaches are not only insulting to us as investors, but they have caused you and me real economic losses. Therefore, I have become so dissatisfied with the behavior and practices of the retail mutual fund industry that Jean, my colleagues, and I no longer tolerate the situation. We've sold all our holdings of retail mutual funds. You should too.

What should you do after you sell your retail mutual funds? You'll find the answer in the next chapter.

You are more powerful than the New York attorney general and the SEC combined . . . Only you can withdraw assets from mutual fund companies.

~ Gary Weiss, author of *Wall Street Versus America:*
The Rampant Greed and Dishonesty That Imperil Your Investments

---

Chapter 5

How to Beat the Retail Mutual Fund Industry at Its Own Game

Deceptive marketing practices. Illegal market timing and late trading. Excessive and hidden fees. All of these are perpetrated on investors by the retail mutual fund industry. If you're as annoyed by this behavior as me, you want to do something about it. So let me show you how you can turn this detrimental situation into a beneficial one.

First, let's not get carried away. Despite the inappropriate business practices and illegal behavior that's going on in the retail mutual fund industry, we must respond realistically. Just because you don't like what's going on in the world of mutual funds doesn't mean you're suddenly qualified to start picking your own stocks and bonds. No matter how amazed or disappointed you are, mutual funds remain the best way to invest. But that doesn't mean we have to keep dealing with the same mutual funds in the same way we did before. It is entirely appropriate that we make important changes — and the opportunity to make those changes is readily available.

When the mutual fund scandal broke in October 2003 with revelations that fund managers at Putnam (then the fourth largest mutual fund company) were personally engaging in market timing and allowing certain customers to do so as well, my colleagues and I at Edelman Financial immediately realized that this story wasn't going to be just about Putnam. We suspected that the entire retail mutual fund industry would become ensnared in a massive scandal unprecedented in the sixty-year history of the mutual fund industry. We quickly concluded, for all the reasons cited in the last chapter, that we needed to sell our investments in those mutual funds, and that we needed an alternative for ourselves and our clients.

Deciding to leave the retail mutual fund world was a relatively easy decision. The harder decision, which we debated intensely in a series of long, sometimes heated meetings, was where to go. I mean, it was one thing to decide to sell the mutual funds we've owned for decades, but what do we buy next?

Like Jean and I did twenty years ago, my colleagues and I started from scratch. Using a clean board and some markers, we considered — and ultimately rejected — every option available.

We considered picking our own stocks and bonds — and rejected the idea as being as foolish as diners who decide they're great cooks merely because they don't like the restaurant.

Or we could hire private money managers and let them pick the stocks and bonds for our clients. We seriously explored that idea and exhaustively researched dozens of money management firms. In the end, we rejected that idea as well, for these reasons:

- **They lack diversification.** These outfits tend to have limited expertise. Most emphasize only one market sector — mid-cap growth stocks, for example. Others provide wider offerings but tend to do so only because clients demand it; they lack the expertise to handle these other asset classes and market sectors effectively. As a result . . .

- **Their performance records are not impressive.** If you compare their investment returns with those of mutual funds, you find little reason to consider these programs.

- **They are complicated.** Private accounts entail statements that are dozens of pages in length — every single month. The tax record keeping alone is quite a chore.

- **Many are run by the same people who manage retail mutual funds — the same funds we're trying to leave.** Talk about jumping out of the frying pan and into the fire! This not only makes the effort pointless, it demonstrates how small the world of money management really is.

- **They are too expensive.** This is the proverbial coffin's final nail. In addition to all the problems noted above, these firms charge fees that often are dramatically higher than what consumers pay to own retail mutual funds.

In the end, we were forced to conclude that mutual funds remain the best answer for us and for our clients. Mutual funds enable you to build a comprehensive investment portfolio quickly, easily, efficiently, and inexpensively. In addition, mutual funds offer you:

- <u>Lower risk</u>. Because mutual funds hold hundreds or even thousands of securities, you avoid the risk that any one stock or bond might become worthless.

- <u>Maximum liquidity</u>. When you place money into a mutual fund, your money remains available to you every day the financial markets are open for business. You can add and withdraw money at any time, usually with no restrictions or expenses (subject, of course, to taxes and current market values). This feature does not exist with many other investments.

- <u>Greater affordability</u>. The brokerage, trading, and custody expenses of buying and managing a portfolio that consists of hundreds or thousands of stocks and bonds would be very expensive to buy and time consuming to manage. Investing in mutual funds reduces these problems.

But not just *any* mutual funds. Indeed, the answer to today's investing puzzle is found in an area of the mutual fund world that is both huge and tiny, long standing and brand new, very familiar yet unknown. Yes, in an investment world filled with contradiction, mutual funds offer both the problem and the solution.

You're probably not aware that there are actually *two* mutual fund industries. You're well aware of *retail* mutual funds, but you probably have never heard of *institutional* funds — and that is where we knew we needed to go.

Institutional shares have been around for a long time. My firm, like many advisors, was quite familiar with them, but until the retail mutual fund scandal exploded, we never bothered with them. First of all, there was no incentive; we'd been using

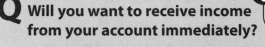

Q **Will you want to receive income from your account immediately?** This is question #5. If you haven't answered questions 1–4, STOP! and turn to page 185.

a) Yes......**ERROR!** In Question #2, you said you'd make additional deposits, but here in Question #5 you say you want immediate withdrawals. Start over on page 192 — and change one of your answers.

b) No.......**Congratulations!** You've completed Part 1 of the Edelman Guide to Portfolio Selection. **Your Letter Score is H.** Return to page 193 and continue to Part 2.

retail mutual funds for decades with a high degree of success; performance was good, risk was within tolerable limits, the behavior of fund management appeared fine, and the cost was acceptable. Well, as we've learned, those days are gone.

Second, the door was shut. Institutional funds typically require that you invest millions of dollars — they serve institutions, after all. Thus, to build a diversified portfolio using a dozen funds, you might need $20 million. That's not a problem for a big pension fund, but I doubt you can cough that up.

Given the situation, we needed to open that institutional door so our clients could invest in the same funds as the nation's biggest endowments and pension plans. Our efforts began in October 2003, and it took us more than two years to gain entry. Along the way, I was forced to completely reshape and reorganize my firm. The effort was well worth it.

To understand why institutional funds are a big part of the solution (there's another important part that I'll explain later), you need to understand how they differ from retail mutual funds.

The biggest — and most obvious — difference between you and an institutional investor is the amount of money you each have to invest. Having more money makes you manage that money differently.

Let me explain: You probably have a five-figure, six-figure, or (if you're really fortunate) seven-figure amount of money to invest; somewhere between $50,000 and $10 million. No matter how much you have, it's chump change compared to institutions — pension funds, endowments, and the cash assets of major corporations.

I've already mentioned David Swensen, who manages the $15 billion endowment at Yale. That's nothing compared to Harvard's endowment of $29.2 billion. And that pales beside the California Public Employees Retirement System, CalPERS, the largest pension fund in America, with $210 billion. Google is sitting on $10.4 billion in cash — but that's nothing compared to Microsoft, which has so much cash on hand that it distributed $75 billion to shareholders in 2004. It has $28.3 billion more. So don't get cocky because you've got some coins in your pocket.

The amount of money these pension fund managers have forces them to approach investments with a perspective that is very different from ordinary retail investors. When you have a limited amount of money to invest, you devote considerable attention to selecting the right investments. But when you have huge amounts of money to invest, you instinctively care more about how you allocate your money.

Let me put it this way. Say I give $1,000 to you and another $1,000 to your best friend. I send you both to Wal-Mart with instructions that you each must spend all the money before you leave the store. What are the odds that you will each leave with the same items? Considering that a typical Wal-Mart store contains seventy thousand products (plus another twenty thousand grocery items), we can be confident that you and your friend will buy completely different items.

Now let's alter the experiment. This time I will send each of you into Wal-Mart with $1 billion. What are the odds that you'll have the same items when you exit this time?

Obviously, you and your friend will leave the store with identical items. That's because, with $1 billion to spend, you'll each buy *the entire store*. You have so much money to spend, you have no choice but to buy everything.

Institutional investors face the same dilemma. With $15 billion at his disposal, do you think David Swensen is trying to decide whether he wants to buy General Electric instead of IBM? Of course not. With all the money at his disposal, he has no choice but to buy both.

Thus, for David Swensen, the question is not "What should I buy?" but, rather, "How much of each should I buy?"

In other words, the key question for institutional investors is not the stock picking decision, but the asset allocation decision. We've come right back to Gary Brinson! (As you learned in chapter 2, he determined the causes of volatility in investment portfolios.)

Indeed, institutions rely extensively on the academic approach to money management, and it explains why they are more successful at investing than retail consumers.

Retail investors — aided by the retail media (*Money*, *SmartMoney*, *Kiplinger's*, CNBC, and so on) and retail stockbrokers (such as Smith Barney, Merrill Lynch, UBS, Ameriprise, and so on) — spend all their time trying to pick stocks that are better than other stocks, or they pick mutual funds that they hope are better than other mutual funds. But investment success isn't about picking investments, it's about allocating your money properly among the many asset classes and market sectors. That's how institutions do it, and that's why they enjoy better results.

The notion of bringing an institutional approach to retail investors isn't new. For years index funds have argued that they offer such an approach, and the debate of index funds versus active managers is well known. I have been a participant in that debate, and in prior books have explained why traditional index funds (led by the poster child of indexing, the S&P 500 Stock Index Fund) are foolish investments.

But academia once again comes to the rescue and now shows us that the issue is more complex than it once was. Previously — and by that I mean as recently as 2002 — retail investors had a simple choice: Pick a retail mutual fund that is run by a retail mutual fund manager who works for a retail mutual fund company and whose job is to pick what he thinks are the best stocks. Or choose an index fund that simply buys every stock in its cat-

Think Picking an Index Fund Is Easy?

Want to buy an index fund? Just answer one question: which index? Wall Street offers tens of thousands of indexes. Which will you pick? Index funds even have their own publication, the *Journal of Indexes* (lower left). And their own conferences — see the brochure, lower right. Sure, you're just going to buy an index fund. Right.

Figure 5.1

Sponsor	Number of Indexes Offered
Morgan Stanley Capital Int'l Barra	80,000[48]
Lehman Brothers	8,000
Dow Jones & Company	4,000
Merrill Lynch	3,000
Standard and Poor's	300
Wilshire Associates	48
Russell Investment Group	23

---

[48] Yes, eighty *thousand*.

egory. Active versus indexing. I won't bother going into each side's arguments here, having done so in *Discover the Wealth Within You*, but I can assure you that it's been one heck of a debate.

The debaters can now go home.

The reason is that both camps have been right, and both have been wrong. The truth, as usual, is found in a combination of the two. You see, the proper question is not

Active versus Indexing

but rather

Active versus Passive

The Active camp has long argued that you should actively select securities, while the Index camp says you should simply buy the securities that comprise an index.

But both camps have ignored an important fact: Investing isn't just about deciding which investments to select; you must also decide what to do after you've selected them. In other words, investing is not merely a question of selection, but selection *and* management. Implicitly, the Active camp has argued for <u>actively</u> selecting securities (demonstrated by picking individual securities based on the merits of each) and then <u>actively</u> managing them (through frequent buying and selling of the securities). Meanwhile, the Index camp says you should <u>passively</u> select securities (by simply buying whichever securities are listed in an index, with no other consideration) and then <u>passively</u> manage them (keep those securities forever, unless there are changes in the underlying index).

In other words, we must parse the debate from one question — Active versus Index — into two questions:

Should your *selection process* be Active or Passive?

<u>and</u>

Should your *management style* be Active or Passive?

As the active proponents (including me) have long claimed, Active security selection is essential. Without it, you wind up buying bad investments or buying too many of some investments and too few of others — resulting in a bad, even wacky, asset allocation model. But once you select those securities, the Index proponents win; you should hold those securities virtually forever.

The Best of Both Worlds: Active Selection Combined with Passive Management

Institutional funds offer this exact approach to investing. They have no choice, because their clients demand it. If you're David Swensen, and you've decided to place, say, 15% of your endowment's assets into mid-cap growth stocks, you want to know that the institutional fund you've picked for that purpose will buy mid-cap growth stocks *only*. You don't want your mid-cap growth fund to suddenly start buying value stocks or large-cap stocks, because you've hired other funds to invest in those categories. If the mid-cap growth fund starts to buy value or large-cap, your overall asset allocation will be affected in ways you can't control and don't want. If that were to happen, you'd pull the assets from the mid-cap growth fund, effectively firing that fund company. If a fund wants to keep David Swensen as a client, it must not deviate from its assignment.

This helps explain why institutional funds are largely immune from the improper behaviors and illegal activities of the retail mutual fund industry:

- **Institutional funds solve the problem of frequent manager changes and manager moonlighting.** Because institutional funds acquire and hold thousands of securities, there's little opportunity for a manager to impact the fund.

- **Institutional funds solve the problem of high turnover.** By owning virtually all the securities in a given asset class, annual turnover is near zero.

- **Institutional funds solve the problems of style drift and bracket creep, as well as excessive cash or margin.** Since turnover is nil, there's virtually no opportunity for a fund manager to alter the fund's makeup. And cash is routinely kept minimal.

- **Institutional funds solve the problems of window dressing, misleading fund names, cosmetic name changes, fund closings and reopenings, and cloning.** For institutional funds, consistency is of primary concern.

Marketing gimmicks that might play well with consumers have no audience among the professionals guiding the assets of the nation's top institutions.

- **Institutional funds solve the problems of closet indexing and fund bloating.** Because institutional funds are *designed* to own virtually every security in a given market sector, they can't be accused of "secretly" doing so. By the same notion, it's impossible to become too big when your mission is to own the entire marketplace.

- **Institutional funds solve the problems of survivorship bias, creation bias, and fund seeding.** Similarly, the experts at the helm of institutional assets cannot be duped by these marketing games.

- **Institutional funds solve the problems of rising costs, hidden fees, stale pricing, confusing share classes, and no economies of scale.** When you're investing billions of dollars, you decide what you're willing to pay. Thus, institutional shares are the cheapest in the entire mutual fund industry, charging as little as one-twentieth the amount that retail funds charge. Now, *that's* economy of scale.

- **Institutional funds solve the problems of illegal market timing, late trading, and personal trading by portfolio managers.** Unlike retail funds, which have millions of investors who each invests small amounts, institutional funds have relatively few clients who each invests millions of dollars. This creates little opportunity for a manager to manipulate the portfolio the way a retail fund manager can.

- **Institutional funds solve the problems of steering business and shelf-space payments.** Institutional funds work directly with their clients. They do not collect assets via broker-dealers like retail funds do. One of the reasons institutional shares are so inexpensive is that they refuse to pay fees to broker-dealers or investment advisors.

! This is question #4. If you haven't answered questions 1–3, STOP! and turn to page 185.

Q What is your age?

a) Under age 70 .... turn to page 123

b) 70 or older .... turn to page 243

In summary, institutional shares have a long-term focus, emphasize extensive diversification, and feature low turnover — matching the investment philosophy I've espoused for twenty years.

> **IMPORTANT!**
>
> **Do not confuse true institutional mutual funds with the "institution class" of shares that are offered by retail mutual funds.**
>
> **As you saw on page 108, retail fund companies offer a bewildering array of share classes. While the underlying portfolios (and their investments) are virtually identical, the share classes themselves differ dramatically in terms of commissions, surrender charges, and ongoing fees. In an effort to attract ultrahigh net-worth investors, as well as pension funds and corporate clients, some retail mutual fund companies offer a special share class that features unusually low fees. This "institution class" of shares typically requires minimum investments of $1 million or more, putting it out of the reach of ordinary retail investors.**
>
> **Although the fees of such institution class shares are more in line with the fees of truly institutional mutual funds, they are still retail mutual funds in every other way. They suffer from the same high turnover, style drift and bracket creep, short manager tenure, and all the other problems described in chapter 4.**

There is no question that institutional funds offer the solution to the problems found in retail mutual funds. At present, we consider Dimensional Fund Advisors to be the best institutional fund family.[49] Founded in 1981 to serve institutional clients, DFA's directors include the most respected names in economics and finance (see Figure 5.2). Since 1990 DFA funds have been available to financial advisors, provided that they complete DFA's training program. To date, only a few hundred of the nation's 225,000 Registered Investment Advisors have completed this training — the advisors of Edelman Financial among them.

DFA will not allow you to invest in DFA funds on your own; you can obtain them only through approved financial advisors. So has this entire book been nothing but a sales pitch?

---

[49]I cringe as I write these words, out of fear that we'll change our opinion before you read this. You might want to check with us to make sure you're getting our most up-to-date advice and information. Just visit RicEdelman.com or call us at 888-PLAN-RIC.

Figure 5.2

Academic leaders affiliated with DFA

Faculty	Affiliation	Area of Expertise
George M. Constantinides, University of Chicago	Board Member of Dimensional's U.S. mutual funds	Asset Pricing, Capital Markets Research
Eugene F. Fama, University of Chicago	Board Member of Dimensional Fund Advisors, consultant for Dimensional's Fixed Income and Value Strategies	Efficient Markets Hypothesis, Random Walk Hypothesis, Capital Markets Research, Multifactor Model, Definitive Finance Text, Tax Research
Kenneth R. French, Dartmouth College	Board Member of Dimensional Fund Advisors, consultant and Head of Investment Policy	Capital Markets Research, Multifactor Model, Tax Research
John P. Gould, University of Chicago	Board Member of Dimensional's U.S. mutual funds	Applied Price Theory, Former Dean of University of Chicago Graduate School of Business
Roger G. Ibbotson, Yale University	Board Member of Dimensional's U.S. mutual funds	Capital Markets Research, Comprehensive Stocks, Bonds, Bills and Inflation Database
Donald B. Keim, University of Pennsylvania	Consultant for Dimensional's Real Estate Securities Strategy and Trading Cost Studies	Capital Markets Research, Real Estate Securities, Small Stock "January Effect"
Robert C. Merton, Harvard University	Board Member of Dimensional's U.S. mutual funds	Asset Pricing Theory, Valuation of Derivative Securities
Myron S. Scholes, Stanford University	Board Member of Dimensional's U.S. mutual funds	Capital Markets Research, Options Pricing Model
Abbie J. Smith, University of Chicago	Board Member of Dimensional's U.S. mutual funds	Capital Markets Research, Financial Accounting Information
Marvin Zonis, University of Chicago	Consultant for International Economics	Corporate Restructuring, Corporate Governance Capital Markets Research, World Political Affairs, Foreign Policy Analysis

I was having a nice day until I started reading this book. I've owned my retail mutual funds for years and thought nothing of it. But then I read these pages, and now I'm convinced that I need to get out of these retail funds. And buy what? Institutional shares, did he say? Fine, where do I get them? From him? <u>Only</u> from him? He's kidding, right?

Yes, I'm kidding.

It would indeed be a rude ploy to suggest that I alone have the only solution to your investment needs. Although some other personal finance writers make such claims, I'm not among them.

It's true that I believe strongly in institutional shares, and it's true that my firm's current answer is DFA. But this could change, and if history is any guide, it's fairly certain that this *will* change at some point, when our continuing research and analysis discovers something better than DFA.

In fact, we're already partway there. You see, we don't use DFA exclusively when constructing portfolios for our clients. In some cases, DFA doesn't offer funds in every asset class or market sector that we want to include in our portfolios, while in other cases we have found that we can obtain the desired asset class even cheaper than we can get it from DFA.

So, yes, there is another source of outstanding shares for you. You can obtain these on your own, without an advisor if you so desire. Like DFA, these shares avoid all the problems of retail mutual funds. That means you can go right ahead and build your portfolio, with nothing standing in your way.

What are these shares that I'm talking about? Turn to the next chapter.

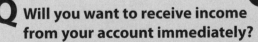

Q Will you want to receive income from your account immediately?

This is question #5. If you haven't answered questions 1–4, STOP! and turn to page 185.

a) Yes......**ERROR!** In Question #2, you said you'd make additional deposits, but here in Question #5 you say you want immediate withdrawals. Start over on page 192 — and change one of your answers.

b) No.......**Congratulations!** You've completed Part 1 of the Edelman Guide to Portfolio Selection. **Your Letter Score is Q.** Return to page 193 and continue to Part 2.

Chapter 6
The Greatest Invention Since Mutual Funds

Allow me to introduce you to Exchange-Traded Funds. First brought to the market in 1993, this newest breed of investment company[50] looks like a mutual fund but has important distinctions. Most important, you don't buy ETFs from a fund company; instead the shares are listed on a major stock exchange (hence its name) where they trade like other securities.

ETFs have six main advantages over retail mutual funds:

1) **ETFs are dirt cheap.** The typical retail mutual fund costs more than three times more than an ETF (the average annual expense ratio for mutual funds is 1.56% versus 0.40% for ETFs, according to Morningstar). ETFs are even cheaper than index funds, which cost an average of 0.70%. And the cheapest ETF charges only 0.07% — just one-tenth the average index fund fee and a tiny fraction of the average retail mutual fund fee. Retail mutual funds cost more because they issue monthly statements and provide other customer services. But ETFs trade like stocks, so the services that retail mutual funds typically provide are instead provided by the brokerage firm or the investor's financial advisor. By avoiding those tasks, ETFs avoid the expenses that go with them.

2) **ETFs enjoy great tax efficiency.** As explained on page 95, mutual funds engage in high turnover, which generates capital gains distributions — forcing investors to pay taxes. But ETFs generally engage in far less turnover (often zero). And even when there is some selling within the

---

[50]Like mutual funds, ETFs are regulated by the Investment Company Act of 1940.

portfolio, it typically doesn't constitute a taxable event for investors. That's because ETFs benefit from a mechanism called *in-kind redemption,* which enables ETFs to redeem shares from baskets of their underlying securities. This avoids taxable distributions, saving the investor money on an annual basis.

3) **ETFs disclose their holdings daily.** With ETFs, you always know what you own. This is in stark contrast to retail mutual funds, which reveal their holdings only twice per year, in tardy filings and often only after considerable manipulation designed to mask what's really going on (see **Window Dressing** on page 180).

4) **ETFs are priced in real time throughout the day.** Mutual funds are priced only once per day, after the market has closed. When buying or selling mutual funds, you don't know the price until the next day. But ETF prices are quoted in real time all day long, just like stocks. Again, this is because ETFs trade on the open exchange.[51]

> *Properly used, ETFs have merit. They enable investors to make long-term bets on the total market or given market segments, or to diversify portfolios.*
>
> ~John Bogle

5) **ETFs tend to be highly specialized.** Retail mutual funds tend to hold securities that are individually selected by the fund's manager. These holdings change constantly, and the fund's holdings at any given moment can be (and usually are) eclectic. But ETFs typically hold only a certain kind of security — say, mid-cap growth stocks — and nothing else. They also tend to hold *every* security in that category; there's no manager trying to pick "which" mid-cap growth stocks to buy. Because this enables investors to own obscure assets that are otherwise too difficult or expensive to buy and monitor. For example, Barclays Bank offers an ETF that holds twenty-four agricultural, energy, and metals futures contracts. Instead of trying to monitor these twenty-four obscure instruments, an investor can merely track one ETF.

---

[51]This also enables ETF owners to short their ETFs, buy them on margin, or purchase options. I don't endorse these ideas, but some investors favor these notions.

6) **ETFs are favored by institutional investors.** Barclays Global Investors, currently the largest issuer of ETFs, reports that 80% of trading in its funds is conducted by hedge funds and other big investors. When you invest in an ETF, you're investing alongside some of the nation's largest investors.

Did I say futures contracts? Indeed. ETFs can acquire, hold, and rebalance any pre-selected group of securities. The first ETFs tracked the S&P 500 Stock Index. But today, thanks to computer technology, you can create an ETF to track virtually any segment of the financial markets. Small manufacturers in the Southwest? No problem. Regional banking stocks? Fine. Aerospace and defense? Sure.

The ability to track specific segments of the market, without the influence (and inconsistencies) of fund managers, with insulation against the scams and abuses found in the retail mutual fund industry, with real-time pricing, dramatically lower costs, and greater transparency — all this explains why exchange-traded funds are so popular among professional investors.

No wonder ETFs constitute the fastest-growing segment of the investment world: Celent, a research and consulting firm, says ETF trading volume more than doubled from 2005 to 2006, and predicts that ETF assets

Shortly after we completed our due diligence on ETFs and had decided to begin incorporating them into our clients' portfolios, a negative article appeared in a trade magazine. The July 2005 issue of *On Wall Street*, a publication written for stockbrokers, featured a cover story proclaiming, "Why Reps Have Soured on ETFs."

That was a scary headline. Here we were, about to introduce ETFs to our clients, and now a major industry publication was saying that stockbrokers don't like ETFs. Why not?

"The fees on these products don't match those on mutual funds and that's giving many advisors pause . . . brokers don't have a lot of incentive to use ETFs . . . [although] for clients, the lower fees associated with ETFs provide a clear advantage to mutual funds."

We knew we were on the right track.

Reprinted with permission from On Wall Street.

will reach $2 trillion by 2010. Considering that ETFs hold only $422 billion in assets (as opposed to $10 trillion in mutual funds),[52] that's really saying something.

Figure 6.1

Investors are already pouring money into ETFs, and assets are projected to grow exponentially.

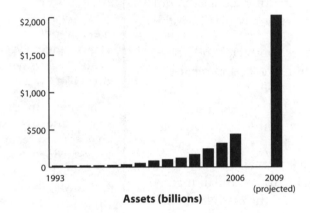

The number of ETFs is also rising dramatically, in response to investor demand. Hundreds more ETFs will be introduced by 2010.

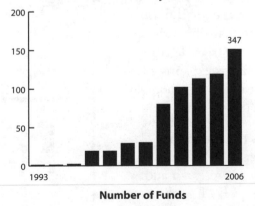

[52]According to the Investment Company Institute, as of December 31, 2006. As if I was making all this up.

As ETFs become more widely available and more ubiquitous, and as consumers learn more about their advantages, ETFs will eventually surpass mutual funds in size and prominence in the marketplace. This is your opportunity to start now.

In the pages that follow, I'm going to help you create a highly sophisticated portfolio based on your personal goals and individual circumstances. Throughout this process, you'll receive an asset allocation model that is similar to those used by the nation's biggest and most powerful institutional investors. You'll have a portfolio that is far more diversified and sophisticated than you ever thought possible, and you'll be able to implement it very easily and at a remarkably low cost.

! This is the end of Part 1. If you haven't answered questions 1–4, STOP! and turn to page 185.

Congratulations! You've finished Part 1 of the Edelman Guide to Portfolio Selection.

Your Letter Score is N.

Remember this Letter Score and return to page 193.

Chapter 7

Creating the Investment Portfolio That's Right for You

Before writing this book, I carefully reviewed other books and websites, to see what asset allocation advice they offer their readers. What I found was disappointing. Almost all of them offer only three options: conservative, moderate, and aggressive. Sometimes a site would offer *five* choices — wahoo!

Do *you* think that every American's investment needs can be addressed by just three (or five) investment portfolios?

I don't think so either. Certainly that's not how we manage money for our clients. So my goal was to provide you with a truly unique service. But that was easier said than done: I had to figure out how to convert a typical two-hour conversation that a new client might have with one of my firm's advisors into a static set of finite questions that would still lead you to an effective portfolio.

It was a daunting challenge, but a fun project. The results are in these pages — in full color to boot. This book features not three, not five, but forty-three portfolios. And to determine which is best for you, you'll use the brand new Edelman Guide to Portfolio Selection®, which I've developed for this book.

The GPS features eight (or nine) questions (depending on your answers). Obviously, asking finite quetions creates a limitation. When we actually talk with new clients, we ask a lot more than that. For example, this book doesn't delve into your tax bracket, or how much of your money you're planning to invest. To be sure, our advisors delve into those issues (and many more).

The GPS is carefully crafted not only to gather the information needed to take you through the process, but to avoid the need for extensive interactivity. This is a book, after all, and there are limitations with the printed page. (For a more dynamic and extensive version of the GPS, visit RicEdelman.com. Thanks to web technology, we were able to design a more sophisticated version there than we are able to do here.)

Still, I invite you to follow the GPS here first (it's fun!). It will take you through the pages of this book, and your unique combination of answers will lead you to one of the forty-three investment portfolios my colleagues and I have designed. Then, if you wish, you can go to my website to take the longer version of the GPS. If you get the same results, you can be highly confident that you're on the right track.

Once you identify your portfolio, you'll be able to purchase investments for it. If you are content to own only exchange-traded funds, you can buy them from any discount broker. If you prefer to include institutional shares, you'll need to work with a financial advisor who offers such funds.

Follow the GPS with Three Points In Mind

Before you begin this exercise, consider these three limitations:

1. My goal is to help you create a portfolio that's suitable and appropriate for you, based on your individual circumstances, goals, and risk tolerance. The forty-three portfolios in these pages are among those used in the Edelman Managed Asset Program, one of the fastest-growing and most popular investment management services in the country. But EMAP offers many more portfolio models, and we are constantly creating new ones (and adjusting current ones) to meet the individual needs of our clients. Therefore, it is entirely possible that none of the portfolios in this book is ideal for your individual financial situation.

2. It's also possible that, by the time you conduct the exercise, we'll have changed the allocation of the model to which you're led, due to changes in the economy, tax law, and other developments in the field of personal finance. Unfortunately, this book is static; I cannot call you or send you an email with important news like we can for our clients. Therefore, I urge you to visit the website, where the information is kept current and up-to-date, or talk with a financial advisor.

3. The GPS in this book assumes that you plan to open just one investment account. But if you're like most investors, you have multiple accounts: joint, trust, IRA, and college savings and retirement plans. You probably plan to

use some of these assets sooner than others (college versus retirement, for example). Also, some accounts should be handled differently than others due to tax law (IRAs versus trust accounts, for example). Printed questionnaires simply cannot deal with such complexity, and this argues for verifying the process through a conversation with a financial advisor. So even though the Guide will steer you toward a specific portfolio, it cannot truly replicate or replace the advice you'd receive by talking privately with a financial advisor.

Despite these limitations, the GPS can help lead you to an effective portfolio model. However, that's as much as I believe a book can do. You might be hoping to receive specific investment recommendations for use with your new investment portfolio, but that information goes beyond the true and legitimate ability of this (or any) book. There are several reasons for this:

1. Even though I have shown that you can build an all-ETF portfolio, we don't do that for our clients, so I don't recommend it for you. Instead you will be better served by including institutional shares, such as those offered by DFA funds. Thus, it would be disingenuous to tell you to buy investments that I do not recommend for our clients.

2. ETFs are being introduced almost weekly.[53] So even if I *wanted* to give you ETF recommendations, I can't do so here. Our recommendations change over time, and as a result, this book obviously omits investment opportunities that weren't available at the time of publication.

3. Changes in the investment world occasionally cause us to change the holdings within the portfolios we provide our clients. If you were to purchase investments listed in this book, you could find yourself buying investments that we might be telling our clients to sell in favor of other choices.

Therefore, you should talk with a financial advisor before you implement the portfolios suggested by this book. An advisor can verify that the portfolio suggested for you in these pages is suitable and appropriate for your situation.

---

[53]At this writing, nearly 300 ETFs are have filed for registration and are awaiting SEC approval. Hundreds more will follow within a few years.

Can a Book Eliminate the Need for an Advisor?

You certainly would appreciate receiving professional advice. But maybe you prefer to avoid the fee that you know an advisor would charge. If that describes you, my advice that you hire an advisor is *doubly important*.

Indeed, you could be guilty of being penny-wise and pound-foolish. Maybe you're a person who can't see the forest for the trees. Got any other applicable clichés?

Although I can understand your desire to avoid an advisor's fee, you need to realize that "avoiding a fee" does not necessarily translate into "saving money." I recall the time a client called us to make a withdrawal from his account. He'd gotten a letter from the IRS saying that he owed $8,000 in taxes, interest, and penalties. Even though we had given him the names of several tax professionals years earlier, our client admitted that he had continued preparing his own returns in order to avoid the cost of paying someone else to do it.

It turns out that his efforts to save a few hundred bucks was about to cost him $8,000 unnecessarily. Fortunately, he called us before he paid that tax bill. Although he assumed that he had to pay the money that the IRS was demanding, we knew better. Knowing his situation, we suspected something was amiss. The IRS letter was triggered by a 1099 form issued by his mutual fund company. As sometimes happens, the IRS computers had confused "gross proceeds" with "capital gains" and mistakenly assumed that our client had failed to pay taxes on tens of thousands of dollars in capital gains. And because our client was trying to handle it on his own, he was about to pay!

We explained the situation to him and convinced him to hire an accountant, as we'd originally suggested, instead of paying the tax. He agreed — at this point, he realized that spending a few hundred dollars wouldn't hurt — and, indeed, his new CPA verified our thought: The IRS made an error. Result: The entire $8,000 liability for taxes, penalties, and interest vanished. It was a perfect example of someone spending thousands in an effort to save hundreds.

Think eight grand is a lot of money? That's nothing. One fall day in 1997, I got a call from an astrophysicist. He had $750,000 to invest; the proceeds of an inheritance. After reviewing his situation, we gave him our recommendations. He chose not to hire us. Instead, he told me, he decided to buy investments himself, saving the cost of my fee. "After all," he said in a comment that I'll never forget, "this isn't rocket science."

Six years later, in 2003, he called again. "Remember me?" he asked. "I'd like to come talk to you, if you're still willing to accept me as a client." He brought me up to date: He had invested all his money in tech stocks, and his portfolio was now worth only $300,000. Yep, in six years he managed to lose more than half of his money. "Remember when I told you that investing wasn't rocket science?" he said. "Well, I was right. *It's harder!* I lost more than four hundred thousand dollars!"

I couldn't resist. "It's even worse than you think," I replied. "If you had accepted our recommendations, your account would currently be worth more than one million dollars."[54] He's been a client of our firm ever since.

My point is this: Anyone can buy mutual funds. Anyone can prepare his or her own taxes. You can shop for your own insurance and select your own mortgage. In many states, you can even write your own will. And if you do all these things on your own, you'll avoid financial advisory fees, tax prep fees, and legal fees.

But buying your own investments, insurance, and mortgages doesn't make you a financial advisor. Preparing your own taxes doesn't mean you're a CPA, and writing your own will doesn't make you a lawyer.

Today's world of personal finance is highly complex. For example, most do-it-yourself investors fret over which investment to buy. They don't realize that the account registration is an equally crucial decision. Will you open a joint account, and if so, what kind? Joint Tenants with Rights of Survivorship, Tenants in Common, or Tenants by the Entirety? Or perhaps you should establish a Transfer on Death account, or even a trust account. If the latter, should that be revocable or irrevocable? Be careful with your answer — each choice has unique tax implications in addition to myriad legal issues.

Most investors don't know the proper answers[55] — in fact, most don't even consider the tax and legal considerations when making investment decisions. So you'll have to excuse me, but as a professional financial advisor, I get a little frustrated when someone tells me that he would prefer to handle his own investments in order to avoid paying our fee. I always wonder if he'll truly be richer by not working with us — especially when you consider that financial advisors do so much more than merely offer advice about investments. College and retirement planning, wills and trusts, employee benefits, real estate and mortgages, paying off debts — the list is quite extensive.[56]

---

[54]Remember: past performance is no indication of future results. This is a true story — like every anecdote in all my books — and it covers a particularly volatile period in the stock market.
[55]You'll find them in *The Truth About Money*.
[56]In a 2007 survey of investors conducted by the Investment Company Institute, 63% said their financial advisor provides five or more services. Yours should too.

Should you really hire an advisor even though (as this is the case with many of our clients) all you need is help with your investments? Well there are really only three reasons to hire an advisor:

1. **You lack the knowledge to handle these matters yourself.** You know you need to invest, but you don't know how to select investments and construct a portfolio. You need to hire an advisor.

2. **You have the knowledge, but you lack the time to manage your own investments.** Jim Cramer says you need to spend one hour per week researching each of your stocks. (If you have fifteen stocks, that's fifteen hours per week. Cramer says you should stop watching football on TV and instead devote that time to your stock portfolio.)

3. **You have the knowledge and the time, but you lack the desire.** You have other things to do with your time. Like, go to work and raise a family — or watch football on TV.

I've just described the clients of my firm; in fact, I've just described *all* the clients of *every* firm: People hire financial advisors when they realize that they lack the knowledge, the time, or the desire to handle their own personal finances.

Make sure you possess all three of the above attributes before you decide to handle your own financial affairs. Otherwise you might cost yourself a lot more than what advisors would charge.

One of my firm's clients is an interesting fellow. He has substantial investment knowledge and experience. He's retired and thus has plenty of time to focus on his affairs. And he considers investing to be a hobby; he enjoys reading the *Wall Street Journal* every day. He hired us anyway.

His reason: to benefit his wife. He realized that she was largely uninvolved (uninterested, really) in their complex financial affairs, and he knew he was likely to predecease her. "If I die," he told me, "I want someone with intimate knowledge of our affairs — someone my wife knows and trusts — to help her and look after her finances after I'm gone." Smart thinking.

Don't avoid advisors merely because you want to avoid their fees. Considering the problems that you might create for yourself, the advisor's fee could be a bargain.

So, decide if you have the *knowledge* to successfully manage all the aspects of your personal finances without the assistance of a professional, objective financial advisor. If you conclude that you aren't an expert, hire one. The cost will be a fraction of the losses you could incur by acting on your own.

Then decide if you have the *time* to successfully manage all the aspects of your personal finances without the assistance of a professional, objective financial advisor. If you conclude that you don't have the time, delegate the tasks to a professional. Sure, you'll incur a fee for the advisor's services; it's an unavoidable result of leading a busy life.

Finally, decide if you have the *desire* to successfully manage all the aspects of your personal finances without the assistance of a professional, objective financial advisor. If you conclude that you'd rather spend your time doing other things, hire one. Sure, you'll incur a fee for the advisor's services, but doing so will enable you to enjoy more fulfilling aspects of your life.

If you conclude that you have the knowledge, time, and desire to manage all the aspects of your personal finances on your own, without the assistance of a professional, objective financial advisor, then proceed — and hope that your skills and abilities match your confidence level.

> Even people who know better sometimes refuse to do what they know they should do.
>
> Tom Stevens put his house on the market in 2005 for more than $1.4 million. His real estate agent told him to lower the price, but Tom refused. A year later, it still hadn't sold. Tom told the *Washington Post*, "What I should have done . . . was listened to my [real estate] agent."
>
> At the time, Tom Stevens was president of the National Association of Realtors.

If you have concluded that you should consider a financial advisor, learn how to choose one by reading Part 13 of *The Truth About Money* (you can also get that information by visiting RicEdelman.com). And, of course, you are welcome to call my firm; we'd be happy to verify that you've selected the right portfolio and that its allocation is the same as what we are currently recommending to our clients.

Building and Managing an Investment Portfolio Using the
Edelman Guide to Portfolio Selection®: A Four-Step Process

Step 1: Suitability Determination

First, you must convince me that purchasing a portfolio of investments is in your best interest. So answer these three questions:

1. Do you have *any* credit card debt?

> It is not appropriate to establish investment accounts (except for IRAs and retirement plans at work) while maintaining credit card debt. You should pay your credit card balances in full, and open taxable investment accounts only after you have done so.

> If you have money in IRAs or retirement accounts at work, continue with this process. Otherwise, proceed no further with this process until you pay off all your credit cards.

2. Do you have *at least* three months' worth of expenses in cash reserves?

> We prefer that you maintain twelve months' worth of spending in cash reserves (in money market accounts, bank certificates of deposit, or other accounts that are insured by the Federal Deposit Insurance Corporation [FDIC]). However, for the purposes of this exercise, you can proceed if you have three months of spending in reserves. If you have less in reserves, proceed no further with this process.

3. Think about the money you're planning to invest. When is the earliest you think you'd withdraw any of this money?

> Mutual funds and exchange-traded funds are long-term investments. You should not purchase these types of investments unless you intend to leave the money invested for at least three years — and the longer the better. If you do, continue. If you don't, proceed no further with this process.

Step 2: Using the GPS to Identify Your Portfolio

Assuming you've made it this far, you're now ready to find out which portfolio is right for you. The GPS is easy and a lot of fun!

It consists of three parts. In the first part, you'll answer five questions that will take you to pages throughout the book, eventually providing you with a letter score (A–R), and returning you here.

You'll then be ready to complete the GPS's second part. You'll answer four questions to obtain a point score (0–10). Then, in the third and final part, you'll simply find your letter and number on a grid to determine which of the forty-three portfolios is best for you. You'll find the portfolios in the full-color insert!

So let's begin.

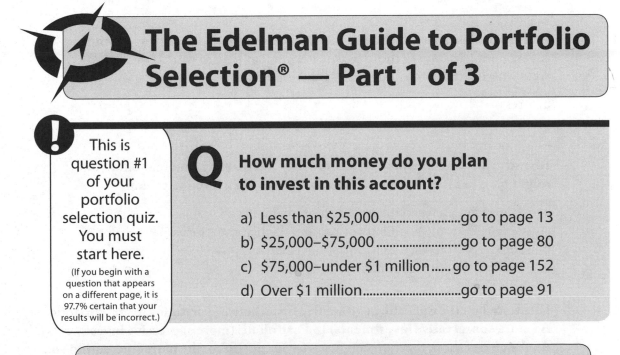

The Edelman Guide to Portfolio Selection® — Part 1 of 3

This is question #1 of your portfolio selection quiz. You must start here.

(If you begin with a question that appears on a different page, it is 97.7% certain that your results will be incorrect.)

Q **How much money do you plan to invest in this account?**

a) Less than $25,000.......................go to page 13
b) $25,000–$75,000 ....go to page 80
c) $75,000–under $1 million......go to page 152
d) Over $1 million............................go to page 91

When you return to this page

ENTER YOUR LETTER SCORE HERE :

Do not turn to the next page until you have obtained your Letter Score.

The Edelman Guide to Portfolio Selection® — Part 2 of 3

Do not answer these questions until you have obtained your letter score from the previous page.

1. **Please elaborate on your answer to the final question from Part One. When is the earliest you think you'd want to receive income from this account?**

   a) Immediately or within the next five years   = 0 points
   b) 5–10 years   = 2 points
   c) 10 years or more   = 3 points

2. **During the last sharp decline in the stock market, did you sell any of your investments (including those in your retirement plan at work) because you were worried that prices might fall further?**

   a) Yes   = 0 points
   b) No   = 2 points

3. **Investment values fluctuate; the more they fluctuate, the more money you might gain or lose. How much fluctuation are you willing to tolerate?**

   a) A lot. I am prepared to lose much of my money in exchange for the possibility of earning the highest returns.   = 1 point
   b) Some. I am prepared to accept some fluctuation in order to earn higher returns.   = 0 points

4. **Illustrated on the opposite page are five hypothetical portfolios, from Portfolio A (more conservative investments) to Portfolio E (more aggressive investments). As the charts show, the more aggressive your portfolio, the more fluctuation you can expect to experience. While all of these hypothetical portfolios end with higher values, some of the charts might have shown losses if they ended at a different point. For this final question, choose the portfolio that shows the level of fluctuation that you would prefer to own.**

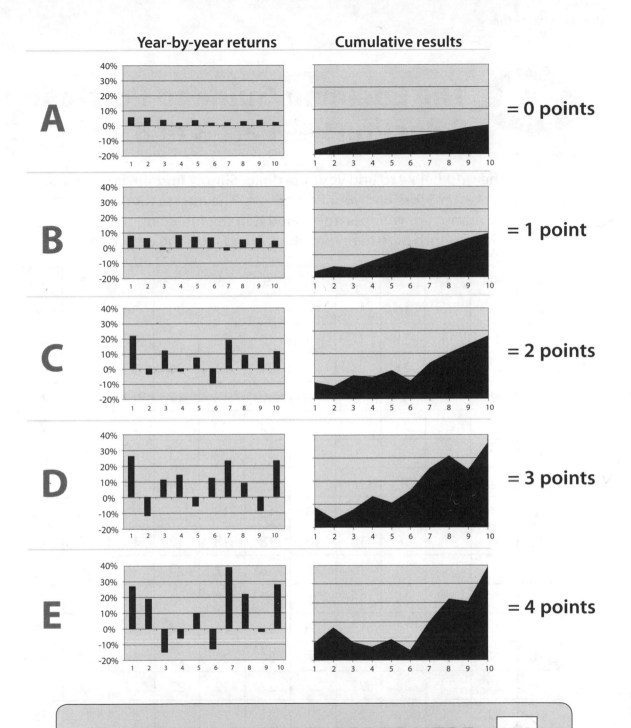

	Year-by-year returns	Cumulative results	
A			= 0 points
B			= 1 point
C			= 2 points
D			= 3 points
E			= 4 points

ENTER YOUR POINT SCORE HERE : 1

Do not turn to the next page until you have obtained
both your Letter Score and your Point Score.

195

The Edelman Guide to Portfolio Selection® — Part 3 of 3

Use the grid below to find your portfolio. Simply find the intersection of your Letter Score and your Point Score. The intersection reveals the number of your portfolio. Find it in the full-color insert!
Then return here to review steps 3 and 4 on the next page.

	0	1	2	3	4	5	6	7	8	9	10
A	1	6	10	10	16	16	27	29	36	36	36
B	11	11	11	17	17	17	28	30	37	39	41
C	21	21	21	21	21	21	21	21	35	35	43
D	2	2	2	2	12	12	12	12	12	12	12
E	23	23	23	23	23	23	23	23	23	23	23
F	7	7	7	7	19	19	33	33	33	33	33
G	4	4	4	4	14	14	14	14	14	14	14
H	3	3	3	3	13	13	13	13	13	13	13
I	18	18	18	18	18	18	18	18	18	18	18
J	1	6	10	10	16	16	27	29	36	38	40
K	25	25	25	25	25	25	25	25	32	32	32
L	5	9	15	15	26	26	26	26	26	26	26
M	8	8	8	8	8	20	20	20	34	34	42
N	22	22	22	22	22	22	22	22	22	22	22
O	21	21	21	21	21	21	21	21	35	35	35
P	8	8	8	8	8	20	20	20	34	34	34
Q	11	11	11	17	17	17	28	30	37	37	37
R	24	24	24	24	24	24	24	24	31	31	31

Step 3: Implementation

Now that you have your portfolio model, you're ready to implement. As mentioned earlier, you can do this in either of the following ways:

1. **Build a portfolio that consists of both institutional shares and ETFs.** Many institutional shares, such as those offered by Dimensional Fund Advisors, are available only through certain financial advisors. This means you must be willing to work with an advisor, and willing to pay his or her fee.

2. **Limit your portfolio to exchange-traded funds**. You can avoid the fees (and the services) of a financial advisor by establishing an account with a discount brokerage firm. To conform to the investment strategy outlined in this book, choose ETFs that:

    i.   focus on a specific asset class or market sector (in accordance with your portfolio model);

    ii. provide extensive diversification within that asset class or market sector;

    iii. have no style drift and or bracket creep (see page 97);

    iv. have extremely low turnover;

    v.   are large enough to support trading volume (many ETFs are so new — and therefore small — that some might be unable to effectively handle periods of dramatic volatility).

Naturally, I recommend the first alternative. I'm biased of course.

Step 4: Maintenance

With your portfolio in place, you must now rebalance it periodically, as described on page 39. If you develop your own portfolio using only Exchange-Traded Funds, you'll have to do this yourself. But if you work with a financial advisor, he or she will perform this service for you. Your advisor will also help you decide whether deposits or withdrawals are best made with taxable accounts or tax-deferred accounts.[57]

You now have your own comprehensive investment portfolio. In the next chapter, you'll get three valuable tips to help you make the most of your new portfolio.

---

[57]Sorry, my bias is showing again.

Chapter 8

Three Important Insights to Insure Your Investment Success

You now you understand the history and science of investing. You've found the alternative to retail mutual funds and have been shown how to build a diversified portfolio that's right for you. Now, pay attention to these three crucial insights for successful investment management. After decades of working with individuals and families, we've come to recognize these principles as essential if you are to achieve success through a long-term portfolio based on diversification and periodic rebalancing.

Insight 1: Never Let Your Investment Decisions Be Determined by Taxes

We see people make this mistake all the time. Often, we come across people who have a substantial amount of money in a single security — an asset they've owned for years that has grown substantially in value. They know they should sell the asset because it represents too much of their net worth, but they refuse because they don't want to pay taxes on their gains. So they continue holding an asset that is no longer appropriate, in a portfolio that is too risky for their situation.

Ironically, refusing to pay taxes sometimes causes investors to lose much more than the tax. I recall a conversation I once had with one of my clients. He wanted to see me because he had recently undergone several significant financial changes in his life, and I agreed that those changes required us to change his portfolio's asset allocation.

I showed him the changes we wanted to make and how we would implement them. Essentially, we needed to move money from some current investments to other investments. He agreed that the changes made sense and gave his approval.

But I wasn't finished explaining everything to him. So I continued, and told him that selling some of the old investments would generate about $60,000 in taxes.

At that point he freaked out.

"SIXTY THOUSAND DOLLARS?!" he yelled, actually jumping out of his chair. "Well, yes," I replied. I then asked why he was so upset. "Where am I going to get sixty thousand dollars?" he demanded.

"From your portfolio," I said. I reminded him that his account was worth more than $1 million, and explained that we'd send him a check from his portfolio to cover the tax liability. But he couldn't be mollified. In fact, if you had walked into my office at that point and seen his face, you might have thought that I had shot his dog.

He decided to leave his portfolio "as is."

About two months later, I called to give him really good news: Most of his tax problem had gone away. "That sixty-thousand-dollar tax liability you were facing is gone!" I said enthusiastically.

"That's great news," he replied. Then a pause, then his question: "How did that happen?"

It was simple, I told him: The stock market had fallen dramatically over the past two months, and when the prices fell, most of his profits evaporated — and so did the tax liability!

I am proud to be paying taxes in the United States. The only thing is, I could be just as proud for half the money.

~Arthur Godfrey

"Look at the good news," I said. "We can now reposition your account without having to pay taxes." Unfortunately, his million-dollar account is now worth only six figures, but, hey, at least he avoided taxes, right?

He didn't appreciate the irony.

It's a sad fact that some people so hate the idea of paying taxes that they will do anything to avoid them

— even to the point of risking investment losses that could be far greater than the taxes would ever be!

Remember: When your investments make money, you will owe taxes. The only way to avoid taxes is to avoid profits. So repeat after me: *Be happy when you pay taxes. The more taxes you pay, the more fortunate you are, because those who pay lots of taxes have made lots of money.*

After all, there *is* something worse than having to pay taxes: not having to pay them. So it's your choice: profits and taxes, or no profits and no taxes.

Keep in mind that federal capital gains tax rates are at their lowest level since capital gains rates were established in 1936. But you'd better hurry, because the current 15% capital gains rate jumps to 20% in 2011. That's a one-third tax increase! So you're better off paying a 15% tax now instead of a 20% tax later.[58]

Taxes matter, but they must never outweigh more important financial considerations, such as risk, income, and liquidity.

Figure 8.1

Get excited: Taxes on investment profits have never been lower!

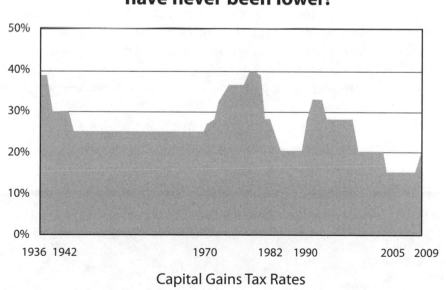

Capital Gains Tax Rates

---

[58]The only exception — and there are *always* exceptions — is if the account owner is expected to die soon. Capital gains pass to heirs free of capital gains tax, so this is worth considering in such cases.

Insight 2: Never Let Investment Decisions Be Determined by Fees

Certainly, it's important to keep fees to a minimum. But fees, like taxes, are an inherent part of investing — you cannot avoid them. Therefore, although fees matter, they should not be a primary determining factor in any decision. After all, investment performance is not determined by fees. Yet when the Investment Company Institute asked investors to name the most important criterion when picking a mutual fund, the majority of responders chose fees over performance or risk.

But fees are the *least* important of these three criteria. After all, if all it took to pick a great fund was to buy the cheapest fund, then that's what everyone would do. There would only be one mutual fund, it would be really cheap, and everyone would own it; there would be no need for a second fund.

Obviously, that can't be right, or there wouldn't be 24,451 mutual funds, according to Morningstar. So try this little experiment: Get a list of those 24,451 funds and rank them three ways, by cost, by performance (pick any time period you wish), and by risk (you can use a variety of risk measures, such as beta, standard deviation, Sharpe Ratio, and more).

You'll discover that the cheapest funds are never the most profitable or the lowest in risk. In other words, buying the cheapest fund doesn't provide you with the best results — and experienced investors know this. That's why you should not focus solely on fees when you search for investments. Sure, fees matter. But to suggest that they matter *more* than performance and risk is foolish — and dangerous.

! This is the end of Part 1. If you haven't answered questions 1–4, STOP! and turn to page 185.

Congratulations! You've finished Part 1 of the Edelman Guide to Portfolio Selection.

Your Letter Score is I.

Remember this Letter Score and return to page 193.

Insight 3: Keep Your Portfolio Consistent with Your Current Circumstances

This book shows you how to build a portfolio based on your current situation. But your circumstances will change over time, and it's vital that your portfolio remain appropriate as your life progresses.

Over time, you'll experience changes in your income, expenses, health, and marital status. You might even change your goals or adopt new opinions about your willingness to tolerate investment risks. For these reasons and more, you must periodically evaluate your current situation to see if your "old" investment portfolio (the one currently in use) is still ideal for your "new" status.

Indeed, investment management is merely part of the overall financial planning process. So although this book is focused on the investment management issue, it's important that you place this subject in context. Remember that making investment decisions without regard to your needs and circumstances can be dangerous. Therefore, instead of blindly rebalancing your portfolio to your original model, consider whether you should make changes to that model in response to changes in your life.

How often should you conduct such a review? That depends on your situation; we provide such reviews for some of our clients annually, while others might go years before a review is needed. If in doubt, conduct a review.

Above all else, remember that investment management should be treated as part of a complete financial plan — not instead of one.

That's it for this chapter. Don't overemphasize fees or taxes, and make sure your portfolio remains appropriate as your circumstances change. In the chapters that follow, you'll learn how to apply your new portfolio and investment strategy to your retirement plan at work, when saving for college, and for generating current income from your portfolio (a common need for retirees). Later, we'll look at insurance and annuities. You'll then get three more insights to help you achieve investment success, and we'll end with a look at the dumbest new lie that's worrying investors.

The following full-color pages contain forty-three investment portfolios modeled after the Edelman Managed Asset Program®.

Chapter 7 shows you how to determine which of these forty-three portfolios is right for you.

Portfolio 1

U.S. Stocks	12%
Large-Cap Value	12%
Large-Cap Growth	0%
Mid-Cap Value	0%
Mid-Cap Growth	0%
Small-Cap Value	0%
Small-Cap Growth	0%

International Stocks	0%
Value	0%
Growth	0%
Emerging Market	0%

Bonds	76%
Government – Short-Term	5%
Government – Intermediate-Term	34%
Corporate – Short-Term	12%
Corporate – Intermediate-Term	14%
Corporate – Long-Term	3%
International	8%

Hedge Positions	12%
Real Estate	8%
Natural Resources	0%
Cash	4%

Portfolio 2

U.S. Stocks	25%
Large-Cap Value	15%
Large-Cap Growth	4%
Mid-Cap Value	1%
Mid-Cap Growth	2%
Small-Cap Value	2%
Small-Cap Growth	1%

International Stocks	7%
Value	3%
Growth	2%
Emerging Market	2%

Bonds	56%
Government – Short-Term	6%
Government – Intermediate-Term	26%
Corporate – Short-Term	8%
Corporate – Intermediate-Term	10%
Corporate – Long-Term	2%
International	4%

Hedge Positions	12%
Real Estate	4%
Natural Resources	4%
Cash	4%

Portfolio 3

U.S. Stocks	27%
Large-Cap Value	15%
Large-Cap Growth	4%
Mid-Cap Value	2%
Mid-Cap Growth	2%
Small-Cap Value	2%
Small-Cap Growth	2%

International Stocks	7%
Value	3%
Growth	2%
Emerging Market	2%

Bonds	56%
Government – Short-Term	6%
Government – Intermediate-Term	27%
Corporate – Short-Term	7%
Corporate – Intermediate-Term	10%
Corporate – Long-Term	2%
International	4%

Hedge Positions	10%
Real Estate	4%
Natural Resources	4%
Cash	2%

Portfolio 4

U.S. Stocks	25%
Large-Cap Value	21%
Large-Cap Growth	0%
Mid-Cap Value	2%
Mid-Cap Growth	2%
Small-Cap Value	0%
Small-Cap Growth	0%

International Stocks	6%
Value	3%
Growth	3%
Emerging Market	0%

Bonds	51%
Government – Short-Term	3%
Government – Intermediate-Term	27%
Corporate – Short-Term	7%
Corporate – Intermediate-Term	7%
Corporate – Long-Term	2%
International	5%

Hedge Positions	18%
Real Estate	4%
Natural Resources	4%
Cash	10%

Portfolio 5

U.S. Stocks	29%
Large-Cap Value	25%
Large-Cap Growth	0%
Mid-Cap Value	2%
Mid-Cap Growth	2%
Small-Cap Value	0%
Small-Cap Growth	0%

Bonds	51%
Government – Short-Term	3%
Government – Intermediate-Term	27%
Corporate – Short-Term	7%
Corporate – Intermediate-Term	7%
Corporate – Long-Term	2%
International	5%

International Stocks	6%
Value	3%
Growth	3%
Emerging Market	0%

Hedge Positions	14%
Real Estate	4%
Natural Resources	4%
Cash	6%

Portfolio 6

U.S. Stocks	31%
Large-Cap Value	25%
Large-Cap Growth	0%
Mid-Cap Value	3%
Mid-Cap Growth	3%
Small-Cap Value	0%
Small-Cap Growth	0%

Bonds	51%
Government – Short-Term	3%
Government – Intermediate-Term	27%
Corporate – Short-Term	7%
Corporate – Intermediate-Term	7%
Corporate – Long-Term	2%
International	5%

International Stocks	6%
Value	3%
Growth	3%
Emerging Market	0%

Hedge Positions	12%
Real Estate	4%
Natural Resources	4%
Cash	4%

Portfolio 7

U.S. Stocks	42%
Large-Cap Value	16%
Large-Cap Growth	14%
Mid-Cap Value	4%
Mid-Cap Growth	4%
Small-Cap Value	2%
Small-Cap Growth	2%

International Stocks	9%
Value	5%
Growth	4%
Emerging Market	0%

Bonds	43%
Government – Short-Term	0%
Government – Intermediate-Term	43%
Corporate – Short-Term	0%
Corporate – Intermediate-Term	0%
Corporate – Long-Term	0%
International	0%

Hedge Positions	6%
Real Estate	0%
Natural Resources	0%
Cash	6%

Portfolio 8

U.S. Stocks	42%
Large-Cap Value	16%
Large-Cap Growth	14%
Mid-Cap Value	4%
Mid-Cap Growth	4%
Small-Cap Value	2%
Small-Cap Growth	2%

International Stocks	10%
Value	5%
Growth	5%
Emerging Market	0%

Bonds	44%
Government – Short-Term	0%
Government – Intermediate-Term	44%
Corporate – Short-Term	0%
Corporate – Intermediate-Term	0%
Corporate – Long-Term	0%
International	0%

Hedge Positions	4%
Real Estate	0%
Natural Resources	0%
Cash	4%

Portfolio 9

U.S. Stocks	36%
Large-Cap Value	25%
Large-Cap Growth	6%
Mid-Cap Value	2%
Mid-Cap Growth	2%
Small-Cap Value	1%
Small-Cap Growth	0%

International Stocks	8%
Value	5%
Growth	3%
Emerging Market	0%

Bonds	42%
Government – Short-Term	2%
Government – Intermediate-Term	22%
Corporate – Short-Term	6%
Corporate – Intermediate-Term	7%
Corporate – Long-Term	2%
International	3%

Hedge Positions	14%
Real Estate	4%
Natural Resources	4%
Cash	6%

Portfolio 10

U.S. Stocks	38%
Large-Cap Value	25%
Large-Cap Growth	7%
Mid-Cap Value	2%
Mid-Cap Growth	3%
Small-Cap Value	1%
Small-Cap Growth	0%

International Stocks	8%
Value	5%
Growth	3%
Emerging Market	0%

Bonds	42%
Government – Short-Term	2%
Government – Intermediate-Term	22%
Corporate – Short-Term	6%
Corporate – Intermediate-Term	7%
Corporate – Long-Term	2%
International	3%

Hedge Positions	12%
Real Estate	4%
Natural Resources	4%
Cash	4%

Portfolio 11

U.S. Stocks	38%
Large-Cap Value	26%
Large-Cap Growth	7%
Mid-Cap Value	2%
Mid-Cap Growth	3%
Small-Cap Value	0%
Small-Cap Growth	0%

International Stocks	8%
Value	5%
Growth	3%
Emerging Market	0%

Bonds	44%
Government – Short-Term	2%
Government – Intermediate-Term	22%
Corporate – Short-Term	6%
Corporate – Intermediate-Term	8%
Corporate – Long-Term	2%
International	4%

Hedge Positions	10%
Real Estate	4%
Natural Resources	4%
Cash	2%

Portfolio 12

U.S. Stocks	43%
Large-Cap Value	23%
Large-Cap Growth	8%
Mid-Cap Value	3%
Mid-Cap Growth	3%
Small-Cap Value	3%
Small-Cap Growth	3%

International Stocks	9%
Value	4%
Growth	3%
Emerging Market	2%

Bonds	36%
Government – Short-Term	4%
Government – Intermediate-Term	17%
Corporate – Short-Term	5%
Corporate – Intermediate-Term	7%
Corporate – Long-Term	1%
International	2%

Hedge Positions	12%
Real Estate	4%
Natural Resources	4%
Cash	4%

Portfolio 13

U.S. Stocks	44%
Large-Cap Value	23%
Large-Cap Growth	8%
Mid-Cap Value	3%
Mid-Cap Growth	3%
Small-Cap Value	4%
Small-Cap Growth	3%

International Stocks	10%
Value	5%
Growth	3%
Emerging Market	2%

Bonds	36%
Government – Short-Term	4%
Government – Intermediate-Term	17%
Corporate – Short-Term	5%
Corporate – Intermediate-Term	7%
Corporate – Long-Term	1%
International	2%

Hedge Positions	10%
Real Estate	4%
Natural Resources	4%
Cash	2%

Portfolio 14

U.S. Stocks	40%
Large-Cap Value	24%
Large-Cap Growth	8%
Mid-Cap Value	2%
Mid-Cap Growth	2%
Small-Cap Value	2%
Small-Cap Growth	2%

International Stocks	10%
Value	4%
Growth	3%
Emerging Market	3%

Bonds	30%
Government – Short-Term	0%
Government – Intermediate-Term	19%
Corporate – Short-Term	2%
Corporate – Intermediate-Term	6%
Corporate – Long-Term	1%
International	2%

Hedge Positions	20%
Real Estate	5%
Natural Resources	5%
Cash	10%

Portfolio 15

U.S. Stocks	43%
Large-Cap Value	25%
Large-Cap Growth	9%
Mid-Cap Value	2%
Mid-Cap Growth	3%
Small-Cap Value	2%
Small-Cap Growth	2%

International Stocks	10%
Value	4%
Growth	3%
Emerging Market	3%

Bonds	31%
Government – Short-Term	0%
Government – Intermediate-Term	19%
Corporate – Short-Term	2%
Corporate – Intermediate-Term	7%
Corporate – Long-Term	1%
International	2%

Hedge Positions	16%
Real Estate	5%
Natural Resources	5%
Cash	6%

Portfolio 16

U.S. Stocks	45%
Large-Cap Value	25%
Large-Cap Growth	9%
Mid-Cap Value	3%
Mid-Cap Growth	3%
Small-Cap Value	3%
Small-Cap Growth	2%

International Stocks	10%
Value	4%
Growth	3%
Emerging Market	3%

Bonds	31%
Government – Short-Term	0%
Government – Intermediate-Term	19%
Corporate – Short-Term	2%
Corporate – Intermediate-Term	7%
Corporate – Long-Term	1%
International	2%

Hedge Positions	14%
Real Estate	5%
Natural Resources	5%
Cash	4%

Portfolio 17

U.S. Stocks	46%
Large-Cap Value	26%
Large-Cap Growth	9%
Mid-Cap Value	3%
Mid-Cap Growth	3%
Small-Cap Value	3%
Small-Cap Growth	2%

International Stocks	10%
Value	4%
Growth	3%
Emerging Market	3%

Bonds	32%
Government – Short-Term	0%
Government – Intermediate-Term	19%
Corporate – Short-Term	2%
Corporate – Intermediate-Term	7%
Corporate – Long-Term	1%
International	3%

Hedge Positions	12%
Real Estate	5%
Natural Resources	5%
Cash	2%

Portfolio 18

U.S. Stocks	53%
Large-Cap Value	21%
Large-Cap Growth	17%
Mid-Cap Value	5%
Mid-Cap Growth	6%
Small-Cap Value	2%
Small-Cap Growth	2%

International Stocks	10%
Value	5%
Growth	5%
Emerging Market	0%

Bonds	27%
Government – Short-Term	0%
Government – Intermediate-Term	27%
Corporate – Short-Term	0%
Corporate – Intermediate-Term	0%
Corporate – Long-Term	0%
International	0%

Hedge Positions	10%
Real Estate	0%
Natural Resources	0%
Cash	10%

Portfolio 19

U.S. Stocks	54%
Large-Cap Value	21%
Large-Cap Growth	18%
Mid-Cap Value	5%
Mid-Cap Growth	6%
Small-Cap Value	2%
Small-Cap Growth	2%

International Stocks	11%
Value	6%
Growth	5%
Emerging Market	0%

Bonds	29%
Government – Short-Term	0%
Government – Intermediate-Term	29%
Corporate – Short-Term	0%
Corporate – Intermediate-Term	0%
Corporate – Long-Term	0%
International	0%

Hedge Positions	6%
Real Estate	0%
Natural Resources	0%
Cash	6%

Portfolio 20

U.S. Stocks	54%
Large-Cap Value	21%
Large-Cap Growth	18%
Mid-Cap Value	5%
Mid-Cap Growth	6%
Small-Cap Value	2%
Small-Cap Growth	2%

International Stocks	12%
Value	6%
Growth	6%
Emerging Market	0%

Bonds	30%
Government – Short-Term	0%
Government – Intermediate-Term	30%
Corporate – Short-Term	0%
Corporate – Intermediate-Term	0%
Corporate – Long-Term	0%
International	0%

Hedge Positions	4%
Real Estate	0%
Natural Resources	0%
Cash	4%

Portfolio 21

U.S. Stocks	55%
Large-Cap Value	21%
Large-Cap Growth	18%
Mid-Cap Value	5%
Mid-Cap Growth	6%
Small-Cap Value	3%
Small-Cap Growth	2%

International Stocks	12%
Value	6%
Growth	6%
Emerging Market	0%

Bonds	31%
Government – Short-Term	0%
Government – Intermediate-Term	31%
Corporate – Short-Term	0%
Corporate – Intermediate-Term	0%
Corporate – Long-Term	0%
International	0%

Hedge Positions	2%
Real Estate	0%
Natural Resources	0%
Cash	2%

Portfolio 22

U.S. Stocks	43%
Large-Cap Value	17%
Large-Cap Growth	14%
Mid-Cap Value	4%
Mid-Cap Growth	4%
Small-Cap Value	2%
Small-Cap Growth	2%

International Stocks	10%
Value	5%
Growth	5%
Emerging Market	0%

Bonds	27%
Government – Short-Term	0%
Government – Intermediate-Term	27%
Corporate – Short-Term	0%
Corporate – Intermediate-Term	0%
Corporate – Long-Term	0%
International	0%

Hedge Positions	20%
Real Estate	5%
Natural Resources	5%
Cash	10%

Portfolio 23

U.S. Stocks	44%
Large-Cap Value	17%
Large-Cap Growth	14%
Mid-Cap Value	4%
Mid-Cap Growth	5%
Small-Cap Value	2%
Small-Cap Growth	2%

International Stocks	12%
Value	6%
Growth	6%
Emerging Market	0%

Bonds	28%
Government – Short-Term	0%
Government – Intermediate-Term	28%
Corporate – Short-Term	0%
Corporate – Intermediate-Term	0%
Corporate – Long-Term	0%
International	0%

Hedge Positions	16%
Real Estate	5%
Natural Resources	5%
Cash	6%

Portfolio 24

U.S. Stocks	46%
Large-Cap Value	18%
Large-Cap Growth	15%
Mid-Cap Value	4%
Mid-Cap Growth	5%
Small-Cap Value	2%
Small-Cap Growth	2%

International Stocks	12%
Value	6%
Growth	6%
Emerging Market	0%

Bonds	28%
Government – Short-Term	0%
Government – Intermediate-Term	28%
Corporate – Short-Term	0%
Corporate – Intermediate-Term	0%
Corporate – Long-Term	0%
International	0%

Hedge Positions	14%
Real Estate	5%
Natural Resources	5%
Cash	4%

Portfolio 25

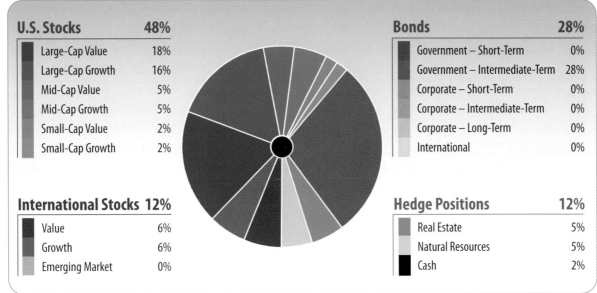

U.S. Stocks	48%
Large-Cap Value	18%
Large-Cap Growth	16%
Mid-Cap Value	5%
Mid-Cap Growth	5%
Small-Cap Value	2%
Small-Cap Growth	2%

International Stocks	12%
Value	6%
Growth	6%
Emerging Market	0%

Bonds	28%
Government – Short-Term	0%
Government – Intermediate-Term	28%
Corporate – Short-Term	0%
Corporate – Intermediate-Term	0%
Corporate – Long-Term	0%
International	0%

Hedge Positions	12%
Real Estate	5%
Natural Resources	5%
Cash	2%

Portfolio 26

U.S. Stocks	47%
Large-Cap Value	27%
Large-Cap Growth	10%
Mid-Cap Value	3%
Mid-Cap Growth	3%
Small-Cap Value	2%
Small-Cap Growth	2%

International Stocks	11%
Value	5%
Growth	3%
Emerging Market	3%

Bonds	26%
Government – Short-Term	0%
Government – Intermediate-Term	15%
Corporate – Short-Term	2%
Corporate – Intermediate-Term	6%
Corporate – Long-Term	1%
International	2%

Hedge Positions	16%
Real Estate	5%
Natural Resources	5%
Cash	6%

Portfolio 27

U.S. Stocks	49%
Large-Cap Value	27%
Large-Cap Growth	10%
Mid-Cap Value	3%
Mid-Cap Growth	3%
Small-Cap Value	3%
Small-Cap Growth	3%

International Stocks	11%
Value	5%
Growth	3%
Emerging Market	3%

Bonds	26%
Government – Short-Term	0%
Government – Intermediate-Term	15%
Corporate – Short-Term	2%
Corporate – Intermediate-Term	6%
Corporate – Long-Term	1%
International	2%

Hedge Positions	14%
Real Estate	5%
Natural Resources	5%
Cash	4%

Portfolio 28

U.S. Stocks	50%
Large-Cap Value	27%
Large-Cap Growth	10%
Mid-Cap Value	3%
Mid-Cap Growth	3%
Small-Cap Value	4%
Small-Cap Growth	3%

International Stocks	11%
Value	5%
Growth	3%
Emerging Market	3%

Bonds	27%
Government – Short-Term	0%
Government – Intermediate-Term	16%
Corporate – Short-Term	2%
Corporate – Intermediate-Term	6%
Corporate – Long-Term	1%
International	2%

Hedge Positions	12%
Real Estate	5%
Natural Resources	5%
Cash	2%

Portfolio 29

U.S. Stocks	53%		Bonds	21%
Large-Cap Value	27%		Government – Short-Term	0%
Large-Cap Growth	12%		Government – Intermediate-Term	12%
Mid-Cap Value	3%		Corporate – Short-Term	1%
Mid-Cap Growth	4%		Corporate – Intermediate-Term	5%
Small-Cap Value	4%		Corporate – Long-Term	1%
Small-Cap Growth	3%		International	2%

International Stocks	12%		Hedge Positions	14%
Value	5%		Real Estate	5%
Growth	3%		Natural Resources	5%
Emerging Market	4%		Cash	4%

Portfolio 30

U.S. Stocks	54%		Bonds	22%
Large-Cap Value	27%		Government – Short-Term	0%
Large-Cap Growth	12%		Government – Intermediate-Term	12%
Mid-Cap Value	3%		Corporate – Short-Term	2%
Mid-Cap Growth	4%		Corporate – Intermediate-Term	5%
Small-Cap Value	4%		Corporate – Long-Term	1%
Small-Cap Growth	4%		International	2%

International Stocks	12%		Hedge Positions	12%
Value	5%		Real Estate	5%
Growth	3%		Natural Resources	5%
Emerging Market	4%		Cash	2%

Portfolio 31

U.S. Stocks	56%
Large-Cap Value	21%
Large-Cap Growth	18%
Mid-Cap Value	5%
Mid-Cap Growth	6%
Small-Cap Value	3%
Small-Cap Growth	3%

International Stocks	15%
Value	8%
Growth	7%
Emerging Market	0%

Bonds	15%
Government – Short-Term	0%
Government – Intermediate-Term	15%
Corporate – Short-Term	0%
Corporate – Intermediate-Term	0%
Corporate – Long-Term	0%
International	0%

Hedge Positions	14%
Real Estate	5%
Natural Resources	5%
Cash	4%

Portfolio 32

U.S. Stocks	58%
Large-Cap Value	22%
Large-Cap Growth	19%
Mid-Cap Value	5%
Mid-Cap Growth	6%
Small-Cap Value	3%
Small-Cap Growth	3%

International Stocks	15%
Value	8%
Growth	7%
Emerging Market	0%

Bonds	15%
Government – Short-Term	0%
Government – Intermediate-Term	15%
Corporate – Short-Term	0%
Corporate – Intermediate-Term	0%
Corporate – Long-Term	0%
International	0%

Hedge Positions	12%
Real Estate	5%
Natural Resources	5%
Cash	2%

Portfolio 33

U.S. Stocks	63%
Large-Cap Value	24%
Large-Cap Growth	20%
Mid-Cap Value	6%
Mid-Cap Growth	7%
Small-Cap Value	3%
Small-Cap Growth	3%

International Stocks	16%
Value	8%
Growth	8%
Emerging Market	0%

Bonds	15%
Government – Short-Term	0%
Government – Intermediate-Term	15%
Corporate – Short-Term	0%
Corporate – Intermediate-Term	0%
Corporate – Long-Term	0%
International	0%

Hedge Positions	6%
Real Estate	0%
Natural Resources	0%
Cash	6%

Portfolio 34

U.S. Stocks	64%
Large-Cap Value	24%
Large-Cap Growth	21%
Mid-Cap Value	6%
Mid-Cap Growth	7%
Small-Cap Value	3%
Small-Cap Growth	3%

International Stocks	17%
Value	9%
Growth	8%
Emerging Market	0%

Bonds	15%
Government – Short-Term	0%
Government – Intermediate-Term	15%
Corporate – Short-Term	0%
Corporate – Intermediate-Term	0%
Corporate – Long-Term	0%
International	0%

Hedge Positions	4%
Real Estate	0%
Natural Resources	0%
Cash	4%

Portfolio 35

U.S. Stocks	66%		Bonds	15%
Large-Cap Value	25%		Government – Short-Term	0%
Large-Cap Growth	22%		Government – Intermediate-Term	15%
Mid-Cap Value	6%		Corporate – Short-Term	0%
Mid-Cap Growth	7%		Corporate – Intermediate-Term	0%
Small-Cap Value	3%		Corporate – Long-Term	0%
Small-Cap Growth	3%		International	0%

International Stocks	17%		Hedge Positions	2%
Value	9%		Real Estate	0%
Growth	8%		Natural Resources	0%
Emerging Market	0%		Cash	2%

Portfolio 36

U.S. Stocks	66%		Bonds	14%
Large-Cap Value	30%		Government – Short-Term	0%
Large-Cap Growth	18%		Government – Intermediate-Term	7%
Mid-Cap Value	4%		Corporate – Short-Term	1%
Mid-Cap Growth	4%		Corporate – Intermediate-Term	4%
Small-Cap Value	5%		Corporate – Long-Term	1%
Small-Cap Growth	5%		International	1%

International Stocks	16%		Hedge Positions	4%
Value	7%		Real Estate	0%
Growth	5%		Natural Resources	0%
Emerging Market	4%		Cash	4%

Portfolio 37

U.S. Stocks	67%
Large-Cap Value	30%
Large-Cap Growth	18%
Mid-Cap Value	4%
Mid-Cap Growth	4%
Small-Cap Value	6%
Small-Cap Growth	5%

Bonds	15%
Government – Short-Term	0%
Government – Intermediate-Term	7%
Corporate – Short-Term	1%
Corporate – Intermediate-Term	4%
Corporate – Long-Term	1%
International	2%

International Stocks	16%
Value	7%
Growth	5%
Emerging Market	4%

Hedge Positions	2%
Real Estate	0%
Natural Resources	0%
Cash	2%

Portfolio 38

U.S. Stocks	59%
Large-Cap Value	27%
Large-Cap Growth	16%
Mid-Cap Value	3%
Mid-Cap Growth	4%
Small-Cap Value	5%
Small-Cap Growth	4%

Bonds	11%
Government – Short-Term	0%
Government – Intermediate-Term	5%
Corporate – Short-Term	1%
Corporate – Intermediate-Term	3%
Corporate – Long-Term	1%
International	1%

International Stocks	16%
Value	7%
Growth	5%
Emerging Market	4%

Hedge Positions	14%
Real Estate	5%
Natural Resources	5%
Cash	4%

Portfolio 39

U.S. Stocks	61%
Large-Cap Value	27%
Large-Cap Growth	18%
Mid-Cap Value	3%
Mid-Cap Growth	4%
Small-Cap Value	5%
Small-Cap Growth	4%

Bonds	11%
Government – Short-Term	0%
Government – Intermediate-Term	5%
Corporate – Short-Term	1%
Corporate – Intermediate-Term	3%
Corporate – Long-Term	1%
International	1%

International Stocks	16%
Value	7%
Growth	5%
Emerging Market	4%

Hedge Positions	12%
Real Estate	5%
Natural Resources	5%
Cash	2%

Portfolio 40

U.S. Stocks	76%
Large-Cap Value	30%
Large-Cap Growth	20%
Mid-Cap Value	5%
Mid-Cap Growth	5%
Small-Cap Value	8%
Small-Cap Growth	8%

Bonds	0%
Government – Short-Term	0%
Government – Intermediate-Term	0%
Corporate – Short-Term	0%
Corporate – Intermediate-Term	0%
Corporate – Long-Term	0%
International	0%

International Stocks	20%
Value	9%
Growth	6%
Emerging Market	5%

Hedge Positions	4%
Real Estate	0%
Natural Resources	0%
Cash	4%

Portfolio 41

U.S. Stocks	78%
Large-Cap Value	30%
Large-Cap Growth	20%
Mid-Cap Value	5%
Mid-Cap Growth	5%
Small-Cap Value	9%
Small-Cap Growth	9%

Bonds	0%
Government – Short-Term	0%
Government – Intermediate-Term	0%
Corporate – Short-Term	0%
Corporate – Intermediate-Term	0%
Corporate – Long-Term	0%
International	0%

International Stocks	20%
Value	9%
Growth	6%
Emerging Market	5%

Hedge Positions	2%
Real Estate	0%
Natural Resources	0%
Cash	2%

Portfolio 42

U.S. Stocks	76%
Large-Cap Value	40%
Large-Cap Growth	36%
Mid-Cap Value	0%
Mid-Cap Growth	0%
Small-Cap Value	0%
Small-Cap Growth	0%

Bonds	0%
Government – Short-Term	0%
Government – Intermediate-Term	0%
Corporate – Short-Term	0%
Corporate – Intermediate-Term	0%
Corporate – Long-Term	0%
International	0%

International Stocks	20%
Value	10%
Growth	10%
Emerging Market	0%

Hedge Positions	4%
Real Estate	0%
Natural Resources	0%
Cash	4%

Portfolio 43

U.S. Stocks	78%
Large-Cap Value	40%
Large-Cap Growth	38%
Mid-Cap Value	0%
Mid-Cap Growth	0%
Small-Cap Value	0%
Small-Cap Growth	0%

International Stocks	20%
Value	10%
Growth	10%
Emerging Market	0%

Bonds	0%
Government – Short-Term	0%
Government – Intermediate-Term	0%
Corporate – Short-Term	0%
Corporate – Intermediate-Term	0%
Corporate – Long-Term	0%
International	0%

Hedge Positions	2%
Real Estate	0%
Natural Resources	0%
Cash	2%

Chapter 9
Applying This Strategy to Your Employer Retirement Plan

With so much emphasis in this book on buying a long-term, highly diversified portfolio, it'd be reasonable if you figured that this is exactly how you should invest the money in your retirement plan at work.

And you'd be wrong.

Yep, it's another example of how complicated it can be to correctly manage your investments. So let me show you how to properly participate in your employer retirement plan.

All plans operate basically the same way, so it doesn't matter where you work. Indeed, the following advice is applicable whether you are:

- a private-sector employee funding a 401(k) plan,

- a nonprofit wage earner contributing to a 403(b) plan,

- a federal employee using the Thrift Savings Plan,

- a municipal employee participating in a 457 plan, or

- a self-employed person investing via a SARSEP, SIMPLE IRA, SEP-IRA, or Solo 401(k).

Pay attention, because the information that follows will help you amass what most Americans would call a fortune.

Ideally, your employer plan will offer institutional mutual funds or Exchange-Traded Funds. But few do. So be it. Work with the choices available to you as best you can.[59]

> 401(k) participants are required to make their own investment decisions, but 69% say they lack investment knowledge, according to a survey by John Hancock. And 67% say their fear of market volatility prevents them from managing their 401(k) properly.

Step 1:
Contribute the Maximum That Your Employer Allows

As you've seen, the more money you save, the more you'll accumulate. But if you feel that you can't afford to contribute the maximum your employer allows, simply start with a smaller amount and increase it every year until you reach the maximum.

Make only pretax contributions, as there's little advantage to contributing money that you can't deduct from your income taxes. (Invest after-tax money in your own investment accounts rather than in your employer's plan.)

Step 2:
Place _All_ Your Contributions into Stock Mutual Funds

If you are at least seven years[60] from using the money in your plan, place _all_ of your contributions (along with your employer's contributions, if any) exclusively in diversified stock mutual funds.

Note the key phrase in that sentence: "using the money." Although most people vaguely understand that they should choose their investments with an eye to the future, most incorrectly focus on their retirement date. They think that if they are retiring in a few years, they need to invest more conservatively than those who are planning to work for many more years.

---

[59]And while you're at it, encourage your employer to make improvements in the choices you're offered. According to the Center for American Progress, typical 401(k) fees reduce the value of employee retirement accounts by 20% to 30%. If your employer were to drop retail mutual funds and annuities and adopt institutional shares and/or Exchange-Traded Funds, your costs would drop dramatically, resulting in as much as 30% more money when you retire.

[60]Why seven years? I choose this somewhat arbitrary number to reduce the risk that market volatility could interfere with your goals. After all, after the S&P 500 peaked in March 2002, it took nearly six years for it to return to its former high.

But such thinking is wrong. Your retirement date is irrelevant. Why? Because you might not need to withdraw money from your plan immediately upon retirement.

Indeed, when our clients retire, they often discover that retirement is not an economic event. Oh, sure, it's one heckuva lifestyle change, but in many cases, that's all it is. Thanks to pensions, Social Security, investment income from nonretirement assets, and, sometimes, income from postretirement work, they don't need to withdraw money from their retirement plans. And because withdrawals from their retirement plans are taxed, they're happy to leave the money untouched. As a result, they do not touch the money in their retirement plan for many years after they've retired.

Therefore, your investment allocation should be based on the date you'll begin to spend some of the money, not the date you'll retire. This can add years to your investment horizon, which enables you to seek higher returns than you otherwise might attempt. This is crucial, because over a thirty-year period (as Figure 9.1 shows), the final five years of your retirement account will produce as much as a third of your account's total accumulated value (thanks to the wonder of compound interest). This is why, if you are at least seven years away from using the money in your plan, you should be placing *all* your contributions (along with your employer's contributions, if any) into diversified stock mutual funds.

Figure 9.1

More than one-third of total retirement assets are created in your final five years of work

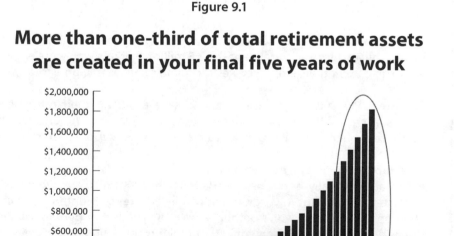

When twenty-year-olds invest like their grandparents, you know something is wrong.

A study of 1.6 million 401(k) participants by Hewitt Associates found that workers ages eighteen to twenty-five (Generation Y) have invested 35% of their retirement assets into fixed-income investments. That's a more conservative approach than workers three times their age, who are nearing retirement. And Fidelity Investments, which manages 401(k) plans for 9 million workers, says 16% of employees in their twenties have no money at all in stocks, while 40% have all their assets in conservative investments, such as "stable value" funds.

Why does Gen Y invest so conservatively? Hewitt says it might be because they graduated at about the time stocks collapsed in 2000–2002, and they're spooked.

Well, they'd better get unspooked — and fast. Investing so conservatively means that Gen Y workers will likely earn 3% to 5% less per year than they would otherwise. And over a forty-year career, every 1% in extra annual return translates into an extra ten years of retirement income, according to research by AllianceBernstein.

To reduce this problem, the Department of Labor has introduced a rule to automatically enroll 401(k) participants in balanced investment options. Although it's not the most effective choice, it's a lot better than the ridiculously conservative approach that so many workers are taking on their own.

It's also worth noting that Hewitt's study didn't focus on 1.6 million workers, but 2.5 million. But it found that of the 2.5 million workers who were eligible to participate in their employer's 401(k) plan, only 1.6 million actually do.

The other 900,000 people are failing to save at all for their retirement. This is a crisis of epic proportions, because millions of Americans will reach retirement age with little to no assets to support themselves.

To reduce that problem, the Pension Protection Act of 2006 enables employers to automatically enroll new workers in their 401(k) plans. Previously, workers had to voluntarily sign up; now they'll have to voluntarily opt out. The hope is that most won't bother — with the result that people will find themselves saving for retirement without taking any action on their own.

Note that I am talking about your *current* contributions. I am not (yet) discussing your account's existing balance in. Still, this notion might disturb you. After all, you know that the stock market is volatile. I agree — and I am telling you to invest exclusively in the stock market, not in spite of the volatility but *because* of it.

There are two reasons for this. First, if your investment horizon is ten, twenty, or thirty years away, volatility is irrelevant. Remember the Crash of '87? One week before the crash, the Dow Jones Industrial Average was 2,471; one week afterward, it was 1,793 — a decline of 38%. As of May 2007, the Dow exceeded 13,200. So who cares about short-term volatility when you have a long-term investment horizon?

Second, when you are adding money to your account on a regular basis — which is exactly what you're doing when you participate in a retirement plan at work — volatility is your friend. By investing a preset amount of money at preset intervals (say, $50 with each paycheck), you're engaging in dollar cost averaging (DCA) — the most successful form of investing ever devised. You can read more about dollar cost averaging in *The Truth About Money*, but suffice to say here that DCA automatically arranges for you to accumulate many shares at low prices and relatively fewer shares at higher prices. The math's efficiency over many decades helps produce long-term profits.

> **What's worse than investing your 401(k) incorrectly?**
>
> Withdrawing the money and spending it! Yet that's what almost half of all workers do when they change employers. Indeed, according to a 2007 study by Hewitt, 45% of workers who leave their jobs cash out and spend their retirement plan assets — effectively destroying their hopes for a secure financial future.

! This is question #5. If you haven't answered questions 1–4, STOP! and turn to page 185.

Q **Will you want to receive income from your account immediately?**

a) Yes .... **Your letter score is E.**

b) No .... **Your letter score is R.**

Congratulations! You're finished with Part 1 of the Edelman Guide to Portfolio Selection. Remember your Letter Score and return to page 193.

But the most fundamental advice in this book is that you should diversify your investments. Isn't this new advice contradictory?

Not at all. You see, there are actually two ways to diversify, not just one. The first way, which we've explored in detail, is to invest a current lump sum into a wide variety of asset classes and market sectors. But the second way involves investing money as you accumulate it (via dollar cost averaging) into a single asset class or market sector. In other words, you can invest *by asset class or market sector* when you have a large amount to invest, or you can invest *by time* when you are investing small amounts over long periods. Both are extremely effective forms of diversification.

That's why we always suggest that our clients place 100% of their retirement plan contributions into stock funds. Often we suggest that 80% be placed into U.S. stock funds (split equally between growth stock funds and value stock funds, or between large-cap funds and mid-cap/small-cap funds) and 20% into foreign stock funds.

This 40-40-20 ratio is merely a suggestion. However, I am adamant that you invest current contributions *only* in stock mutual funds (even if you use only one fund). Never dollar cost average into bonds — and that includes bond funds, government securities, fixed accounts, and money market funds. History tells us that over long periods, stocks have always earned more than all of those. I can't promise that this will occur in coming decades. But still.[61]

One final point: Once you pick your mix of stock funds, stick with it. For years. No matter what. Reject all temptation to switch into other stock funds that might appear to be doing better, or bond funds and money markets that might be experiencing less volatility at one time or another. (Refer back to the lessons of being a long-term investor in chapter 1.)

Dollar cost averaging demands (*demands*, mind you) that you own your stock funds throughout periods of poor stock-market performance; if you sell or stop contributing while prices are down, you'll guarantee that you'll enter retirement broke. So stick with your chosen funds as though they're tattooed to you.[62]

Actually, that tattoo metaphor is appropriate. You should pick investments with the expectation that you might own them *permanently*. Realize that removing

---

[61]Remember, so far we're talking only about your current contributions, not your existing balance.
[62]If a given choice underperforms for many years, you can consider swapping it for another stock fund, but this should be a rare event, executed reluctantly and only after substantial research and deliberation. I mean, how often do you remove a tattoo?

them will be painful and expensive — and it can leave scars that will stay with you for life.

So I'll say it again: <u>Pick your mix of investments and then stick with them for years. Never switch into other funds simply because they appear to be earning more or losing less</u>. If you follow only *one* piece of advice from this entire book, this is it.

Step 3:
Diversify Your Existing Account Balance

If you're clever, you might have figured out that investing all your contributions in stock funds creates an unintended side effect: After you've been doing this for a number of years, you'll have so much money in your stock funds that your next paycheck contribution will be insignificant. As a result, your dollar-cost-averaging strategy will no longer be able to offset the impact of market volatility — the very volatility I earlier told you to ignore.

To solve this problem, you must diversify the existing balance of your retirement account — adding other asset classes and market sectors in accordance with your portfolio model as explained earlier in the book — with particular attention paid to your model if you are planning to tap into your retirement accounts within the next seven years.

If You Can Invest in L Funds, Don't

Many employer retirement plans now offer so-called L funds, short for Lifecycle or Lifestyle.

I have a different word for them: *Lousy. Lazy* and *Loser* come to mind too.

L funds emanate from the basic concern that most workers don't know how to build properly diversified portfolios. So these funds are intended to do it for them. Thus, L funds are actually portfolios featuring different combinations of ordinary mutual funds. In other words, L funds are funds that own other funds. A fund of funds.

This is why L funds can be called Lazy: They offer workers an easy way to obtain asset allocation. Instead of picking your own combination of mutual funds, you just select one L fund. The most conservative L funds invest mostly in government bond and money market funds; at the other end of the risk spectrum, L funds invest primarily in stock funds.

To help you decide which L fund to choose, look at the names:

- **Lifecycle funds** typically feature a year in their name. The 2030 Portfolio, for example, has an asset allocation designed for a person who plans to retire in 2030. Its construction would differ from a 2010 fund, a 2020 fund, and a 2040 fund. These types of funds are also called **Target Funds.**

- **Lifestyle funds** typically reference risk in their name. The Conservative Portfolio invests in lower-risk securities, while Moderate and Aggressive portfolios invest more, most, or even all of their money in stocks.

Using the literature you get from your retirement plan administrator, you select the fund that most closely matches your risk tolerance or the time you will need money from your account. It's that simple!

Yeah, right.

> A fund has fees. If a fund invests in other funds, does that mean you're paying fees on fees? Yes. An L fund is essentially a mutual fund that invests in other mutual funds. Therefore, you not only incur the fees of the underlying funds, you pay the costs of the fund wrapper too. The total cost of the typical L fund is twice as much as the typical mutual fund, according to *Money Management Executive.*
>
> The SEC is now requiring fund-of-funds — which essentially describe L funds — to disclose the underlying cost of the funds they invest in. Prior to 2007, such funds only had to disclose their overall expense ratios.

Q Will you want to receive income from your account immediately?

This is question #5. If you haven't answered questions 1–4, STOP! and turn to page 185.

a) Yes......**ERROR!** In Question #2, you said you'd make additional deposits, but here in Question #5 you say you want immediate withdrawals. Start over on page 192 — and change one of your answers.

b) No.......**Congratulations!** You've completed Part 1 of the Edelman Guide to Portfolio Selection. **Your Letter Score is C.** Return to page 193 and continue to Part 2.

As you might suspect, proper asset allocation isn't that simple. As a result, these asset allocation models are a sucker's bet. That's why L funds might also be called Losers.

Here's why: Imagine you hire me as your financial advisor. After we have been introduced, you say, *"Ric, I would like you to invest my life savings in a way that creates a diversified portfolio appropriate for my circumstances."*

So I ask, "How old are you?" When you tell me your age, I hand you an asset allocation model and say, "Here's the investment portfolio that's right for you."

You probably wouldn't be happy if I gave you investment recommendations based on nothing other than your age. Yet this is what L funds do. It makes no sense! In fact, if I tried to pull a stunt like that, you'd walk out the door — and rightfully so. Before giving recommendations to a client, my colleagues and I ask about your income and expenses, assets and debts, marital status and family situation, health, goals, objectives, attitude about risk, and other important information. Such information helps insure that we're building a portfolio that truly is suitable and appropriate for you.

Even in this book, where I try to make the process as easy as possible while still providing effective advice, it still took eight (or nine) questions! Yet L funds somehow are supposed to be OK solely because they ask, "When will you retire?" They don't ask "When will you need the money?" It's an absurd approach to financial planning and asset allocation. In fact, it's Lazy.

Here's another, even more troubling problem: Most workers don't know that L funds are comprised of other funds. As a result, most of those who use L funds use them incorrectly — leading to ironic results.

You see, you're supposed to put all your money into one L fund. Sound scary? It's not. Remember that these funds contain other funds, mixed together to form a specific asset allocation. They are not designed to be used in conjunction with other funds — L or otherwise.

If you do that, your actual asset allocation model will be nonsensical. And that could cause workers a lot of harm — turning Lazy workers into Losers. And that's exactly what's happening. According to the Thrift Savings Board, which oversees the retirement plan used by employees of the federal government, 55% of plan participants who are using the plan's L funds also have money in other funds offered by the plan — and 16% have money in *every* fund offered. That's not what the Thrift Board intended.

(It's even worse in private-sector plans. According to Vanguard, which offers its own version of L funds to 401(k) plans nationwide, 63% of plan participants use L funds in addition to other funds.)

A final problem: Many L funds are poorly constructed. For example, professional advisors generally would tell a thirty-year-old worker to invest 100% of his or her retirement assets in U.S. and international stocks. But many 2040 funds — such as the one offered by the federal Thrift Savings Plan — place 15% of their assets in bonds. This is a poor allocation strategy.

Indeed, an AllianceBernstein study of target-date funds found that "the primary flaw in most is that they invest too conservatively . . . they hold too little in equity and too much in fixed income and cash to generate the growth required to fund participants' spending over what may be several decades in retirement."

Yep, L funds are Lousy. Don't invest in them.

Step 4:
Rebalance Your Account

Participating in your retirement plan isn't enough. You must also pay attention to it. Left alone, your allocation model will change due to varying performances of the investments you've selected. For that reason, you must review your allocation periodically.

! This is the end of Part 1. If you haven't answered questions 1–4, STOP! and turn to page 185.

Congratulations! You've finished Part 1 of the Edelman Guide to Portfolio Selection.

Your Letter Score is D.

Remember this Letter Score and return to page 193.

Yet 32% of workers say they never do. Not surprising: 61% told a poll sponsored by AllianceBernstein that they lack confidence in managing their investments, don't enjoy it, and give them minimal attention.

These sentiments might describe you. Tough. Pay attention anyway and rebalance periodically — as if your retirement depended on it.

What to Do with Your Retirement Account after You Leave Employment

You retired, got fired, or quit. What did you do with the money in your 401(k), 403(b), 457, or Thrift Savings Plan?

Don't leave it there. Even if you left an employer years (or decades) ago, transfer any money that's still inside that plan to an IRA. There are lots of reasons for this, including:

- You can do this without incurring any taxes or IRS penalty, and usually without any fees or expenses.

- Most employer retirement plans offer only a limited number of investment choices. Those choices often aren't very good. But in an IRA, you have virtually unlimited investment opportunities.

- By moving your money to your IRA, you enjoy complete control over it. You'll never have to deal with the bureaucracy of your former employer's human resources department or the outside administrator that handles the retirement plan.[63]

- Tax rules governing IRAs are friendlier than the rules pertaining to employer plans. Both you and your heirs will benefit if your assets are in an IRA instead of an employer plan.

- Life is much more convenient when you have one IRA instead of a dozen old 401(k) plans. Considering that the average worker changes jobs every

---

[63]If you think dealing with your HR department is no problem now, just wait twenty years. By the time you need to fuss with your account, you won't know anyone who works at the company. And that assumes the company still exists. Thanks to corporate mergers and bankruptcies, it might not.

The Lies About Money

four years, a married couple could find themselves with twenty retirement accounts over the course of their careers. Imagine all the mail and record-keeping chores! By comparison, all that money can be placed in just two IRA accounts — one for you and one for your spouse. This dramatically reduces your administrative burden, while boosting the likelihood that you'll remain fully compliant with all IRS rules.

Speaking of IRS rules, here are just two examples of how IRAs are superior to employer plans:

1. When you reach age 70½, you must begin to make annual withdrawals. The IRS says you need to make only one withdrawal from one IRA, even if you have many IRA accounts. But if you still have assets in multiple 401(k) plans, you must make a separate withdrawal from each 401(k) account. That is quite an administrative chore. If you accidentally miss one, you'll be forced to pay the IRS a 50% penalty — even if you withdrew plenty from other accounts. This can't happen with IRA accounts.

The three-year bear market that occurred from 2000 through 2002 proves the value of long-term investing, dollar cost averaging, and investing in employer retirement plans. Those years will be remembered as one of the worst three-year periods in the history of the stock market. In those thirty-six months, the S&P 500 Stock Index fell 43%. And yet, three years after that debacle, millions of investors found themselves substantially richer than they were at the beginning of the decade. If you weren't among them, you have only yourself to blame.

Indeed, a study of seventeen million 401(k) accounts from 2000 through 2005, conducted by the Employee Benefit Research Institute and the Investment Company Institute, revealed that workers who made no changes to their investment strategies through the six-year period had 50% more in their accounts at the end of 2005 than they did at the start of 2000. By contrast, those who stopped contributing when market prices declined and those who switched from stock funds to other investments fared much worse. In some cases, account values gained little, and in a great many cases, account values at the end of 2005 were still lower than they were when the stock market reached its nadir in October 2002.

The rich get richer by doing what they are supposed to do: They invest, and they continue to invest, no matter what the economic environment. If you want to be like them, you need to act like them.

2. If there's still money in your IRA when you die, your spouse can continue to withdraw money from the account over his or her lifetime. This spreads the tax liability over many years. And later, when the spouse dies, your children can continue to do the same — stretching the taxes over many decades. But your kids won't be allowed to do this if the money is still in your 401(k). Instead they'll be forced to pay taxes on the money almost immediately, creating a huge tax bill and hurting their ability to let that money grow tax-deferred for their future.[64]

Clearly, for all these reasons, IRAs are far superior to employer retirement plans. So don't delay: If you have money in a former employer's plan, move it to an IRA. To learn how, read *The Truth About Money.*

If You're Not Saving for Retirement

Is it possible that you are *not* saving for retirement? Just in case, let me add a commentary on this point.

Ahem.

I'm not sure if you've noticed, but you are living and working in the twenty-first century, not the 1950s. Back then, all you had to do was go to work each morning for forty years. When you retired, your company presented you with a gold watch and a pension. Workers didn't have to know anything about retirement planning, because their employers took care of it. The employers funded the pension and managed it, and sent retirees checks every month for as long as they lived.

You don't live in that world. Instead your retirement depends solely on you. To assist you, most employers allow you to place some of your paycheck into a retirement plan. There are many types of plans, but they all work pretty much the same: You choose how much of your money to invest, and you decide where to invest

---

[64]*Ha!* you're saying to yourself, *Ric doesn't know that the tax law changed in late 2006, giving children the same ability as spouses to "stretch out" the deceased's 401(k).* Nice try, but you'll have to try harder to stump me. It's true that Congress conveyed this benefit to children via the Pension Protection Act of 2006. But the IRS trumped Congress in early 2007. Congress's amendment to the tax code requires employers to amend their plans; the agency declared that employers may do so <u>at their option.</u> Because of the cost involved, most employers aren't bothering to make the change. Result: Children enjoy no such benefit. And you thought we lived in a democracy. We don't. We live in a bureaucracy.

it (using the choices offered by your employer). When you retire, the money is yours. Some employers contribute money to workers' accounts, but many don't.

I often meet people who are not participating in their retirement plan at work simply because their employer doesn't contribute to the account. If this describes you, put this book down. Look at your spouse (or look in the mirror if you have no spouse or partner) and say out loud that you will have no money at age sixty-five and that *it's all your boss's fault.* Then call your children or your siblings, or both, and tell them that you will have *no* money when you're sixty-five because your boss has refused to put some of *his* money into *your* retirement plan.

That mean old nasty boss!

Listen up. You can either deal with the situation or just complain about it. Either way, the amount of money you end up with in retirement is up to you, not your boss. Sure, your boss should offer you a retirement plan. Many do. And your boss should contribute to your account. Plenty do. If yours doesn't offer a plan or doesn't

Are you accidentally losing some of your employer's match? A quirk in your employer's accounting system could be causing this. This is particularly true if you contribute the maximum to your account each year.

Without question, the employer match — that's where the boss adds money to your account only if you do — is a great deal. After all, it's free money! But if you are among those who contribute the maximum, watch out: Your excellent savings habits could be hurting you. You see, many employers — including the federal government — match employee contributions in a very literal sense, and this methodology can hurt good savers.

Here's what I mean: Suppose you contribute $15,000 to your plan each year, at the rate of $1,500 per month. That means you finish contributing to your plan by October. Further suppose that your company matches your contributions, under a policy that matches "50% of contributions, up to 6% per year."

You might take this to mean that if you contribute 12% of your pay, your boss will add 6%. But that's not necessarily how it works. Instead your boss might contribute a maximum of 0.5% per month, provided that you put in 1% or more each month. In this case, completing your contributions in October means that you will not get the boss's November and December contributions! You lose some of your employer's match simply because you don't spread out your contributions over the entire calendar year.

Workers lose lots of free money this way. Watch out for this trap. If your employer matches your retirement plan contributions, find out whether the match is based on the *amount* of your contributions, or the *timing* of your contributions. Don't lose a nickel of that free money.

contribute on your behalf, find a job with an employer that does. Regardless, start saving for retirement — now.

This means you are not allowed to complain that you "can't" save for retirement because your employer doesn't offer a retirement plan. You don't need an official "retirement plan" in order to save for retirement. And you certainly aren't prevented from saving for retirement merely because your employer isn't helping you save for retirement. Saving for retirement is *your* responsibility. The task belongs to no one else.

Thus, you have a choice. You can handle your retirement account the right way and enter retirement with as much as $3 million. Or you can handle it the wrong way and amass only $700,000.[65] Your choice.

These figures are based on:

- a forty-year career;

- a starting salary of $40,000;

- an annual raise of 2%;

- an annual contribution of 10%;

- an employer contribution of 3% per year;

- an average annual return of 10%.

These assumptions produce an account value of $3,078,162. If you eliminate the employer contribution, you'll still amass $2,367,817. So stop saying that there's no point in saving for retirement merely because your boss doesn't contribute to your account.

If you mishandle your account — by saving less, starting later, or earning lower returns — you'll end up with far less.[66]

---

[65]Or you can be a complete moron by saving nothing, so you enter retirement with nothing.
[66]Which means you're pretty depressed right now if you haven't been saving much, or if you didn't start saving in your twenties or thirties, or if you haven't been earning stock market–like returns. Sorry. But look at the bright side: You can start now, and you'll make a huge difference going forward. You can also talk to your kids so they can avoid the mistakes you've made. See? There's always lemonade. . . .

Chapter 10
Applying This Strategy When Saving for College

The best way to save for college is to establish a College Savings Plan, based on Section 529 of the Internal Revenue Code (not to be confused with Tuition Prepayment Plans, which also are covered by Section 529).

This is assuming that you should be saving for college in the first place.[67] College planning, and its role in the broader financial planning spectrum, is covered in-depth in *The Truth About Money*, so I won't cover that here (other than the footnote you've just read). However, a recap of 529 plans is in order.

Section 529 plans are sponsored by each of the fifty states and the District of Columbia. Virtually no two plans are the same: Fees and contribution limits vary, as do the investment options. Some plans require you to select a portfolio based on the child's age, while others allow you to construct your own portfolio using the funds available in the plan. In some state plans, you invest without the aid of a financial advisor, while others have you work through an investment advisor, brokerage firm, or bank, generally paying a sales charge or fee.

You're permitted to enroll in any state's plan, regardless of where you or the child lives. Therefore, if you're interested in establishing a 529 plan, you must choose either a state plan (accepting whatever funds that plan offers) or a fund company (and enroll in whichever state plan that offers it). Investors also must decide whether to work with an advisor or handle this effort on their own. (Some advisors work only with certain plans.)

---

[67]Actually, no one should save for college in the first place. You should save for college in the *second* place. The first place you should be saving is in your retirement plan. Don't save for college without first saving for retirement.

One factor to consider is taxes: You may get a state income tax deduction if you invest in the plan offered by the state where you live. (Some state residents enjoy a state income tax deduction regardless of which state's plan they select, and a case currently before the Supreme Court may extend this benefit to all Americans.) In our opinion, the tax deduction is not enough of an incentive to choose your state's plan over another state's plan that you feel is superior. The tax deduction is relatively small because it's merely a *state* tax deduction; there is no tax break on your *federal* tax return. Since state income tax rates are rather low compared to federal tax rates, the savings tend to be rather low.

> If you own a 529 plan and have decided it is not the ideal plan, you can transfer the account to another state's plan, always tax-free and usually with little or no cost.

Selecting a 529 plan, as with all investment decisions, involves choices. It's important that you consider all aspects and avoid decisions that are based on only one criterion. Consider the plan offered by your state and read the prospectus carefully for complete information on fees and expenses. Remember that choosing a plan offered by a different state might be in your best interests even though you don't get the tax deduction. To compare different plans, go to www.collegesavings.org.

As with employer retirement plans, you're limited to the investment choices offered by each 529 plan. Depending on the plan you select, this means you can't always create a portfolio in conformance with the portfolio model you've identified in this book. Worse, many state plans allow you little to no investment flexibility. Instead they force you to use predesigned portfolios based on the child's age — the very problem outlined in my description of L funds in chapter 9.

(As if that's not bad enough, the portfolio models used by many states are downright nonsensical. Would you want to place 20% of your college savings in a money market account for a two-year-old? That's what some plans do!)

Oh, well — as with your employer retirement plan, do the best you can within the constraints. Rebalance periodically. And remember to reallocate your portfolio as the child gets closer to college.

> At this writing, no 529 plan offers Exchange-Traded Funds. However, DFA funds are offered by the SMART 529 Select plan, sponsored by West Virginia.

If You're Not Saving for College

Is it possible that you have college-bound children but are *not* saving for college?

Everyone knows how expensive college is, but many parents believe their kids will go to school for free, thanks to scholarships and grants. Their spending habits show that saving for college is not a priority. As a result, many parents — including you? — are not saving enough and are rationalizing why that's OK. Most parents don't have a financial plan, and some actually believe in myths!

These are pretty strong accusations, and I have equally strong evidence to support them. A 2006 survey on college planning by AllianceBernstein found parents saying — and doing — shocking things. To wit:

Many Parents Think Their Kids Will Go to School for Free!

- 72% of parents believe their children have special or unique talents that will earn them scholarships.

- 68% believe colleges will design an aid package that they can reasonably afford.

- 31% of those who plan to help fund their children's undergraduate education haven't started saving yet.

Meanwhile:

- 97% of aid administrators think parents have a false sense of security that colleges will help them cover costs.

! This is the end of Part 1. If you haven't answered questions 1–4, STOP! and turn to page 185.

Congratulations! You've finished Part 1 of the Edelman Guide to Portfolio Selection.

Your Letter Score is G.

Remember this Letter Score and return to page 193.

- 92% of aid administrators say parents overestimate the amount their children will receive in scholarships.

- 66% believe that scholarships and grants are less available than they were in the past.

Most Parents Are Not Trying to Save for College!

- 58% of parents spend more on restaurants or takeout than they save for college.

- 49% spend more on vacations.

- 38% spend more on consumer electronics.

- 31% spend more on allowances.

- 74% admit they could be saving significantly more for their children's education if they limited the amount they spent on:

  - traveling,

  - entertainment,

  - electronics,

  - impulse purchases, and

  - toys, clothes, and entertainment for their children.

Most Parents Are Not Saving Enough!

- The typical parents will only save enough to pay for 23% of their children's undergraduate expenses.

- Parents with children ages fourteen to seventeen plan to have (on average) $12,000 saved by the time their child reaches college age. But the projected cost is $54,882 for a public university and $131,361 for a private college.

- Parents with children ages five and under plan to save $25,000, but the cost is forecast to be $98,561 for a public university and $235,905 for a private college.

Most Parents Are Rationalizing!

Many parents say debt is good; they say it helps students focus on their studies, value their education, and become more financially responsible. But a variety of studies conducted by *USA Today*, Experian, the National Endowment for Financial Education, and others show that of college graduates ages twenty-one to thirty-five who have college debt:

- 42% are living from paycheck to paycheck.

- 34% have sold personal possessions to make ends meet.

- 27% have delayed a medical or dental procedure.

- 22% have taken a job they otherwise wouldn't have taken.

- 29% have refrained from continuing their education.

- 11% have delayed getting married.

As if the cost of a college degree isn't bad enough, tomorrow's college students are more likely than prior generations to need a postgraduate degree. That means even more debt, according to the website FinAid, which says the average graduate degree saddles students with $54,000 in additional college-related debt.

Figure 10.1

Type of Program	% of students who incur debt	average graduate debt	average total debt (grad & undergrad)
Master's degree	60%	$26,895	$32,858
Doctoral degree	58%	$49,007	$53,405
Professional degree	51%	$82,688	$93,134
MBA	53%	$35,525	$41,687
MSW	77%	$27,136	$37,028
PhD	40%	$36,917	$41,540
EdD	53%	$49,050	$47,725
Law (LLB or JD)	88%	$70,933	$80,754
Medicine	95%	$113,661	$125,819

- 28% have delayed having children.

- 44% have delayed buying a house.

- 67% pay out more in college loans than they place into savings.

- 40% don't have a savings account that they contribute to on a regular basis.

- 55% don't participate in their retirement plan at work or have an IRA.

- 44% have already defaulted on a debt.

- 28% receive money from their parents.

- 58% of new grads moved back into their parent's home following graduation; of these, 32% were still there after a year, and 19% of those twenty-one to thirty-five were still living at home.

- 76% "worried about money a lot" while they were in college; 64% still worry about money.

- 91% agree with the statement "People who graduate without any college debt have a big advantage in life."

> You can now save money while spending money.
>
> All you have to do is sign up with BabyMint (www.babymint.com) or Upromise (www.upromise.com). Then shop with hundreds of participating vendors around the nation to buy everything from cellular phone service to gasoline, from everyday products found in supermarkets to restaurants and retailers.
>
> The deal is simple. By making a purchase with a participating retailer, a portion of the money you spend is diverted into a Section 529 college savings account on behalf of your child or grandchild.

Most Parents Don't Have a Financial Plan!

- 70% of parents don't have a financial plan that takes college savings into account.

- 42% have not even had a serious conversation with their children's other parent about how they will pay for college.

- 80% of parents have not sought the help of a financial advisor.

- 45% are not familiar with 529 college savings plans.

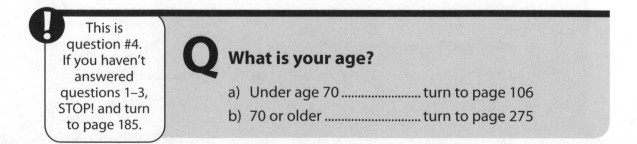

This is question #4. If you haven't answered questions 1–3, STOP! and turn to page 185.

Q **What is your age?**

a) Under age 70 .... turn to page 106
b) 70 or older .... turn to page 275

- Even among the 56% of parents who are specifically saving for their children's education, the majority are not using a 529 plan.

Even those who do have a plan, have one that stinks!

- 18% say they have not begun saving for their children's college costs because their kids are still young.

- 75% plan to save the same amount for each child.

- 31% prefer to take little or no risk (16% have all of their college savings funds in checking and savings accounts).

- 53% of parents plan to take out loans.

- 62% intend to draw on money they have saved for other purposes.

Most Parents Believe in Myths!

- Parents think the total cost of college will be four times the freshman cost. But due to annual increases of 6% to 7%, the senior year will cost 22% more than the freshman year. More than 90% of aid administrators say that parents lowball college costs.

- Parents think financial aid is money that doesn't have to be paid back. This is true only 44% of the time. But 56% of aid is comprised of loans (federal or private) that must be repaid.

Sadly, parents who fail to plan properly for their kids' education will find that they are punishing not just their children — but their *grandchildren*. (Yes, the ones they don't yet have.) When the time comes for their kids to start saving for their own

> Today the number-one reason that students drop out of college is cost, according to the College Board, the organization that administers the SAT exam to college-bound students. In 1980 the number-one reason was failing grades.

> The average student at a four-year public college now takes 6.2 years to obtain a degree, while the average student at a four-year private college takes 5.3 years, according to the College Board. Cost is cited as the primary reason it takes longer to graduate: Students can't afford to pay for a full course load in each semester.

children's college educations, those who graduated with debt will be far less able to do so.

If you're not saving for college yet, start now by opening an account in a 529 College Savings Plan.

Why Grandparents Should *Not* Save for College for Their Grandchildren

No one disputes that saving for college is primarily the responsibility of the parents. But many parents claim they lack the ability to save, due to household expenses and the other costs of childrearing.

Fortunately, grandparents are often in a perfect position to help. They tend to have more money and fewer expenses than parents — and they love doting on their grandkids. So it's no wonder that more than half of grandparents are helping to save or pay for college for their grandkids, according to AARP.

But in many cases, that's not the wisest action.

If you're the grandparent, think carefully before you write checks to a 529 College Saving Plan — or any other account that benefits a child (such as a Coverdell Education Savings Account or a custodial account formed under the Uniform Transfer to Minors Act). Allow me to offer a strong case against the idea of your helping to save for a grandchild's college education.

Five Reasons Why You Shouldn't Chip In

First, there's no assurance that the grandchild will need your money. The kid might not go to college at all. Or he or she might win scholarships or grants that alleviate the need for the family's financial support.

Second, you might not *like* the kid by then (or his parents). Oh, sure, he's a bundle of fun at age four, and you see him almost daily. But by age eighteen, he might be a drug addict, a car thief, or a high-school dropout. His parents might have divorced by then, and your former in-law might have moved across the country, taking the child. By the time that kid is eighteen, you might not have seen him or her in years. This is someone to whom you want to give thousands of dollars?

Third, the kid's parents might develop troubles of their own: business failure, job loss, alcohol abuse, medical problems, or the already mentioned marital issues. The parents might raid the college account, grabbing the cash for their own purposes. Imagine how you'd feel if your money got diverted that way.

Fourth, you might discover that you need the money yourself! As you get older, you may decide to travel in style or buy a beach house — or pay for that heart operation. You'll regret having given money away if you later need it.

Fifth, you might end up with too many grandkids! Magnanimously establishing a trust fund with $10,000 for your first grandchild is a fun and loving act, and when the second baby arrives, you'll do the same in order to treat everyone fairly. But this could become a problem when you become a grandparent for the ninth time.

Yeah, yeah, none of this will ever happen in your family. But we've seen all of the above time and again among our clients.

A Better Way to Help

For all these reasons, let's consider the idea that you *don't* help your kids save for college for your grandchildren. Don't fret — I'm not being as heartless as it might seem. You see, I'm simply suggesting that you keep your money in your name. Then, when a grandchild goes to college, you evaluate the situation — taking into consideration all the above issues. Based on the child's needs, the needs of other family members, your financial ability, and, most of all, your attitude toward the child, you simply (if you wish) write a check at that time.

But you won't write a check to the grandchild or his parents. Instead you'll write a check directly to the college or university. There's no gift tax limit when checks are payable to an institution; by contrast, gifts to people cannot exceed $12,000 per year.

If you're concerned that you might die before a grandchild reaches college, well, that's what wills are for. Simply amend your estate planning documents so that a stated sum of money will be placed into a trust fund upon your death, to help pay for college for the grandkids. Any good estate attorney can draft the language for you.

If you follow this suggestion and refrain from contributing to the parents' current college savings efforts, be aware of two downsides. First, by not placing money into a college savings plan, you lose the opportunity to shift assets out of your estate. If your net worth exceeds $2 million, this eliminates an opportunity to reduce estate taxes. Second, you deny yourself the joy of contributing to savings plans for the kids and grandkids. But you can solve that problem by helping them in other ways, such as buying them bicycles and cars and taking them on trips they couldn't otherwise afford.

So be a great grandparent, but be a wise one.

Q Will you want to receive income from your account immediately?

This is question #5. If you haven't answered questions 1–4, STOP! and turn to page 185.

a) Yes......**ERROR!** In Question #2, you said you'd make additional deposits, but here in Question #5 you say you want immediate withdrawals. Start over on page 192 — and change one of your answers.

b) No.......**Congratulations!** You've completed Part 1 of the Edelman Guide to Portfolio Selection. **Your Letter Score is K.** Return to page 193 and continue to Part 2.

Chapter 11
Applying This Strategy When Investing for Income

At some point — and perhaps you or your parents are already there — you'll want to begin receiving income from your investments.

Often, retirees focus exclusively on the preservation of principal (you'll read more about the Eleventh Commandment in chapter 15). But you do that only by sacrificing your income.

Figure 11.1 shows the results of placing all $100,000 in a one-year bank CD as opposed to a diversified portfolio as outlined in this book. As you can see, the CD's interest income fluctuates annually. Over the ten-year period ending December 31, 2006, you would have received a total of $41,250 in annual income — but that income would have ranged from $1,220 to $6,610. That's a level of unpredictability that no retiree can easily tolerate.[68]

By comparison, say you obtained a more diversified portfolio. For fun, I turned to Ibbotson Associates for data on a portfolio containing equal portions of the following asset classes and market sectors:

- Long-Term Bonds (as measured by the Lehman Brothers Long-Term Bond Index)

- Intermediate-Term Bonds (Lehman Brothers Intermediate-Term Bond Index)

---

[68]Couldn't you avoid this volatility simply by investing in a ten-year CD instead? Theoretically, yes, but in practice, no retiree would ever do this. You'd be afraid to lock up your money for such a long period, and you'd further fret that *next year's* rate might be higher. For these reasons, most retirees place their money into shorter-term CDs, where they get whipped by the winds of fluctuating interest rates.

- Real Estate (Dow Jones Wilshire Real Estate Securities Index)

- U.S. Growth Stocks (S&P/BARRA 500 Growth Index)

- U.S. Value Stocks (S&P/BARRA 500 Value Index)

- International Stocks (Morgan Stanley Capital International European, Australian, and Far East Index)

- Precious Metals (Gold Index, as reported by Ibbottson Associates)

> **Note that this allocation is purely hypothetical. I do not recommend the above portfolio, and we have never placed any client in such an allocation. It is offered here solely to illustrate the income potential of a diversified portfolio.**
>
> **The portfolio you would actually use to generate income should be determined based on the evaluation process provided for you in chapter 7. Furthermore, if you are in the "accumulation" phase of your life (meaning you are adding to your savings), your portfolio is likely to be quite different from one you'd use once you enter the "distribution" phase in retirement. Therefore, when you are ready to begin withdrawing money from your portfolio, revisit chapter 7 and obtain a new portfolio, for your current portfolio is almost certainly not the one you should be using to generate monthly income designed to last a lifetime.**

Had you invested in that portfolio and withdrawn the same annual income as the bank CD, you too would have enjoyed $41,250 over the ten-year period. But unlike the CD, which was still worth the same $100,000 as it was in 1997, your diversified portfolio would have grown 67% — to a total value of $167,065!

In other words, the diversified portfolio would have allowed you to boost your income by 67% after ten years, because you could begin to withdraw money based on your new account value instead of your original value. This would dramatically

! This is question #5. If you haven't answered questions 1–4, STOP! and turn to page 185.

Q **Will you want to receive income from your account immediately?**

a) Yes .... **Your letter score is E.**

b) No .... **Your letter score is R.**

Congratulations! You're finished with Part 1 of the Edelman Guide to Portfolio Selection. Remember your Letter Score and return to page 193.

offset the otherwise devastating effects of inflation, which can significantly erode the buying power of your retirement income.

Indeed, based on the Consumer Price Index, the federal government's measure of inflation, you would have needed $127, 244 in 2006 to buy what $100,000 would have bought ten years earlier. In other words, your money held in "safe" CDs would actually have fallen 27% in real economic terms! Talk about "safely" going broke!

Instead of waiting ten years to boost your income, you could have used the diversified portfolio to double your annual income (compared to the bank CD). If you had done that, you would have enjoyed $82,500 in income, and at the end of ten years, your portfolio value would be almost $102,000.[69]

Figure 11.1

If you had invested $100,000 10 years ago

Year	into a 1-year CD:		into a diversified portfolio and...	
	You would have received annual interest income of . . .	. . . and the year-end value of your CD would have been:	. . . withdrawn the same amount as offered by the CD, the year-end value of your account would have been:	. . . withdrawn TWICE AS MUCH as the CD, your year-end value would have been:
1997	$5,590	$100,000	$107,093	$101,503
1998	$5,740	$100,000	$114,980	$102,938
1999	$5,700	$100,000	$122,327	$103,219
2000	$5,390	$100,000	$127,191	$101,092
2001	$6,610	$100,000	$124,508	$90,992
2002	$4,400	$100,000	$116,876	$79,831
2003	$1,840	$100,000	$113,830	$75,327
2004	$1,220	$100,000	$139,240	$90,509
2005	$1,440	$100,000	$156,412	$99,728
2006	$3,320	**$100,000**	**$167,065**	**$101,997**
Total income:	**$41,250**		**$41,250**	**$82,500**

[69]Note, however, that if you had taken such a large amount of income from your portfolio each year — 8.2% — you would have had to tolerate substantial volatility in your account value. Notice that by 2003, the portfolio's value had fallen to $75,000. That's why we caution our clients who want to take large annual withdrawals.

Your annual income would still have fluctuated wildly. For this reason, we recommend that you instead choose to receive a steady monthly income. If you had withdrawn a flat 5% per year from your portfolio, your annual income would have been $5,000 per year and your ending account value would have been $157,791.

Figure 11.2

Year	If you had invested in a diversified portfolio and...	
	withdrawn 5% per year, your income would have been ...	... and the year-end value of your account would have been:
1997	$5,000	$107,683
1998	$5,000	$116,385
1999	$5,000	$124,591
2000	$5,000	$130,035
2001	$5,000	$129,050
2002	$5,000	$120,700
2003	$5,000	$114,455
2004	$5,000	$136,231
2005	$5,000	$149,441
2006	$5,000	$157,791
Total income:	**$50,000**	
Ending value:	**$157,791**	

Note: assumes withdrawal of 5% of the original balance

It's important to note that these figures reflect only the ten years ending December 31, 2006. Different time periods would produce different results, and past performance is no indication of future results. However, we have executed such systematic withdrawal programs for thousands of clients over the past twenty years, and we've seen how they performed in every kind of market environment (from the Crash of '87, to the dot-com bubble burst to the Chinese market decline of 2007). There is no doubt that this approach to money management is far superior to placing your money entirely (or even largely) in fixed-income investments such as bank CDs, U.S. Treasury Securities, or municipal bonds.

It's also worth noting that the income you receive from your portfolio is not necessarily taxable. Taxes are due on the dividends and capital gains your portfolio produces, which may be different from the income you receive.

So rely on the investment strategy outlined in this book. It's not only going to help you accumulate wealth, but it will help you generate income from that wealth when you're ready for it.

Should You Adjust Your Portfolio Model Due to a Pension?

I am addressing this specifically to those who currently receive a pension or will upon retirement. If this describes you or a friend or family member whose finances you assist, keep reading. Otherwise, feel free to skip the rest of this chapter.

Chances are, you're still here. I'm not surprised, because pensions are extremely common; one-third of the nation's retirees receive one. That includes 2.4 million who used to work for the federal government. State and local governments currently provide pensions to 4 million retirees, including former firefighters, police officers, and school teachers. Colleges and universities provide pensions to millions of retired faculty and staff, and the military pays pensions to 1.4 million retirees. Tens of millions of union members and other retirees receive pension checks every month as well. And then there's the elephant of all pensions: Social Security. The Social Security Administration provides $33 billion in retirement income to 33 million Americans every month.

Ordinarily, it wouldn't occur to me that you might consider altering your investment portfolio merely because you now or will receive income from a pension. But I've had enough phone calls to my radio and television shows from folks asking about it, so there are clearly some pundits touting the idea. Considering the subject of this book, advice on the matter is warranted.

The short answer is *no*, you should not alter your investment portfolio merely because you receive a pension — and *especially* not for the reason that people say you should. Frankly, having said that, I'd prefer to end the chapter right here. But if I don't elaborate, somebody will send me an email demanding to know *why not*.

So, fine, here's the explanation. It's a bit long, but, hey, you asked for it.

Say you're retired, and you've decided (quite arbitrarily) to invest your $200,000 life's savings equally into bonds and stocks — a fifty-fifty split.[70] You do this because you know that bonds are safer and generate income, while stocks are riskier and grow in value. So you figure that combining the two allows you to enjoy current income that won't be eroded by inflation, with relative safety.[71]

Thus, you're content with placing $100,000 into stocks and $100,000 into bonds.

But wait! Let's say you also have a pension that pays you $5,000 per month. Isn't receiving pension income the same thing as receiving bond income?[72] After all, both pensions and bonds are considered safe, and both provide predictable, stable income.[73] So getting income from a bond is equal to getting income from a pension.

In mathematical terms, that means getting $60,000 annually from a pension is the same thing as getting $60,000 from bonds. To get your bonds to pay that much, assuming you can invest in bonds or CDs that pay 5% in annual interest, your bonds would be worth $1.2 million.

In other words, a pension that pays $60,000 per year is the same as having a $1.2 million bond portfolio. This means your portfolio is not really 50-50, but 93-7. Here's the math:

Figure 11.3

Treating a pension like bonds is like playing seesaw with an elephant.

	Stocks	Bonds	Total
From your investments	$100,000	$ 100,000	$ 200,000
Equivalent value of your pension	(0)	$1,200,000	$1,200,000
Total	$100,000	$1,300,000	$1,400,000
Percentage Allocation	**7%**	**93%**	**100%**

Therefore, according to this nonsense,[74] you should place *all* your money into stocks; because of the pension, you already have too much in bonds!

---

[70]Having read this far, you know that such a portfolio would be dumb, but let's move on.
[71]Boy, talk about oversimplifying diversification. For a more complete review, re-read *all* of chapter 1.
[72]No, but you insisted on talking about this.
[73]And dogs and cats both have four legs. Doesn't make them the same.
[74]Hey, *you* wanted to keep talking about it, not me.

All this is utterly absurd. It might sound clever to suggest that pension income is the same as receiving interest from a bond, but stupidity is often disguised as cleverness. In fact, pensions and investments are wildly different, as shown in Figure 11.4:

Figure 11.4

Don't pretend your pension is similiar to an investment. They have nothing in common.

Pension	Investment
You have no control over the income you can receive.	You have complete control over your income.
You are limited to monthly income, and your employer determines the amount.	You can receive income whenever you want. You decide the amount and frequency.
Once the income begins, you can never change it; you'll never be able to receive a lump-sum payment.	You can increase, decrease, start, or stop your income whenever you wish. While receiving income from your investments, you continue to be able to withdraw money in lump sums at any time, in any amount.
There is nothing you can do to boost the monthly income you'll receive.	You can add to your investments so that your future income will be higher.
The income does not rise with inflation.[75]	Because you control the income, you can receive more to compensate for higher expenses.
The income ceases upon your death.[76]	Whatever money you don't spend during your lifetime will pass to your spouse and children or other heirs.[77]
You are guaranteed to receive income for as long as you live.	If you withdraw too much money too quickly, or if your investments fall in value, you might run out of money before you die.

---

[75]Even if your pension does offer a cost-of-living adjustment, you have no control over the frequency or amount of these increases.
[76]If your pension continues after your death, for the benefit of your spouse or children, that's because you've agreed to receive less income during your lifetime.
[77]And some of it, maybe, to the IRS.

As if the differences in the chart were not enough, there is an even more trouble-some implication to the whole idea. If you accept the premise that you don't need to own bonds because you have a pension, you will, as a result, place *all* your money into stocks! A retiree foolish enough to have placed his $200,000 life savings into the S&P 500 Stock Index at the end of 1999 would have seen his portfolio fall in value by 43% in just three years. And if he had withdrawn just $1,000 per month to supplement his income, his account would have been worth only $112,067 by December 31, 2002. There isn't a jury or arbitration panel in the world that would have agreed with the "expert" that a retiree should place all of his liquid investments exclusively into stocks — despite the existence of a pension.[78]

So be happy that you receive (or are due to receive) a pension. But don't let that fact cause you to alter your portfolio model.

> If you can receive your pension in a lump-sum payment upon retirement instead of a series of payments over your lifetime, do so. By investing that money in accordance with chapter 7, you'll be able to generate income to replace the pension. This is a much better choice than the pension, for these reasons:
>
> 1. By taking the lump sum, you are no longer at risk if your employer later lowers its retiree benefits — because you'll have already received all the money that's due you.[79]
>
> 2. By taking the lump sum, you can invest the money as you wish. You have no such flexibility when agreeing to receive a pension; instead your employer handles the investments.
>
> 3. Once pension payments begin, you can never change the income you receive. This is a particular problem because inflation erodes the pension's purchasing power. But through the lump sum, you remain in complete control. You decide how much income you want to receive, and you can change this income at any time as your needs change.
>
> 4. With pensions, all you ever get is this month's payment. But when you've chosen the lump sum, you have full access to the entire lump sum, which you can use at any time for any purpose. That's a big help if you incur a major medical expense or other family need.

---

[78] I am a member of the NASD Board of Arbitrators. Trust me on this one.
[79] According to the Pension Benefit Guaranty Corporation, sixty thousand retirees today are receiving payments that are lower than what they were promised.

> 5.   Income from a pension ends upon your death.[80] But when you take the lump sum, you can give to your spouse, children, or other heirs all the money you don't spend during your lifetime.

Can we stop talking about this now? Good. Because what I really want to talk about are three more tips to help you achieve investment success. You'll find these in the next chapter.

---

[80]Pension income can continue for your spouse. But for that to happen, you must agree to receive a lower pension income than you'd otherwise receive. And in no case will there be any benefit available for children or grandchildren.

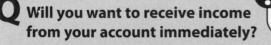

Q Will you want to receive income from your account immediately?

This is question #5. If you haven't answered questions 1–4, STOP! and turn to page 185.

a) Yes......**ERROR!** In Question #2, you said you'd make additional deposits, but here in Question #5 you say you want immediate withdrawals. Start over on page 192 — and change one of your answers.

b) No........**Congratulations!** You've completed Part 1 of the Edelman Guide to Portfolio Selection. **Your Letter Score is C.** Return to page 193 and continue to Part 2.

Chapter 12

Three More Important Insights to Insure Your Investment Success

It's not enough that you develop the proper investment strategy. It's equally important that you build an effective financial plan around that strategy. Otherwise you could find that your efforts fail to reward you with a secure financial future. So consider these three additional insights into financial planning and portfolio management.

Insight 4: You *Will* Retire One Day, and Probably Sooner than You Anticipate, No Matter How Much You Protest

It is extremely unlikely that you will die at your desk. Even if you never want to stop working, you might have to: 40% of retirees say they were forced to retire because of either poor health or layoffs.

You might have to quit much sooner than you want too. Sun Life Financial found that 22% of retirees quit working seven years sooner than they expected. As a result, most retired before they were eligible for Social Security benefits, and they had accumulated only about half as much in retirement assets as they'd hoped. The result: a dismal retirement scenario. (An analysis by Guardian Life Insurance Company of America found that being out of work for just two years reduces future retirement savings by $61,000; a five-year hiatus results in a $137,000 shortfall.)

Perhaps you think you'll solve the problem by working after you retire; 77% of working Americans say this. But only 12% of current retirees actually work, and only 27% have *ever* worked in retirement, according to the Employee Benefit Research Institute and Pew Research Center.

So do not develop an investment strategy with a cavalier attitude. The truth is that you are highly likely to become dependent one day on the income that your investments can provide.

Insight 5: Do Not Underestimate the Amount of Income You'll Need in Retirement

Americans are confident people. As with most things, we're confident about our prospects for retirement.

Every year the Employee Benefit Research Institute co-sponsors a public opinion poll called the Retirement Confidence Survey. The 2007 RCS found that 70% of workers are confident they'll have enough money to live comfortably in retirement; only 10% are "not at all confident" about their financial futures. These statistics have remained stable since 1993 as shown in Figure 12.1 — demonstrating that Americans remain confident regardless of what's happening in the economy.[81]

Figure 12.1

Americans are consistently confident about their ability to retire in comfort.

	1993	1997	2000	2002	2003	2004	2005	2006	2007
Confident	73%	65%	72%	70%	66%	68%	65%	68%	70%

Confidence in Having Enough Money to
Live Comfortably Throughout Retirement, 1993–2007

---

[81]In 1994, stocks returned less than 2%; but prices soared during the tech boom of the late 1990s. But from 2000 through 2002, the S&P 500 Stock Index lost nearly half its value. Through it all, Americans remained confident about their ability to retire in comfort.

But confidence isn't always well placed. Sometimes confidence can be more accurately described as arrogance or ignorance. I mean, how can 70% be confident that they'll enjoy a comfortable retirement when, according to the Employee Benefit Research Institute, only 48% are participating in a workplace retirement plan? And 44% of workers who have not saved for retirement nonetheless feel confident that they will have a comfortable retirement!

> Women are more acutely aware than men of the need to save for retirement. So if you're a woman, give yourself a pat on the back. Next, give yourself a swift kick in the behind, because you're no better than men at doing anything about it. In a 2003 survey by Prudential, 53% of the baby-boom women surveyed said they intended to save and invest more money over the next two years. But when Prudential checked back two years later, it learned that only 11% of the women actually did so.
>
> **Good intentions are not enough.**

Obviously, much of this confidence is misplaced. No wonder that the Economic Policy Institute predicts that 27% of households approaching retirement are likely to have retirement incomes that are less than half of their working incomes. (EPI also notes that Social Security replaces only 43% of the average worker's preretirement income — about two-fifths of what is needed.)

Despite having read all this, you're nevertheless feeling cocky — er, ah, confident — right now. That's because you think you are saving plenty for retirement, unlike the misguided masses. And, based on your confidence, you're certain that the portfolio you've selected earlier in this book will help provide you with the financial security you want in retirement.

But are you, in fact, saving enough? Don't be so sure: Workers in the RCS survey said they expect their savings to provide them with a large portion of their income

---

! This is question #5. If you haven't answered questions 1–4, STOP! and turn to page 185.

Q **Will you want to receive income from your account immediately?**

a) Yes .... **Your letter score is L.**

b) No .... **Your letter score is A.**

Congratulations! You're finished with Part 1 of the Edelman Guide to Portfolio Selection. Remember your Letter Score and return to page 193.

in retirement. Six in ten savers — and even two in ten nonsavers — say that personal savings will supply them with their largest source of retirement income.

But this is mathematically impossible. According to RCS data, shown in Figure 12.2, half of all workers have less than $25,000 in savings and investments. No wonder the Center for Retirement Research at Boston College says that 25% of workers in their fifties will have to work two years longer than they plan because retirement will not be affordable.

Figure 12.2

Half of all workers have saved almost nothing.

	All Workers	Ages 25–34	Ages 35–44	Ages 45–54	Ages 55+
Less than $25,000	49%	68%	52%	35%	32%
$25,000–$49,999	10%	9%	10%	11%	9%
$50,000–$99,999	13%	10%	14%	15%	11%
$100,000–$249,999	15%	9%	15%	19%	20%
$250,000 or more	14%	5%	9%	21%	28%

Reported Total Savings and Investments
(not including primary residence or retirement plans)

Imagine you are sixty-five years of age, and you want to withdraw $25,000 from your savings every year for the rest of your life. Assuming you live to age ninety and that your savings earn 5% per year, guess how much money you need in savings at age sixty-five?

You need more than $350,000. That's assuming you never increase your income — meaning you'll receive the same two grand per month at age eighty-five that you're receiving at age

You figure you'll have enough money to retire when you reach retirement age. But will you? Lots of today's retirees had the same confidence. It's worth your time to find out if things worked out for them — because you're traveling the same path.

And it turns out that you can learn a lot from current retirees. According to the 2006 Financial Well-being Index, created by the Principal Financial Group, 32% of retirees say their biggest financial planning regret was that they started saving too late.

sixty-five. If you want to adjust your income for 4% inflation, you'll need nearly $650,000 — or almost twice as much!

Thus, it's clear that abysmally low-interest savings accounts cannot possibly constitute your "largest source of retirement income." Instead your largest source of income will be . . . Social Security.

Do you even know when you're eligible for Social Security retirement benefits?

Many people don't. The 2006 Retirement Confidence Survey showed that only 19% of working Americans can correctly state the age when they'll be entitled to receive benefits. An astonishing 49% of workers think they'll get benefits sooner than they actually will.

Figure 12.3 shows when your benefits can begin:

Figure 12.3

If you were born in	You can receive full Social Security benefits at age
1937 or earlier	65
1938	65 and 2 months
1939	65 and 4 months
1940	65 and 6 months
1941	65 and 8 months
1942	65 and 10 months
1943–1954	66
1955	66 and 2 months
1956	66 and 4 months
1957	66 and 6 months
1958	66 and 8 months
1959	66 and 10 months
1960 and later	67

Note: Partial benefits can begin at age 62
(age 60 for widows and widowers.)

Indeed, according to the Social Security Administration, Social Security is the major source of income for most of America's elderly: 65% of those age sixty-five or older receive more than half of their annual household income from Social Security.

> The problem is particularly acute for the forty-three million Latinos living in the U.S. They comprise the fastest-growing portion of the population — 14% and rising — but 8 in 10 Latinos have less than $5,000 saved for retirement, and 60% work at companies that do not offer a retirement plan, according to a poll by Americans for Secure Retirement and the Latino Coalition.

In fact, among Social Security beneficiaries, 54% of married couples and 74% of unmarried people receive half or more of their household income from Social Security. For 21% of married couples and 43% of unmarried people, Social Security provides an astonishing 90% or more of their income.

Yet only 20% of workers think Social Security will be their largest source of income in retirement, as shown in Figure 12-4.

Figure 12.4

Largest Expected Sources of Retirement Income

		Have Saved for Retirement	
	All Workers	**Yes**	**No**
Personal savings (net)	50%	60%	31%
A workplace retirement savings plan, such as a 401(k)	28%	32%	21%
Other personal savings or investments	22%	28%	10%
Social Security	14%	7%	26%
A employer-provided traditional pension or cash balance plan	13%	16%	9%
Employment	11%	7%	19%
The sale or refinancing of your home	2%	2%	1%
Real estate income	1%	1%	0%
Other	2%	2%	4%
Don't know	5%	5%	7%

The maximum that someone turning sixty-five in 2007 can receive in Social Security retirement benefits is $2,053 per month. Therefore, unless you're saving a heck of a lot more than you currently are, you can expect this to be your dominant (or even sole) source of income in retirement.

That assumes, of course, that Social Security benefits will still exist when you retire. I have no doubt that benefits will indeed continue to be paid, but it is highly unlikely that you will receive the same high benefits that current retirees receive, or that you will start to receive them as early as they did.

You know this, of course. You're simply confident that you'll be fine anyway.

According to the 2006 RCS study, only 42% of workers said they had completed a retirement-needs calculation — the basic planning step in determining how much money you're likely to need in retirement and how much you need to save to meet that goal. And most of those who claimed to have made the calculation really hadn't. Only 19% of these respondents actually asked a financial advisor for help. Almost as many made their own estimate, while 44% admitted that all they did was guess!

Yep, my retirement is secure, you say.

How do you know, I ask?

Because, you reply with confidence and a puffed-out chest, *I guessed!*

Figure 12.5

When it comes to calculating retirement needs, most people just guess!

	Total
Guess	44%
Ask a financial advisor	19%
Do your own estimate	17%
Read or hear how much needed	11%
Fill out a worksheet or form	5%
Use an online calculator	3%
Base on cost of living/desired retirement lifestyle	3%
Other	4%

Method of Determining Savings Needed for Retirement,
by Doing a Retirement Needs Calculation

No wonder, then, that nearly a third say they won't even need $250,000 — an amount that would give you only about $800 per month after taxes, assuming we adjust for inflation and that you live to age ninety.[82]

Figure 12.6

Amount of Savings Workers Say
They Need for Retirement

	Total
Less than $250,000	26%
$250,000–$499,999	18%
$500,000–$999,999	20%
$1 million–$1.9 million	11%
$2 million or more	8%
Don't know/Don't remember	18%

Maybe those who say they won't need a lot of money in retirement figure they'll simply spend less in retirement than they do currently. Some people even rely on the "rule of thumb" that you will spend 30% less after you retire.

At first, this seems to make sense because retirees avoid several big expenses that workers incur. First, workers spend about 7.5% of their pay on Social Security taxes; retirees don't incur this cost. Second, workers place money into retirement plans and IRAs; again, retirees don't. Finally, workers spend lots of money on commuting, wardrobe, lunch, and other office-related costs. These expenses easily add up to 10% to 15% of pay annually. Thus, workers typically spend 30% of their pay on costs that disappear once they retire.

Retirees are filing for bankruptcy at a faster rate than any other age group in America, and poverty among the elderly is likely to increase, according to the Center for Retirement Research at Boston College. The richest one-third of households may not be able to sustain their standard of living, it says, and 45% of the poorest one-third risk poverty. The reason: They lack pensions and 401(k) savings and are less likely to own a home, but incur disproportionately high health care costs compared to the rest of society.

---

[82]When calculating run-out-of-money scenarios for our clients, we presume that they will live to age ninety-five or one hundred.

Therefore, the reasoning goes, you'll be fine even if your retirement income is 30% less than your preretirement pay. So if you're earning $100,000 in your final year of work, you should plan on spending $70,000 per year in retirement.

This is utter nonsense.

The wizards who figured out the above have clearly never actually provided financial advice to real people. But I have, and I can assure you that retirees don't spend less in retirement because they avoid employment-related expenses. They spend less in retirement *because they have no choice!* If they had done a better job at saving money, they'd have more money to spend, and they'd be happily spending it. It's a lie[83] to suggest any other reason.

Having developed thousands of financial plans for individuals and families over the years, I can tell you that virtually none of my clients spends less in retirement than he or she did while working — at least, not voluntarily. It is foolish to consider otherwise. Although retirees avoid many expenses that workers incur, there's a flip side to consider: Your job actually *prevents* you from spending money. After all, from the time you leave your house in the morning until the time you get home, you generally spend no money (except for coffee and lunch) because you are at work.

But as soon as you retire, you'll have a newfound ten hours each day.[84] No matter what you decide to do with those ten hours, you're going to spend money. Gardening and puttering around the house will result in trips to Home Depot. Lunch with friends won't be free. Going to the movies, traveling — all these activities cost money.

---

[83]Remember? This book is called *The Lies About Money*.
[84]Worried about the prospect of having to fill your day? Don't fret. Many of our clients facing retirement wonder what life will be like, and six months after they've retired, they all report the same happy news. *"I don't know how I ever found the time for work!"* they say. They're busier than ever and having the time of their lives. You will too.

 This is question #5. If you haven't answered questions 1–4, STOP! and turn to page 185.

Q **Will you want to receive income from your account immediately?**

a) Yes .... **Your letter score is F.**
b) No .... **Your letter score is M.**

Congratulations! You're finished with Part 1 of the Edelman Guide to Portfolio Selection. Remember your Letter Score and return to page 193.

Certainly life will be different in retirement, but it will not be *cheaper*. You might not spend money on 401(k) contributions, but you'll spend money in other ways. This is borne out by a study by the consulting firm McKinsey & Company which showed that while 32% of workers say they'll cut their expenses in retirement, only 10% of retirees actually spend less than they did in their working years. Those data are confirmed by the Employee Benefit Research Institute, which found that 55% of retirees spend as much or more in retirement as they did while working — even though half of current workers think they'll be able to cut their income in retirement by 15% to 50% (Figure 12.7).

Figure 12.7

Workers underestimate the amount they need for retirement

	Workers (Needed in Retirement)	Retirees (Current Income)
Lower (don't know percentage)	NA	6%
Less than 50%	14%	17%
50%–70%	36%	13%
70%–85%	28%	6%
85%–95%	7%	1%
95%–105% (about the same)	6%	34%
105% or more (higher)	6%	21%
Don't know/Refused	3%	1%

Percentage of Preretirement Income in Retirement

Q Will you want to receive income from your account immediately?

This is question #5. If you haven't answered questions 1–4, STOP! and turn to page 185.

a) Yes......**ERROR!** In Question #2, you said you'd make additional deposits, but here in Question #5 you say you want immediate withdrawals. Start over on page 192 — and change one of your answers.

b) No.......**Congratulations!** You've completed Part 1 of the Edelman Guide to Portfolio Selection. **Your Letter Score is B.** Return to page 193 and continue to Part 2.

If you believe the lie that you'll spend less in retirement, you won't save as much as you really should. Say you earn $100,000 at age sixty-five (your final working year), and you think you'll spend only $70,000 per year once you're in retirement. If that were true, you would need to enter retirement with about $1.1 million in your investment portfolio. This assumes the portfolio grows 8% per year, you increase your spending 3% annually to keep pace with inflation, and that you live to age ninety-five. With these assumptions in place, you will enjoy a happy retirement lifestyle.[85]

But what happens if, after you enter retirement, you discover that your projections were wrong? If you spend as much in retirement as you spent while working, you could be broke by age eighty-one. And don't even get me started about the fact that some of the other assumptions might fail too. If your investments earn less than expected, if inflation is higher, if you live longer, or if you incur higher expenses due to health care needs, you'll wish you'd saved even more.

So do yourself a favor and assume that you will spend in retirement as much as you're spending now. After all, we haven't even mentioned the kids. Even though your children will be grown and on their own by the time you retire, we have found that many of our retired clients are providing financial assistance to their grown children. You may too. And let's not forget about the *grandkids*.

And what about health care costs, or the costs of long-term care? More than half of the U.S. population will require some type of long-term care during their lives — meaning that even if you won't ever need the care, your spouse or another family member probably will.

Half of all adult children already provide financial support to their parents, according to the National Alliance for Caregiving. And a study by John Hancock found that, of such family members, 36% pay more than $1,000 per month while 11% pay more than $3,000 per month. Furthermore:

- 27% used money they had set aside for immediate goals such as vacations or a new car.

- 15% used money they had set aside for retirement.

- 13% used current income.

- 12% gave up a job in order to provide care.

---

[85]This example assumes significant — even total — erosion of principal. Although you'd be fine well into old age, your heirs would get little or nothing.

The average annual cost for a one-bedroom unit in an assisted living facility is now $33,000, according Genworth Financial's annual survey of nine thousand nursing homes, assisted-living facilities, and home care providers. It found that the average cost for a home health aide is $25 per hour and that the average cost of a private room in a nursing home is $71,000 per year. The U.S. Department of Health and Human Services says that the average stay is two and a half years.

That means you can count on spending $175,000 for yourself, your spouse, your parents, and/or your spouse's parents. Or maybe you or a member of your family will be among the 10% who stay in a nursing home for five years. That brings the tab to $350,000. *Ka-ching!*

Maybe no one in your family will need long-term care services for another twenty years. By 2030, says the American Council of Life Insurers, the average annual cost is expected to exceed $190,000 per year.[86] That's $475,000 for a typical nursing home stay of two and a half years. And you think your retirement expenses will *decline?*

The bottom line is that you will want or need to spend money, and you'll regret not having it. So you'll enter retirement in one of two conditions:

You'll have too little money and wish you'd saved more

or

You'll have more money than you'll need.[87]

Which would you prefer?

---

[86]After all, since 1990 the cost of nursing home care has increased at an average annual rate of 5.8% — almost double the overall inflation rate.

[87]What's that? You want *just enough, no more than you need but no less, either?* That's great, but your name isn't Goldilocks, and this isn't a fairy tale. In the real world, you'll either accumulate too much or too little. You won't get it "just right."

Insight 6: Do Not Overestimate Your Investment Returns

Even if you do everything right — even if you do everything this book tells you to do — you run the risk of disappointment if your expectations are unrealistic. From 1926 to 2006, the stock market (as measured by the S&P 500 Stock Index, according to Ibbotson Associates) gained an average of 10.4% per year, while the bond market (as measured by the performance of U.S. Long-Term Government Bonds, says Ibbotson) gained 5.9% per year. These figures were remarkably consistent for virtually every twenty-year interval you might choose to examine.

These statistics show us that (over long periods) the stock market generates higher returns than the bond market. Thus, the highest returns are likely to come from an all-stock portfolio, while the lowest returns can be expected from an all-bond portfolio. Logically, then, it's reasonable to assume that a portfolio that contains both stocks and bonds can be expected to generate an average annual return somewhere between 5.9% and 10.4% — depending largely on how much of your portfolio is placed into bonds versus stocks.

Yet investors surveyed by JP Morgan Chase said that they expect to earn an average of 13.1% per year from their investments. If you adopt that attitude, you'll be setting yourself up for failure.

There is, in fact, a huge difference between annual returns of 13.1% and 10.4%. Say you invest $500,000 for twenty years. At 13.1% per year, you'll end up with $5.8 million, while 10.4% will produce only $3.6 million — or 38% less. If your annual return is 8%, you'll end the twenty years with just $2.3 million.

Q **Will you want to receive income from your account immediately?**

This is question #5. If you haven't answered questions 1–4, STOP! and turn to page 185.

a) Yes......**ERROR!** In Question #2, you said you'd make additional deposits, but here in Question #5 you say you want immediate withdrawals. Start over on page 192 — and change one of your answers.

b) No.......**Congratulations!** You've completed Part 1 of the Edelman Guide to Portfolio Selection. **Your Letter Score is K.** Return to page 193 and continue to Part 2.

Maybe you can't relate to someone who invests a half million bucks for twenty years. So let's suppose instead that you invest $100 per month for forty years. At 13.1%, you'll end up with $1.7 million. Based on the S&P 500's long-term historical return, the stock market can be expected to produce only $715,000, while an 8% return would produce $349,000.

Someone who earns 10.4% per year for twenty or forty years ought to celebrate. But if you're expecting 13.1% per year, you're likely to feel like a failure. Worse, if your retirement expectations depend on earning 13.1% per year, you not only will feel like a failure, you actually will be a failure. You won't be able to retire as young as you'd hoped, you won't be able to live in that expensive house you bought, you won't be able to travel as extravagantly as you'd planned, you won't be able to pay for your grandkids' college educations as you'd promised, and you won't be able to drive a car as new or luxurious as you'd wanted.

And that's where the trouble will begin. If you expect 13.1% per year, you'll consider lesser investment returns to be inadequate — to the point that you'll believe that something must be wrong if your investments are earning "only" 10.4%. You'll figure that there must be investments out there that can provide you with the 13.1% that you want, so you'll sell your investments and buy others. They'll be easy to find — the financial press is always bragging about some investment or other that generated a huge return over the past few months or couple of years. You'll buy those investments just in time to watch them fall sharply in value — ironically, resulting in returns that are far less than even the CD rates that uneducated investors manage to obtain.

You can avoid this disaster by setting realistic expectations. What's realistic? Well, when JPMorgan asked institutional investors what they expected their portfolios to earn per year, the average answer was 8.2%. My colleagues and I agree with that consensus.[88]

Allow me to summarize. Despite your intentions, expectations, and desires, you will likely retire one day, you'll need more money in retirement than you need now, and your investments are not likely to generate returns as high as you might hope.

---

[88]But it's not a target. If the markets deliver double-digit returns (as they did through much of the 1990s), our clients will enjoy those gains. We're simply not counting on it, and we suggest that you don't either.

If you build an investment strategy based on these principles, you'll be much more likely to enjoy a happy and financial secure future.

Figure 12.8

Why it's important to earn competitive returns — and equally important to set realistic expectations.

At these rates of return . . .	You'll accumulate this amount if you invest . . .	
	$500,000 for 20 years:	$100 per month for 40 years:
1.25% per year (CD portfolio)	$641,019	$62,236
5.5% per year (all-bond portfolio)	$1,458,879	$174,104
8% per year (blended portfolio)	$2,330,479	$349,101
10.4% per year (all-stock portfolio)	$3,617,025	$714,616
13.1% per year (unrealistically high expectation)	$5,864,380	$1,670,731

In the next two chapters, we'll explore the roles of insurance and annuities in your investment strategy.

Chapter 13

Implementing This Strategy with Life Insurance

This entire book has been devoted to showing you how to build a comprehensive investment portfolio designed to meet your individual needs. You now have a specific portfolio, thanks to the Edelman Guide to Portfolio Selection® you have already completed.

Can you build that portfolio by placing your money in a life insurance policy? No, and at the risk of offending some life insurance agents and financial planners, I want to tell you that anyone who says life insurance is a great investment is a liar.

Therefore, this chapter's message is simple: Do not try to implement the investment strategy described in this book by purchasing a cash-value life insurance policy. In fact, don't try to implement *any* investment strategy by purchasing life insurance. Now feel free to skip the rest of this chapter.

Still with me? OK, paddle on.

Insurance is not an investment. In fact, the word *investment* is overused. Anytime people refer to something as being to your benefit, they refer to it as an investment. A good education is an "investment" in your future. Volunteering at a homeless shelter is a worthy "investment" of your time. So let's put boundaries on our conversation: The *American Heritage Dictionary* defines *investment* as "property or another possession acquired for future financial return or benefit."

Doesn't insurance fall under this definition? It might seem so. After all, you give a relatively small amount of money to an insurance company, and, later, your beneficiaries receive a large amount upon your death. Isn't that a good investment?

No, it's a good financial plan and a good insurance practice.

The distinction is important. You see, you purchase an investment to increase your wealth, while you purchase insurance to *protect* the wealth or income you currently have.

For example, if you want to turn $1,000 into $20,000 so that you can make a down payment on a house, you would purchase investments. But if you already live in the house, you would purchase insurance to protect yourself from financial losses you'd incur from a fire.

Here's another example: You get a job in order to earn an income. But to protect that income, you buy disability insurance. Got it?

It's obvious that people buy investments to make a profit. But did you know that making a profit from insurance is a crime? It's true: You are permitted to use insurance only to recover losses. For example, if your spouse earns $50,000 a year, you can probably buy a $1 million policy on his or her life. But no insurance company would let you buy a $10 million policy.[89]

Keep this in mind when an insurance agent says that life insurance is an excellent investment. When he makes that statement, he's either speaking colloquially or he is flat-out lying.

What about Cash Value Policies?

You've certainly heard of life insurance policies that feature *cash value* or an *accumulation account*. Don't these constitute investments?

No, they don't. Instead such features are merely part of the internal workings of a life insurance policy. Here's how it works:

Your insurance premium is based on your age; the younger you are, the less likely you are to die, and, therefore, the lower the cost of your policy. But as you age, the probability of death increases, and so does the cost of the insurance. As a result, insurance is cheap when you're young, but it becomes very expensive when you're older — so expensive that it's likely unaffordable. To prevent you from being unable to pay for the policy in future years, some policies allow you to pay more today than necessary so you can pay less later.

---

[89]The insurer would assume that the only reason you want to buy a $10 million policy is so you can kill your spouse to get the insurance proceeds. Sounds like a great idea for a movie. Oh, wait, it *was* a movie: *Double Indemnity*. In this classic 1944 thriller, an insurance salesman helped his lover kill her husband so she could collect on her husband's policy.

With these types of policies, some of the money you pay covers the cost of today's premium, while the rest is placed into interest-bearing accounts (often called the accumulation account) or *subaccounts* that are, essentially, mutual funds. Retail mutual funds. In future years, as the cost of insurance rises (because you're getting older), the insurer uses the money in the accumulation account to cover the increased insurance costs. This way, you don't have to pay more for the policy than you were paying when you were younger.

That's why it's highly misleading to suggest that the accumulation account generates a profit for you: The "profit" is actually part of the policy's overall design. If you try to collect on it, you'll destroy the policy.[90] Indeed, the cash in that accumulation account is needed to keep the policy in force; without it, the policy will terminate unless you pay additional money.

The surface of my refrigerator door is very shiny, and I can see my reflection in it. But the guy who sold me the refrigerator never suggested that one of the refrigerator's added features is that it also serves as a mirror. The same is true of life insurance. Maybe your policy, or one being pitched to you, features an accumulation account. But that does not mean your insurance is an investment, and it certainly doesn't mean that your policy is a *good* investment.

There's an easy way for you verify this. Since the goal of any investment is to produce a profit, the higher the profit, the better the investment — right? So let's compare two strategies and see which one produces the better result.

I asked one of the nation's oldest, largest, and best-known life insurance companies to provide me with an illustration for a forty-year-old nonsmoking male in good health who purchases a $500,000 variable universal life insurance (VUL) policy.

---

[90]If you have one of these policies, and you don't believe me, tell the insurer to send you a check for the amount that's in your policy's accumulation account. The insurer will do that — and your policy will either terminate or you will be required to pay much higher premiums.

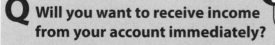

Q Will you want to receive income from your account immediately?

This is question #5. If you haven't answered questions 1–4, STOP! and turn to page 185.

a) Yes......**ERROR!** In Question #2, you said you'd make additional deposits, but here in Question #5 you say you want immediate withdrawals. Start over on page 192 — and change one of your answers.

b) No.......**Congratulations!** You've completed Part 1 of the Edelman Guide to Portfolio Selection. **Your Letter Score is H.** Return to page 193 and continue to Part 2.

As Figure 13.1 shows, the annual cost is $5,630, and at age sixty-five, if the gentleman is still alive, his policy will have a cash value of $243,222 — if (and that's a big *if*!) the underlying subaccounts grow as projected. (The policy guarantees a surrender value of only $9,554 at age sixty-five — after you've "invested" more than $135,000!)

Figure 13.1

If you examine the details of any insurance policy, you'll see that it's a very poor investment.

Year	Annual Cost of Policy	Total Cost of Policy	Hypothetical Surrender Value	Guaranteed Surrender Value
1	$5,630	$5,630	-0-	-0-
2	$5,630	$11,260	-0-	-0-
3	$5,630	$16,890	$1,233	-0-
4	$5,630	$22,520	$6,754	$2,106
5	$5,630	$28,150	$2,585	$5,640
6	$5,630	$33,780	$18,738	$8,996
7	$5,630	$39,410	$25,240	$12,176
8	$5,630	$45,040	$32,113	$15,169
9	$5,630	$50,670	$39,385	$17,972
10	$5,630	$56,300	$47,076	$20,566
11	$5,630	$61,930	$56,947	$24,543
12	$5,630	$67,560	$67,193	$28,133
13	$5,630	$73,190	$77,670	$31,132
14	$5,630	$78,820	$88,382	$33,482
15	$5,630	$84,450	$99,334	$35,118
16	$5,630	$90,080	$109,826	$35,263
17	$5,630	$95,710	$120,886	$34,857
18	$5,630	$101,340	$132,682	$33,974
19	$5,630	$106,970	$145,292	$32,578
20	$5,630	$112,600	$158,800	$30,628
21	$5,630	$118,230	$173,292	$28,054
22	$5,630	$123,860	$188,862	$24,774
23	$5,630	$129,490	$205,618	$20,684
24	$5,630	$135,120	$223,684	$15,654
25	$5,630	$140,750	$243,222	$9,554

Now let's compare this to someone who buys a thirty-year term life policy instead. The annual cost, provided by another old, large, well-known company, is $825 per year, or $4,805 less than the VUL policy. Assuming the gentlemen invests the savings in a stock mutual fund, and assuming his investment earns the same 10% per year that the VUL policy projects, his investment would be worth $519,813 by age sixty-five. After paying 15% in federal capital gains taxes and 6% in state taxes, he would net $435,879.

$243,222 vs. $435,879

You tell me: Which is the better choice?

> **If you still need convincing, notice in Figure 13.1 that the VUL policy's surrender value is virtually $0 for the first three years.[91] And it takes at least twelve years for the surrender value to equal what you'd pay in premiums![92]**

At this point, some insurance agents may try to cry, *"Foul!"* They'll try to tell you that my example is merely hypothetical, that the policy *they* are proposing won't do so poorly.

Granted, Figure 13.1 is based on projections. So let's look at actual results, shown in Figure 13.2. This data, published in April 2007 by *National Underwriter,* shows the actual historical performance of whole life insurance policies issued by thirteen major life insurance companies ten and twenty years ago, as of December 31, 2007. Over the ten-year period, the actual return for the cash value of these policies ranged from -3.8% to 4.8%. During that period, the S&P 500 Stock Index gained 8.4% per year. For the twenty-year period, the policies' actual returns ranged from 3.4% to 6.1%, compared to 11.8% for the S&P 500. So who exactly is entitled to cry, *"Foul!"* ???

These are compelling reasons to choose a low-cost term policy and invest the difference.

---

[91] That's because such policies are front loaded. The insurance company incurs substantial expenses to issue a policy, from the agent's commission to underwriting costs. All these expenses are on top of the annual mortality charges, administrative fees, and other expenses. Thus, it takes years for the insurance company to recoup its costs of issuing policies, and until it does, it awards no growth in the accumulation account.
[92] So if life insurance really *is* an investment, it's a really bad one!

Figure 13.2

Whole Life Historical Performance
as of December 31, 2007

Actual Internal Rate of Return		
	Policies issued 10 years ago	Policies issued 20 years ago
Assurity Life	-3.79%	3.60%
Country Financial Life	1.92%	3.68%
Guardian Life	-0.37%	4.20%
Massachusetts Mutual Life	-0.93%	4.03%
Metropolitan Life	1.03%	3.57%
Mutual Trust Life	-0.89%	3.80%
National Life	-2.26%	3.37%
New York Life	-0.28%	4.76%
Northwestern Mutual Life	1.29%	5.43%
Penn Mutual Life	-0.59%	3.52%
Savings Bank Life of MA	4.82%	6.14%
Security Mutual Life of NY	-2.17%	3.56%
State Farm Life	-1.09%	3.56%
S&P 500 Stock Index	**8.4%**	**11.8%**

Note: data based on $250,000 policy issued to male nonsmoker Preferred Class, age 45.

I once got a question on my radio show from a caller that, well, let's just say it wasn't exactly the kind of question you'd expect an ordinary consumer to ask.

"Ric, what do you think of using Equity Index Universal Life Insurance as a way to fund my retirement savings?"

I was taken aback. This question, I realized, could have come only from someone who had spent time with an insurance salesperson — and, most likely, a person who doesn't call himself an insurance salesperson.

A good salesperson can make the pitch sound attractive: You buy a life insurance policy that pays money to your family if you die prior to retirement. And while you're alive, you can withdraw money from the policy. *Yessir*, you can withdraw from the policy, the very dollars you've been paying over the years. *You betcha.*

Here's another sales pitch: If you withdraw the money from your policy's accumulation account, you do so free of federal and state income taxes!

That sounds enticing, but you need to know why that is true. There's no tax simply because the money is a *loan*. You're supposed to repay it with interest. If you die before doing so, your beneficiary will get the death benefit *minus* the loan amount and its accumulated interest.

This provides further evidence that insurance policies don't produce profits. Profits are taxable. Loans, which must be repaid, are not.

It's also worth noting that the ability to borrow on a tax-free basis from your policy is not a force of nature but an act of Congress. Might Congress change the tax law between now and the time you'd want to "borrow" the cash from your policy?

Not only that, the pitch continues, your account value will grow year after year. By how much? *Wellsir*, we're glad you asked, and, *by golly*, you're just gonna love this. If the stock market rises, your cash value rises too. But if the stock market falls, your account value will not fall: in fact, it will rise 3%.

If all this sounds too good to be true, that's because it is. The agent doesn't tell you that the annual cost of the policy is very high — often ten times more expensive than term life insurance — because you're paying for both the cost of insurance and the cost of an investment. The investment portion goes into the accumulation account.

The accumulation account is then invested into an Equity Index Annuity, which pays you a portion of the return earned by the S&P 500 Stock Index. Yes, you get only *a portion* of the stock market's gains, but in exchange, the policy guarantees that the amount placed there will not drop in value even if the stock market does. That sounds good, but it's really a sucker's bet: By its very nature, you'll own the policy for decades, yet since 1926 the stock market has *never* lost money in any fifteen-year time period or longer. In other words, the policy is protecting you from something that has never happened!

Once you realize this, you begin to understand the scam associated with the product. Since you're not likely to lose money, the policy's profit potential is very low — and the "missed profits" constitute a huge expense in missed wealth. You see, the sales agent might tell you that your account will earn, say, 70% of the stock market's returns (for example, if the market earns 10%, you earn 7%). But cutting your returns 30% per year results in a huge cut in profits.

How big a cut? Say your policy costs $10,000 per year, and you're entitled to 70% of the S&P 500. Let's further say your return will be 0% in any year in which the

S&P 500 loses money. And let's use actual S&P returns from 1986 to 2005 — a twenty-year period that includes 2000 through 2002, the stock market's worst three-year performance in a generation. In this example, a $10,000 annual investment would have grown to $709,320, but the policy would have $60,677 less. That's a big price to pay for a so-called guarantee.

How rampant is this type of bad advice? Very, judging from the number of emails I get from listeners of my radio show. Here's an example:

> *My wife and I are considering refinancing. One person suggested we take a variable interest loan for $600,000 that is fixed at 1.25% for five years. He suggested we invest $300,000 in whole life insurance and get a guaranteed rate of return. After five years we could apply the money made in the whole life policy to the principal. What makes this attractive is we would not have to pay tax on the earnings, as it would be washed in the equity. This sounds good, as my wife and I plan to retire in about five years, but I have never heard of such a plan.*

This is scary stuff. I count ten problems with the "advice" offered by the insurance agent. They are as follows:

1. The "fixed" rate of 1.25% refers only to the payment calculation; the loan's actual interest rate is 6.75%.

2. The difference between making payments based on a 6.75% rate and a 1.25% rate will be added to the mortgage balance, meaning the client will owe the bank much more in five years than the $600,000 originally borrowed.

3. Refinancing to cash out $300,000 for investment purposes presents a big tax problem. Interest is tax-deductible only on the first $100,000; interest paid on the excess $200,000 is not tax-deductible. This dramatically impacts the effectiveness of the strategy.[93]

---

[93]It's also worth noting that under tax law, you cannot invest mortgage proceeds into tax-deferred or tax-exempt investments. This includes annuities, municipal bonds, and Section 529 college savings and tuition prepayment plans. If you violate this rule, the mortgage interest you pay is not tax-deductible.

4.   The whole-life policy indeed offers a "guaranteed" rate of return, but the guarantee is not 6.75%, which is what borrowing the money will cost. As a result, the future value of the account will be less than the amount the client pays in interest — making the strategy a failure.

5.   The "guarantee" applies only if the money is left in the policy for at least fifteen years. If the client takes the money from the contract in the fifth year, there will be substantial penalties that dramatically reduce the proceeds.

6.   There is no assurance that the client will be permitted to withdraw the money from the policy in five years without tax liability. This is a function of tax law, which could change over the next five years.

7.   Assuming a tax-free withdrawal is indeed permitted, that is simply because the withdrawal is considered a loan; it must be repaid. If it is not repaid, the money placed into the contract will be lost. The death benefit will also be lost, and the prior withdrawals will be subject to taxes and penalties.

8.   The cost of the policy (underwriting expenses, mortality charges, commissions, policy fees, and so on) will prevent the policy from accumulating as much value as investments in mutual funds could produce.

9.   The commission on this product is as much as one hundred times more than the commissions for investing in mutual funds.

10.   Securities regulators caution stockbrokers and investment advisors about encouraging consumers to invest mortgage proceeds without substantial disclosure and suitability determinations. But life insurance is outside the jurisdiction of these regulators, giving insurance agents free reign to pitch anything they want, without explaining to consumers the regulatory issues involved.

None of the above was disclosed to the consumer. How often do agents, some of whom masquerade as financial planners, make such a pitch to unsuspecting consumers? Too often. Here's one more email I received, along with my comments.

No legitimate financial advisor would endorse the idea of reducing 401(k) contributions in order to "invest" in life insurance.

There's no such thing as "investment grade" life insurance! This is just hyperbole.

Has he explained how "guaranteed" and "ceiling" are calculated? How much must the stock market grow in order for you to receive returns?

His comments are worthless. The only thing you can rely on is what the contract says — and it's difficult for consumers to understand the legalese.

I am looking to refi my current mortgage, take out equity, and invest it in investment grade life insurance contract with a guaranteed rate (1–2%) and a ceiling rate (10–12%). I will reduce my 401k contribution to pay the higher mortgage. He says the policy will grow at an average of 8% and I will be available to draw in 20 years tax-free and the policy can be cancelled with equity returned minus fees and expenses and surrender fees.

Do you really believe that he is able to predict what the tax code will say 20 years from now?

Have you seen in writing from the contract exactly how much of your money you'll be able to get back? (In the first several years, it's going to be virtually nothing.)

By now, you're convinced: Buying life insurance as an investment is a bad idea. But if that is true, why do so many life insurance agents and financial planners recommend these policies for their clients? The reason, I'm afraid, is simple: They promote the idea because they're paid handsomely to do so.

If your financial advisor suggests that you invest $10,000 in a retail mutual fund, his commission would be $600 or less. An advisor like us using institutional shares and ETFs on a fee basis would earn $50 to $200. But if you place that same $10,000 in a variable universal life insurance policy, the commission could be as much as $12,000.[94] Which product do you think an advisor would rather recommend?

I've been in the financial planning profession for more than twenty years, and I have never read — or even heard of — an academic study or independent research report that endorses the use of insurance for investment purposes. But I have come upon a substantial number of articles, brochures, advertisements, seminars, and

---

[94]Yes, twelve thousand dollars.

even entire books written, created, presented, or distributed by insurance companies, insurance agents, and financial planners that tout the investment benefits of life insurance. Their motivation is clear.

So instead of buying expensive life insurance, buy cheap life insurance. It's called term insurance. The name reflects the fact that its cost remains the same throughout the term (or period) you select; ten, fifteen, twenty or thirty years. Shorter terms are cheaper, but longer terms maintain their prices longer.

To figure out which term length is best for you, determine how long you need the protection. If your children are young, you might consider a twenty-year policy to insure their ability to pay for college. If you want to protect a spouse, a thirty-year policy might be appropriate, so you have coverage until you retire (by which time you'll theoretically have enough in savings to eliminate the need for life insurance). Or perhaps you're worried about signing a big office lease as part of starting a business. In that case, a ten-year policy might be plenty.

> **What's the difference between an insurance agent and an insurance broker?**
>
> An agent works for one insurance company and sells products offered only by that company. But a broker is licensed with many insurance companies and shops for the best product for his client.
>
> Therefore, you have a choice: You can talk to many agents to compare each company's products, or you can work with an insurance broker who will do the shopping for you.

When trying to decide between two terms (ten or fifteen), choose the longer term. Although it will be somewhat more expensive, it avoids the risk that you might need the coverage for a bit longer than you anticipate. You see, you never want to keep a policy beyond its initial term, because the cost skyrockets.

For example, I asked my staff for the cost of a $250,000 twenty-year term policy for a thirty-five-year-old nonsmoking woman in good health. After checking with dozens of insurance companies, we received quotes as low as $145 per year. Meanwhile, the cost of a thirty-year policy was $227.

! This is question #5. If you haven't answered questions 1–4, STOP! and turn to page 185.

Q **Will you want to receive income from your account immediately?**

a) Yes ....**Your letter score is F.**
b) No ....**Your letter score is P.**

Congratulations! You're finished with Part 1 of the Edelman Guide to Portfolio Selection. Remember your Letter Score and return to page 193.

Is the twenty-year policy the better choice? Yes, but only if you're sure you don't need the policy in the twenty-first year. That's because the cost of that policy jumps to $3,115 in year twenty-one! Meanwhile, the thirty-year policy will still cost just $227. So make sure you select the proper term for your policy.

Be careful when shopping for life insurance on the Internet. It seems so easy: You input the amount of insurance you want, your age, gender, health status, and other information, and the sites tell you how much the insurance will cost. But a study of six insurance websites by the National Underwriter Company found that prices vary dramatically from website to website. At one site, the cheapest policy costs $299 a year, while another site says the cheapest cost for the same coverage is $180.

The Consumer Federation of America examined twenty-five life insurance websites and found that some sell insurance directly to you, earning commissions for doing so, while others are designed to generate leads for insurance agents. CFA discovered that 40% of the sites were difficult to use, not yet operational, didn't communicate in plain language, or didn't offer quotes online. Only six quoted the least expensive policies. So if you insist on shopping for insurance on the Web without the aid of an advisor, proceed with caution.

If you currently own cash-value life insurance, consider canceling that policy and replacing it with a new term policy.[95] Take the cash value and use the money to pay off credit cards, build cash reserves, or invest in mutual funds. Important: Do not cancel current coverage until *after* you obtain the new policy!

To learn more about determining how much life insurance your family needs, read chapter 74 of *The Truth About Money;* Rules 79, 80, 82, and 83 of *The New Rules of Money*, and chapter 4 of *What You Need to Do Now*.

Aren't you glad you didn't skip the entire chapter?

---

[95]A whole-life policy is appropriate if you need life insurance for your, uh, whole life. (Such policies are particularly effective for estate planning considerations; see chapter 64 of *The Truth About Money*.) Just don't consider these policies to be "investments."

! This is question #3. If you haven't answered questions 1–2, STOP! and turn to page 185.

Q How much cash do you have in reserves?

a) Less than 12 months of expenses.........turn to page 84

b) 12 months of expenses or more.........turn to page 112

Chapter 14

Implementing This Strategy with Variable Annuities

Are variable annuities bad for you? If you don't think so, consider these comments:

I cannot imagine a situation where I'd recommend a variable annuity.

~John Biggs, former chair of TIAA-CREF pension funds

You rarely find me so deeply angry at a common investment product that I dream of blowing it to smithereens. But stand back, I'm going to light the fuse. My target: tax-deferred, variable annuities — a name that hints of probity, with a soupcon of tax savings on the side. What a laugh. It will cost you more in taxes and possibly risk your security, too.

~Jane Bryant Quinn, personal finance columnist
and author

The marketing efforts used by some variable annuity sellers deserve scrutiny . . . Sales pitches for these products might attempt to scare or confuse investors . . . NASD is issuing this Investor Alert to help seniors and other prospective variable annuity buyers to make informed decisions about how to invest for their retirement. This Alert focuses solely on deferred variable annuities and the unique issues they raise for investors.

~NASD, the chief regulator of the brokerage industry

My colleagues and I are currently seeing a proliferation of noteworthy schemes in three related areas: "senior specialists," variable annuities, and unlicensed individuals selling unregistered securities to seniors.

~Patricia Struck, president of the North American Securities Administrators Association, the oldest international organization devoted to investor protection

---

Variable annuities are ranked #3 on California's Top 10 Investment Schemes and Scandals for 2004.

~Department of Corporations, California's Investment & Financing Authority

---

Variable annuities are patently unsuitable investments for senior citizens.

~Florida Department of Elder Affairs

Variable annuities appear on Pennsylvania's list of Top Financial Scams.

~Pennsylvania Securities Commission

Smoke and mirrors can't disguise the simple truth about variable annuities: Most investors can do better elsewhere.

~*Kiplinger's Personal Finance* magazine

Wow. Such an onslaught of criticism cannot possibly be wrong. Variable annuities *must* be horrible.

But guess what variable annuities consist of? Something called "subaccounts." Yep, when you place your money in a variable annuity, you choose one or more subaccounts to hold your money. If your subaccount grows in value, you make money, and if it falls in value, you lose money.

Guess what subaccounts are? Clones of mutual funds. So you can invest in a mutual fund directly, or you can invest in one via a variable annuity. Either way, you get the same manager and similar results. If you doubt this, take a look at chapter 14 of *Discover the Wealth Within You*.

How can it be that mutual funds are OK, while annuities that invest in mutual funds are not OK?

The primary reason, say the critics, are fees.

As you've already learned from chapter 4, all mutual funds charge fees. But when you invest in an annuity, you pay the fund's fee *plus* the annuity company's fee. This extra layer of fees can double or even triple your total costs.

What a rip-off.

Or is it? Doesn't common sense suggest that, if they are charging an extra fee, annuities must be providing an extra service or benefit? Yep. As usual, common sense prevails.

As we've seen, there's no difference investment-wise between mutual funds and annuity subaccounts. But there is a major difference safety-wise. That's because annuities offer guarantees that mutual funds lack. This difference is worth exploring, because it explains (at least partly) why annuities are more expensive than mutual funds.

Are Principal Guarantees Worthwhile?

If you invest in a mutual fund that loses money, you lose money. But if you invest in a variable annuity, and its subaccount loses money, you might not lose any money at all. That's because, unlike mutual funds, many annuities offer performance guarantees. They come in three forms:

- <u>Death benefits</u>. At the time of your death, if your investment is worth less than its original value, the annuity company will pay your beneficiaries the amount you had invested (minus any withdrawals you had made). If the account is worth more, your beneficiaries get the higher amount.

- <u>Living benefits</u>. If your investment falls in value during your lifetime, you will be permitted to withdraw an amount equal to your original investment. Each annuity company offers its own version of this benefit, but here's an example. Say you invest $100,000 in a stock subaccount, and the market then crashes, causing the value of your investment to be worth only $60,000. If you withdraw the entire $60,000, you'd have a loss of $40,000. But if you withdraw no more than 7% of your original investment amount per year ($7,000 in this example), the annuity company will let you receive that income for more than fourteen years — effectively returning 100% of your original investment back to you.

- <u>Lifetime income</u>. When you're ready to receive income from your annuity (presumably in retirement), the annuity can provide you with monthly income that's guaranteed to last as long as you live (or as long as you *and* your spouse live). Mutual funds cannot make this promise.[96]

Certainly there's a value to these benefits, and that value is reflected (at least partly) by the fee that the annuity charges you. But are these guarantees really worth the fees that annuities charge for them?

---

[96]There is substantial fine print associated with these lifetime income streams. Among other things, the annuity will tell you how much you can receive, based on the account's value and your life expectancy. Once you start receiving income (called *annuitizing)*, you can't ever change your mind. The income will not rise, meaning that inflation will erode its value over time. You'll never have access to your principal again, and when you die, the payments stop; you cannot leave what's left to the children. Make sure you get good advice from a professional advisor before you agree to annuitize an annuity.

Maybe. Maybe not. As is the case in so many areas of personal finance, the answer depends on the client.

I remember a client who needed to place some of his money in the stock market, but he was too spooked to do so. As a child, he'd heard stories of how his grandfather lost everything in the Great Depression, and as an adult he saw friends wiped out when the dot-com bubble burst. He was terrified of losing money; as a result, his money was in bank accounts, earning low returns. With his limited income and meager savings, he wouldn't have enough to support himself in retirement, which was fast approaching. He needed to earn higher returns, and that meant he needed to place some (*some*, mind you, not *all*, not even *most*) of his money in stock mutual funds, where he'd have the potential of earning higher returns. But he couldn't bring himself to do it because he knew that stock funds can lose money. Ironically, his fear of financial failure was causing him to invest in a way that would virtually guarantee financial failure!

So we recommended a variable annuity to him. Thanks to the annuity's promise that he would not lose principal, he was able to bring himself to invest where he needed to invest.

Thus, the guarantees are worthwhile when they help you invest the way you should but otherwise wouldn't. They are also of value for people who would rather not worry about market volatility and who don't mind paying an extra 1% or 2% per year for the protection against market losses.

But for most long-term investors, the guarantees are not very worthwhile. That's because the annuities are insuring you against something that is not likely to occur. So why reduce your returns by the cost of the guarantee if you're unlikely to need it?

Q Will you want to receive income from your account immediately?

!

This is question #5. If you haven't answered questions 1–4, STOP! and turn to page 185.

a) Yes......**ERROR!** In Question #2, you said you'd make additional deposits, but here in Question #5 you say you want immediate withdrawals. Start over on page 192 — and change one of your answers.

b) No.......**Congratulations!** You've completed Part 1 of the Edelman Guide to Portfolio Selection. **Your Letter Score is O.** Return to page 193 and continue to Part 2.

Still, if you feel better wearing suspenders with your belt, by all means proceed.

Even if you don't want or need the principal guarantee that the annuity offers, you might find annuities worthwhile for a different reason: taxes. You don't pay them when you own annuities — or, rather, you don't pay them right away. Let's explore this area further, for it is perhaps the most touted of all benefits that annuities offer.

Is Tax-Deferral All That Valuable?

If you invest in a mutual fund (outside of a retirement plan), you will incur a tax liability almost every year. The explanation, long and complicated, is fully covered in *The Truth About Money*, so I'll avoid that discussion here. But here are the key points, to help you understand the crucial tax differences between mutual funds and annuities.

All investments (stocks, bonds, real estate — you name it) are designed to generate income (interest or dividends) or grow in value (appreciation). Some do both. If your investment generates income, you pay taxes on that income in the year it is earned. If your investment grows in value, you pay taxes on that appreciation in the year you sell the investment.

- If your mutual fund owns an investment that generates income, your fund will pass along the income to you. This is called a *dividend distribution,* and most fund investors reinvest their distribution back into the fund. But the IRS doesn't care if you reinvest your dividends; you still have to pay taxes on them.

- If your mutual fund made money selling investments during the year, your fund will pass along to you the net appreciation. This is called a *capital gains distribution.* Again, even if you reinvest this distribution, you have to pay taxes on it. And because most retail mutual funds sell all (or almost all) of their investments every year, most funds trigger annual capital gains distributions.[97]

Most funds generate income *and* capital gains, and this forces most mutual fund shareholders to pay taxes annually. But annuities don't incur this problem. That's

---

[97]This frequent buying and selling is called turnover and is a major problem with mutual funds today. Read more about it in chapter 4.

because all the profits earned by annuities — whether income or growth — are tax-deferred. This means you don't pay taxes on your annuity's profits until you actually withdraw money from your account.

Avoiding annual taxes on investment profits is a big advantage. But it works only if you leave the money in your annuity for eighteen to twenty years or longer. Tax law is to blame: When you pay taxes annually on your mutual funds, most profits are taxed (at the federal level) at 15% or less. But when you withdraw profits from your annuity, you're taxed at your top marginal tax bracket, which can be as high as 35%. So the only way to justify paying 35% instead of 15% is to pay it much, much later — like, twenty years later. Letting the money remain in the account allows it to compound, producing higher profits that compensate for the higher tax rate.

Does tax deferral really work? Are you really better off paying a higher tax later instead of a lower tax now? The financial community debates this question endlessly; I, too, offer extensive analyses in *The Truth About Money* and *Discover the Wealth Within You.*

Proponents argue that, from a tax perspective, annuities are superior to mutual funds because:

1. If you move money from one mutual fund to another, you'll trigger taxes. But you can move money from annuity to annuity — or from subaccount to subaccount — with no tax liability.

2. It's a myth that all the withdrawals you take from your annuity will be taxed at 25% or higher. Annuity withdrawals are taxed as "ordinary income"; thus, depending on your federal income tax bracket, some of your withdrawal might be taxed only at the 15% tax rate.

Q **Will you want to receive income from your account immediately?**

This is question #5. If you haven't answered questions 1–4, STOP! and turn to page 185.

a) Yes......**ERROR!** In Question #2, you said you'd make additional deposits, but here in Question #5 you say you want immediate withdrawals. Start over on page 192 — and change one of your answers.

b) No.......**Congratulations!** You've completed Part 1 of the Edelman Guide to Portfolio Selection. **Your Letter Score is Q.** Return to page 193 and continue to Part 2.

3. If you "annuitize" your withdrawals (that is, you agree to receive money in equal payments over the rest of your life), part of the income you receive is actually a return of your original investment and therefore completely tax-free.

4. Mutual fund distributions rarely enjoy the 15% capital gains tax rate, because many capital gains distributions are classified as "short-term," meaning you pay taxes at the ordinary income rate of 28% to 35%. Since this is the same rate you'd pay on annuity withdrawals, mutual funds offer no advantage.

5. Having to report annual mutual fund distributions can cause you to lose other tax credits, deductions, or exemptions. (Fund distributions could even cause retirees to pay taxes on their Social Security income.) So even if you pay the IRS only 15% on your fund's distribution, your overall taxes could be higher.

6. Your annuity might one day become completely tax-free. If Congress replaces our tax code with a flat tax, value-added tax, or some other tax system, you'd no longer pay taxes on income. In that world, all distributions from annuities would be tax-free, making people who had paid annual taxes on their mutual funds feel quite stupid.

But those who think mutual funds have tax law on their side offer equally compelling arguments:

1. Even though you plan to leave your investments untouched for twenty years, let's face it: Life happens. If you incur a job loss or major expense (medical expenses, college, and weddings come to mind), you could be forced to make a withdrawal. If so, you'd be better off tax-wise if your money was in mutual funds.

2. When you withdraw money from your annuity,[98] the IRS presumes that you are withdrawing profits first; only after you've withdrawn all the profits do you then withdraw principal. This means you're paying taxes on 100% of your initial withdrawals. But with mutual funds, you have greater

---

[98]I'm referring to annuities purchased since 1982. Annuities purchased prior to this date, known as *pre-TEFRA annuities*, are subject to a different set of tax rules.

flexibility. As a result, many mutual fund owners can take withdrawals without paying any taxes — and sometimes they actually get tax deductions![99]

3. If you withdraw money from your annuity prior to age 59½, you'll pay taxes plus a 10% penalty on the earnings. There is no such penalty with mutual funds.

4. Congress has threatened to remove tax-deferral from annuities. Doing so would increase federal revenue — and leave annuity holders stuck with more expensive investments that offer no tax benefits over mutual funds.

5. If you pick mutual funds with very low turnover (such as the institutional shares and ETFs described in this book), you dramatically reduce annual distributions — effectively making most or all of your profits tax deferred. Yet when you sell your shares, your federal tax rate will be no higher than 15%.

6. If you own mutual funds at your death, the profits pass to your heirs tax-free. This *step up in basis* does not apply to annuities.

Which camp is right? It's hard to say definitively, but our conclusion is that annuities make sense if:

- you are highly confident that you won't touch the money for twenty years or more;

- you like one or more of the principal guarantees that annuities offer; or

- you hate paying taxes, and you enjoy the idea of deferring your taxes for decades, even if your eventual tax is higher than it might have been otherwise.

Does the above seem rather narrow to you? It does to me too, and this probably explains why less than 7% of the $4 billion in assets that my firm manages is held in annuities. What I'm saying is that annuities usually aren't the best choice, but in some cases they are, and in such cases, we use them. For example, the higher your tax bracket, the more benefit you get from tax deferral. Thus, we do not believe in any dogma — no "annuities are always horrible" or "annuities are always the

---

[99]To see how this can happen, read chapter 60 of *The Truth About Money*.

greatest" mantra. We're not drinking anyone's Kool-Aid, and you shouldn't, either. Instead recognize that annuities are worthy of consideration, and if they are suitable and appropriate for you, use them.[100]

And keep in mind that maybe, just maybe, all the negative comments you read about variable annuities aren't as negative as you might think. Consider Jonathan Clements, the well-regarded *Wall Street Journal* columnist. Over the years, Jonathan has written often about variable annuities:

November 11, 2001	If you hear [this] from a broker or planner, you should probably grab your money and run fast in the opposite direction: . . . "This variable annuity is perfect for your IRA." . . . Advisors will talk up the annuity's usually useless insurance feature. The real reason: Annuities generate lucrative commissions for the advisor.
April 14, 2003	Why do some advisors use their clients' individual retirement accounts to buy variable annuities? . . . You guessed it: It is all about the advisor's take.
August 13, 2003	Yes, variable annuities . . . can make sense as part of an investment plan. But all these strategies are classic ways of squeezing fat commissions out of unsuspecting investors. Consider yourself warned.
January 21, 2004	Lately, conservative investors have flocked to variable annuities.But as I see it, sales ought to be slumping and the only buyers should be young cheapskates and graying gamblers . . . these [are] oddball investments . . . a dubious proposition . . . no bargain. . . .

---

[100]Here's one way to tell if you've invested in annuities inappropriately: By the time you invest in an annuity, you should already be contributing the maximum to a retirement plan at work as well as an IRA (assuming you're eligible for both). People who place money in annuities instead of a retirement plan or IRA are making a mistake.

Some readers might conclude that Jonathan hates annuities. But consider his September 16, 2004, column:

> I manage three variable annuities, one for each of my children and one for myself. Surprised? . . . I purchased a variable annuity for myself because I was maxing out on both my IRA and my company retirement plans, and I wanted to sock away even more money on a tax-deferred basis. Meanwhile, I opened variable annuities for my kids as a way of getting investment compounding on a grand scale. Think about it: My children are fifty years from retirement, which means they will get fifty years of tax-deferred growth. Yeah, I suspect they will remember their old man fondly.

Thus, Jonathan doesn't think that *all* annuities are bad. Rather, he frets that some (many? most?) annuities are too expensive and that they are purchased by (sold to?) too many people for whom they are unsuitable. Those are valid concerns, but it does leave open the possibility that, given the right circumstances, annuities can be appropriate investments for some people.

> **At this writing, no variable annuity offers exchange-traded funds. However, DFA funds are offered in a product called Advisor's Edge, sponsored by Peoples Benefit Life Insurance Company, a subsidiary of AEGON, one of the world's largest insurance companies. The Advisor's Edge variable annuity is available only through select financial advisors.**

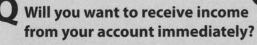

Q **Will you want to receive income from your account immediately?**

This is question #5. If you haven't answered questions 1–4, STOP! and turn to page 185.

a) Yes......**ERROR!** In Question #2, you said you'd make additional deposits, but here in Question #5 you say you want immediate withdrawals. Start over on page 192 — and change one of your answers.

b) No.......**Congratulations!** You've completed Part 1 of the Edelman Guide to Portfolio Selection. **Your Letter Score is K.** Return to page 193 and continue to Part 2.

Should You Invest in a Variable Annuity in Your Retirement Plan at Work?

Consumers invested $37 billion in variable annuities in the third quarter of 2006, according to the National Association of Variable Annuities. How could this be, if annuities are beneficial only in limited circumstances?

The answer is that annuities are sold, not bought. Annuities pay higher commissions to stockbrokers and insurance agents than mutual funds, so that's what many salespeople prefer to sell.

This is a big concern to securities regulators, who are investigating the industry's sales practices. For example, Ameriprise Financial paid a $350,000 fine in 2002 for improper annuity sales practices.

Pay attention if you or someone you love participates in a 403(b) retirement plan at work, such as a school, hospital, university, charity, or religious organization. Nominally, 403(b) plans look like 401(k) plans. But whereas 401(k) plans typically allow workers to choose mutual funds, many 403(b) plans restrict you to annuities.

On its face, the notion is absurd. The main benefit of annuities is tax-deferral. But when you invest in a 403(b) plan, your money grows tax-deferred anyway — no matter what investment you choose. Therefore, putting a tax-deferred annuity into a tax-deferred 403(b) account is redundant: The annuity doesn't give you any tax benefit that the plan isn't already giving you — but you're paying more in fees than you would with mutual funds. (The same problem exists with IRAs. The money in IRAs grows tax-deferred too, so why place IRA assets into an annuity?)

Tax-wise, there's no point to using annuities in a tax-deferred account. But as we've seen, there's more to annuities than just tax-deferral. They also offer principal guarantees; mutual funds don't. Considering that many people have the bulk of their money in IRAs and employer retirement plans, investing these monies in annuities might — *might*, mind you — make sense.

What to Do If You Want to Get Rid of Your Variable Annuity

If you own an annuity and have concluded that the benefits of tax-deferral and performance guarantees are insufficient to justify its expenses, liquidate the annuity and move the money to institutional mutual funds and exchange-traded funds as outlined in this book.

If your annuity is worth more than the amount you invested, you'll owe taxes on the profits. If you're under age 59½, you'll incur a 10% IRS penalty on those profits as well. The annuity company might even assess a surrender charge. These costs might dissuade you from acting.

You know from chapter 8 that you should proceed anyway. But you might regard selling to be an acknowledgment that you should not have invested in the variable annuity in the first place. You might not sell merely so you don't have to admit that you've made an error.[101]

This is a common psychological mistake that investors make. To see if this might be affecting you, and to learn how to overcome such behavior, read "Mind Over Money" in my book *Ordinary People, Extraordinary Wealth*. But in the meantime, sell the investment that's not best for you and buy the one that is.

In these past two chapters, you've learned about some pretty big lies people tell you about insurance and annuities. Next, in our final chapter, you'll examine one of the biggest lies being told today — and why you need to recognize it as such.

---

[101]If you feel this way, relax. You didn't err. At the time, tax law strongly favored the use of annuities. It's only in recent years that tax law has reduced their allure. So there's no need to beat yourself up.

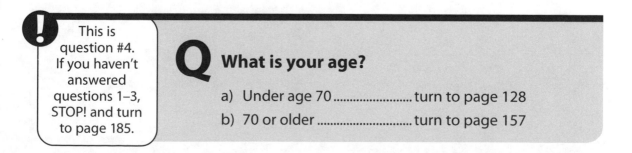

! This is question #4. If you haven't answered questions 1–3, STOP! and turn to page 185.

Q **What is your age?**

a) Under age 70 .... turn to page 128
b) 70 or older .... turn to page 157

Chapter 15
Should You Adjust Your Portfolio Because Baby Boomers Are Retiring?

Supposedly, the stock market will crash sometime between 2017 and 2024.

The alleged reason: The Baby-Boom Generation will sell its stocks to generate income as it enters retirement. Since there are so many Boomers relative to the rest of the population, there aren't enough people to buy all the stocks that Boomers will be selling. With more sellers than buyers on a massive, unprecedented scale, the stock market will crash.

Sounds plausible, doesn't it?

Everyone knows that Boomers comprise the largest portion of our population — of three hundred million Americans, seventy-seven million were born between 1946 and 1964. That's 26% of the total population.

We also know that Boomers comprise the biggest group of investors, right? After all, their youngsters — Generation X — and *their* offspring, Generation Y, have little income or assets (relatively speaking), and thus don't have much money invested in the stock market. Ditto for the Depression Babies who are already 70+ years old (those folks are already well into retirement, and 10% of them are poor, according to the U.S. Census Bureau. Clearly, Depression Babies, as a whole, have little money in the stock market.)

So, yes, it's the Boomers who own most of this country's stocks, right? They've been dutifully building their wealth for as long as forty years, preparing for the future by saving in employer retirement plans and investing in stocks and stock mutual funds. Currently, 83% of Boomers — sixty-four million people — are still working or living with a wage earner, and as a result they haven't yet needed to touch their savings.

But just wait! say the pundits. *The Boomers will soon retire!* And when they do, they'll stop putting money into the stock market. Instead they'll begin to take money out. *They'll switch from being buyers to sellers!*

My goodness. This sounds scary.

Well, you can relax, because this is a ridiculous theory. Allow me to give you several reasons why:

First, the idea is absurdly oversimplified. Of all the incredible complexities governing worldwide economics, some idiot is actually predicting what the stock market will do *ten or twenty years from now* based on just *one* consideration?! Hey, fellas, let's completely ignore corporate profits, worker productivity, inflation, taxes, interest rates, social issues, environmental concerns, politics, war, public health, public policy, regulation, and more, and simply conclude that *the entire stock market will collapse solely because Uncle Fred and his classmates are all turning sixty-five.*

A person who claims that retiring Boomers will cause a market crash is revealing that he is not a financial advisor. I say this because I *am* a financial advisor, and have been counseling individuals and couples for more than twenty years. I've helped thousands of people prepare for retirement and maintain their lifestyles in retirement. And through my experience — which *every* financial advisor can confirm — I can tell you that there is *one* fundamental fact about retirees:

They never liquidate their investments.

Think about it. Can you imagine a sixty-five-year-old guy coming home from work and saying to his wife, *"Hey, honey, I've just retired. Quick, let's liquidate our entire stock portfolio!"*

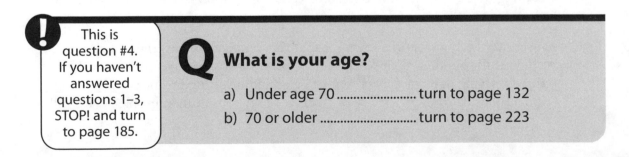

! This is question #4. If you haven't answered questions 1–3, STOP! and turn to page 185.

Q **What is your age?**

a) Under age 70 .... turn to page 132

b) 70 or older .... turn to page 223

Such a conversation would be absurd and thus would never happen. Everyone who counsels real people knows this. Only some nut playing with spreadsheets in an ivory tower could concoct the fairy tale that retirees will sell all of their investments.

But this doesn't mean retirees won't *touch* their investments. They will: As they approach and enter retirement, they will reallocate their portfolios, to lower their investment risks and generate investment income.

And investment income is indeed a big deal to retirees. It has to be. After all, they're not earning a paycheck anymore. So they seek a "paycheck" from their investments instead. And that's a healthy, reasonable thing to do.

Indeed, selling is the *last* financial act a retiree would ever take. This fact is so fundamental that we financial advisors have made a joke of it: We laugh that retirees obey the Eleventh Commandment: **Thou Shalt Not Spend Principal**.

Retirees will do *anything* to avoid spending principal. They'll get a job greeting shoppers, they'll cancel their cable TV subscription, they'll drive a fifteen-year-old car, they'll even cut muffins in half and buy half as many. *But they won't spend principal.*

Retirees observe the Eleventh Commandment because they are smart people. They know that the money they have is *all* the money they will *ever* have, and they know it must last their remaining lifetime. They realize that they (or their spouse) might live twenty or thirty more years, and they know (and fear) that medical expenses will increase as they get older. They might even need to pay for care in a nursing home. So the last thing they want to do is put themselves into a position where they might run out of money.

I call it the Bag Lady Syndrome. No matter how much money one of my retired clients might have — it could be millions — she nonetheless fears that she might become penniless. As any real financial advisor can tell you (anyone who really works with retirees, that is, not just those who write books and have talk shows and *pretend* to be advisors), there's no point in trying to convince a retiree that he or she is fine financially; no matter how "fine" they are, they fear going broke. Frankly, it's a healthy fear, for it really does help them avoid such an outcome.

Therefore, the only person who might suggest that Boomers will cause the stock market to crash is a person who does not understand retiree psychology. But real financial advisors truly know how real retirees behave.

Therefore, instead of suggesting that stock prices will fall when the Boomers retire, I can argue that stock prices will actually *rise*. I can offer two reasons for this:

- Affluent retirees often have more income than they need, so they invest their excess money. They *buy* instead of sell, causing stock prices to rise.

- Gen Xers, who are now trying to save for their own retirements, want to invest in stocks. But most of the stocks are owned by Boomers, who refuse to sell. This forces Gen Xers to bid up the prices, to compel Boomers to part with their securities. Result: Stock prices rise. (A 2006 study by Eaton Vance showed that retirees were moving their assets into *dividend-paying* stocks. This provides additional support to the notion that retirees don't sell assets in retirement. Instead they generate income from them.)

If you like this theory, great — but keep in mind that it's as ridiculously oversimplistic as the one offered by the liars who say Boomers will cause prices to fall. My point is that it's silly to draw *any* conclusion about what will happen in the stock market twenty years from now.

But let's take this a step further, anyway. Let's say you don't buy my theory that Boomers will hold their stocks. Let's say you still believe Boomers will sell.

To whom?

> **But won't Boomers *have* to sell their IRAs and retirement accounts when they reach age 70½?**
>
> No, and the pundits who cite this IRS rule to support their claim are showing how little they know about investor psychology. It's true that you generally must begin to distribute money from your IRA and other retirement accounts after age 70½. However, there's a big difference between making a distribution from your account and actually spending the money.
>
> When our clients reach the age of mandatory distributions, we usually just move the required amounts from their IRA or some other retirement account into a taxable investment account. By doing so, they meet the IRS requirement (paying taxes on the distribution, which is the point of the rule), but the bulk of the money remains fully invested as before.
>
> So, no, the RMD rule (for required minimum distributions) does not support the ridiculous assertion of the worrywarts.

This question is the basis of the market crash theory: Boomers will sell, and although Gen Xers will buy, there aren't enough of them to buy all the shares that Boomers will be selling. With a market filled with more sellers than buyers, prices will collapse, says the theory.

Even if you believe the premise, the theory still fails. Why? Because the pundits are thinking only about Gen Xers in the United States. They have completely forgotten about the rest of the world!

There are 618 million Gen Xers living in China and India alone — that's twice the population of the entire United States — but the average annual income in China and India is $8,000 and $3,500, respectively, according to the United Nations. As these nations continue their industrial development, billions of people will have newfound money to invest. With relatively few investment opportunities in their own nations, U.S. securities will be of prime appeal. If indeed American Boomers want to sell, they'll have a ready audience. Again, the stock market will not fall. Instead it will likely rise.

Still convinced that this so-called Age Wave is something to fear? Then consider a 2006 report by the U.S. Government Accountability Office. It says Boomers will not cause a stock market decline when they retire, for a very simple reason. It's not because Boomers won't sell, says the GAO. It's not because there are plenty of buyers, either.

It's because most Boomers don't own stocks in the first place.

Indeed, according to the GAO's examination of the Federal Reserve Board's 2004 Survey of Consumer Finances, 52% of all the assets owned by Boomers are held by the wealthiest 5%; two-thirds are held by the top 10%. A full third of Boomers own absolutely no stocks, bonds, mutual funds, or retirement accounts at all!

Well, you can't sell what you don't own — and the majority of Boomers own little or nothing. In fact, wealth is so highly concentrated that the Boomers who do own stocks own so much that they have no need to sell — they'll be able to support themselves just by living off their dividends!

> The GAO's study was supported by research by the Securities Industry Association, which found that while 10% of Boomers currently live in poverty, 20% will be in poverty after they retire. The reason: When you retire, you lose your paycheck. Without it, millions who have no savings will enter poverty.

The GAO study further supports the arguments I've made:

- Retirees do not sell assets. Instead some slowly spend their assets over their lifetimes, while others actually continue accumulating assets.

- Boomers will enter retirement over a nineteen-year span. This extended timeline makes it unlikely that the U.S. stock market will experience a sharp and sudden decline.

- Boomers are more willing than prior generations to use their home equity as a source of income, further reducing pressure for them to sell securities.

- Studies show that past changes in the U.S. population's age structures had little to no effect on stock market returns and bond yields.

- The minority of Boomers who own the majority of stocks are more likely to bequeath their securities than sell them. Tax law bolsters this prediction, because Boomers pay taxes when selling assets, but they can transfer some or all of their wealth to heirs tax-free.

- Finally, says the GAO report, "macroeconomic and financial factors have explained more of the variation in stock returns from 1948 to 2004 than shifts in the U.S. population's age structure . . . such factors could outweigh any future demographic effect on stock returns."

So ignore the sensationalists who say the Age Wave will cause a financial panic. Those people are just trying to get on TV so they can sell their books. But one thing is sure: Somewhere between 2017 and 2024, you'll be wondering, Whatever happened to the guys who made that prediction?

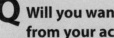

Q Will you want to receive income from your account immediately?

This is question #5. If you haven't answered questions 1–4, STOP! and turn to page 185.

a) Yes......**ERROR!** In Question #2, you said you'd make additional deposits, but here in Question #5 you say you want immediate withdrawals. Start over on page 192 — and change one of your answers.

b) No.......**Congratulations!** You've completed Part 1 of the Edelman Guide to Portfolio Selection. **Your Letter Score is O.** Return to page 193 and continue to Part 2.

Epilogue
Lessons Learned

As disturbing and disheartening as it is to learn that the retail mutual fund industry is now at odds with everyday investors, it is reassuring and revitalizing to know that alternatives are available.

By using the information and guidance offered in this book, you will be able to regain control of your investments and your financial future. So let's recap all the information contained within these pages — consider it a checklist to help you manage your investments, starting today!

Chapter 1

1. Save, save, save. There is no substitute for investing as much money as you can, as often as you can. Regardless of your investment strategy, the more you save, the more wealth you'll accumulate.

2. Maintain a long-term investment horizon. Don't let current events or market activity sway you into making changes in your portfolio. Remember to stay focused on your long-term goals, not the daily news.

3. Build a highly diversified portfolio using a wide variety of asset classes and market sectors. Investing isn't just about being "in" or "out" of the market. It's about being in every market, all the time.

4. Rebalance your portfolio periodically. Left untouched, even the best portfolio design will unravel due to fluctuating market performance. By rebalancing, you reduce your investment risks and increase the likelihood that you'll achieve your goals.

Chapter 2

5. Remember that *risk* is as important as *return*. Always evaluate the risk involved in seeking potential returns.

6. Reduce your investment risks by diversifying and by giving your investments the time they need to generate the returns you seek.

7. Ignore the current investment fad, hottest tip, and latest prediction. Those claiming to know what the future holds never have your best interests in mind.

Chapters 3–7

8. Sell your retail mutual funds wherever possible, and replace them with institutional shares and exchange-traded funds.

9. Design an investment portfolio that's suitable and appropriate for your situation. Avoid the temptation to buy investments merely because you think they'll "make money."

Chapter 9

10. Contribute as much to your employer retirement plan that your employer allows on a pre-tax basis.

11. Place all of your current contributions (and all of your employer's contributions, if any) in diversified stock mutual funds.

12. Diversify your existing account balance, and rebalance it periodically.

! This is the end of Part 1. If you haven't answered questions 1–4, STOP! and turn to page 185.

Congratulations! You've finished Part 1 of the Edelman Guide to Portfolio Selection.

Your Letter Score is I.

Remember this Letter Score and return to page 193.

13. Encourage your employer to offer institutional shares and/or ETFs in your retirement plan at work.

14. When you separate from service, (that is, quit, get fired or retire), move the money in your former employer's retirement plan to an IRA.

Chapter 10

15. Establish a 529 College Savings Plan. Do not assume that you must choose a plan offered by your state of residence. Instead choose the plan that offers the investments you prefer most.

16. If you are a grandparent, think twice before contributing to a grandchild's college savings account. It might be wiser to help pay the actual tuition bills when the child enters college.

Chapter 11

17. When investing for current income, create a diversified portfolio and generate systematic withdrawals. This will offer better protection against inflation than a portfolio that is predominately or exclusively invested in bonds or CDs.

18. Never adjust your portfolio's holdings merely because you have or will receive income from a pension.

Chapter 13

19. Never purchase life insurance for investment purposes.

20. If you own a life insurance policy that you purchased primarily for investment purposes, talk to a financial advisor (not the agent who sold you the policy) for an independent opinion as to whether you ought to keep, replace, cancel, or sell the policy.

Chapter 14

21. Do not assume that annuities are always horrible or always perfect. The truth is somewhere in between, and suitability always depends on one's individual circumstances.

22. Do not invest in an annuity in an employer retirement plan or IRA. If you already have, talk to your employer or a financial advisor about moving the money to mutual funds.

Chapter 15

23. Do not let claims that Baby Boomers are retiring scare you into altering your long-term investment strategy.

Insights (Chapters 8 and 12)

24. Never let tax considerations determine your investment strategy. Taxes are the by-product of successful investing.

25. Never let expenses determine your investment strategy. Investing is about achieving results, not avoiding fees.

26. Make sure your portfolio reflects your current situation. Even a well-crafted portfolio will become outdated as your life changes. Review your portfolio periodically to make sure it remains suitable and appropriate for you.

27. Act as though you will retire one day, and build a financial plan and investment strategy around that assumption — even if you swear you'll never retire. You might change your mind or be forced to retire, and you'll be glad you've built a strategy that anticipates such a scenario.

28. Do not underestimate the amount of money you will need in retirement. It is highly unlikely that you will want to live on less in retirement than you do currently.

29. Do not overestimate your investment returns. Assume modest returns and save accordingly, to boost the likelihood that you will achieve your goals.

And Finally

30. Listen to *The Ric Edelman Show* on the ABC Radio Networks. (Sorry, couldn't resist.)

Sources

Figure 1.1: Standard & Poor's.

Figures 1.3–1.12: Performance of the S&P 500 Stock Index from Jan. 1, 1998 through Dec. 31, 2006. Source: Ibbotson Associates.

Figure 1.13: Lehman Brothers Long-Term Government Bonds, Lehman Brothers Long-Term Corporate Bonds, Lehman Brothers Intermediate-Term Government Bonds, Lehman Brothers High-Yield Index, Federal Reserve, S&P/BARRA 500 Growth Index, S&P/BARRA 500 Value Index, S&P/BARRA MidCap 400 Growth Index, S&P/BARRA MidCap 400 Value Index, Fama-French Small Value Index, Fama-French Small Growth Index, S&P/IFCI Emerging Composite Index, MSCI World ex U.S. Index, DJ Wilshire Real Estate Securities Index, Wall Street Journal, London Closing Price, Dow Jones-AIG Commodity Index.

Figure 1.14: Standard & Poor's.

Figure 1.15: S&P 500 December 1997–December 2006, Ibbotson Associates. Equity Mutual Fund Net Cash Flows, December 1997–December 2006, Investment Company Institute.

Figure 2.1: Morningstar data as of December 31, 2006

Figure 2.2: Ibbotson Associates.

Figure 2.3: "Determinants of Portfolio Performance," *Financial Analysts Journal*, 1986.

Figure 2.4: Journal of Finance.

Figure 2.5: Ibbotson Associates.

Figure 2.6: Lipper Analytical Services.

Figure 2.7: "Popular Culture and the Stock Market," www.socionomics.net, Robert R. Prechter, Jr., 1985.

Figure 3.1: *Financial Planning* magazine, March 2007.

Figure 4.1: Investment Company Institute, Morningstar 2004 data are for all funds that had reported as of October 31, 2004.

Figure 4.3: Center for Research in Securities Prices; John Bogle; 2005, CFA Institute.

Figure 4.4: Morningstar as of December 31, 2006.

Figure 5.1: Morgan Stanley Capital International, Lehman Brothers, Dow Jones and Company, Merrill Lynch, Standard and Poor's, Wilshire Associates, Russell Investment Group.

Figure 5.2: Dimensional Fund Advisors.

Figure 6.1: Investment Company Institute.

Figure 8.1: U.S. Treasury Department.

Figure 9.1: Assumes $40,000 starting salary at age 25, with 2% annual salary increases, and that you contribute 10% of pay to a retirement plan with a 3% employer match, earning 8% per year.

Figure 10.1: FinAid.

Figures 12.1–12.2; 12.4–12.8: Employment Benefit Research Institute and Mathew Greenwald & Associates, Inc., 2006–2007 Retirement Confidence Surveys. Reprinted with Permission.

Figure 13.1: undisclosed.

Figure 13.2: National Underwriter.

! This is the end of Part 1. If you haven't answered questions 1–4, STOP! and turn to page 185.

Congratulations! You've finished Part 1 of the Edelman Guide to Portfolio Selection.

Your Letter Score is N.

Remember this Letter Score and return to page 193.

For Further Reading

If you'd like to learn more about the academic research pertaining to portfolio management, consider these books and articles.

Adriaans, P., and D. Zantinge. *Data Mining*. Harlow, Eng.: Addison Wesley Longman, 1996.

Agrawal, R., et al. *Modeling Multidimensional Databases*. Research Report, IBM Almaden Research Center, San Jose, CA, 1997.

Agrawal, R., et al. *Mining Association Rules Between Sets of Items in Large Databases*. Proceedings of the 1993 ACM SIGMOD Conference, Washington, D.C., May 1993.

Agrawal, S., et al. *On the Computation of Multidimensional Aggregates*. Proceedings of the 22nd VLDB Conference, Bombay, India, 1996.

Ang, James S., and Jess H. Chua. "Composite Measures for the Evaluation of Investment Performance." *Journal of Financial and Quantitative Analysis* 14(2) (1979), 361–384.

Balzer, Leslie A. "Measuring Investment Risk: A Review," *Journal of Investing* 3(3) (1994), 47–58.

Bawa, Vijay S. "Optimal Rules for Ordering Uncertain Prospects," *Journal of Financial Economics* 2(1) (1975), 95–121.

Bernstein, Peter S. *Capital Ideas: The Improbable Origins of Modern Wall Street*. New York: The Free Press, 1993.

Bernstein, Peter S. *Against the Gods: The Remarkable Story of Risk*. New York: Wiley, 1996.

Bey, Roger P. "Estimating the Optimal Stochastic Dominance Efficient Set with a Mean-Semivariance Algorithm." *Journal of Financial and Quantitative Analysis* 14(5) (1979), 1059–1070.

Bookstaber, Richard, and Roger Clarke. "Problems in Evaluating the Performance of Portfolios with Options." *Financial Analyst Journal* 41(1) (1985), 48–62.

Boyce, W. E. and R.C. DiPrima. *Elementary Differential Equations*, 5th ed. New York: Wiley, 1986.

Brinson, Gary P., L. Randolph Hood, and Gilbert L. Beebower. "Determinants of Portfolio Performance." *Financial Analyst Journal*, July–August 1986, 39–44.

Cabena, P., et. al. *Discovering Data Mining: From Concept to Implementation*. Upper Saddle River, NJ: Prentice Hall, 1997.

Cavallo, R.E., and G. J. Klir. "Reconstructability Analysis of Multi-dimensional Relations: A Theoretical Basis for Computer-aided Determination of Acceptable System Models." *International Journal of General Systems* 5 (1979), 143–171.

Chen, Peng, and Sherman Hanna. "Small Stocks vs. Large Stocks: It's How Long You Hold That Counts." *The Journal of American Association of Individual Investors*, July 1999.

Christensen, R. *Analysis of Variance, Design and Regression*. London: Chapman& Hall, 1996.

Efron, B. "The Efficiency of Logistic Regression Compared to Normal Discriminant Analysis." *Journal of the American Statistical Association* 70 (1975), 892–898.

Elton, Edwin J., Martin J. Gruber, and Manfred W. Padberg. "Simple Criteria for Optimal Portfolio Selection." *Journal of Finance* 31(5) (1976), 1341–1357.

Elton, Edwin J., Martin J. Gruber, and T. Urich. "Are Betas Best?" *Journal of Finance* 33 (1978) 1375–1384.

Fama, Eugene F., and Kenneth R. French. "The Cross Section of Expected Stock Returns." *Journal of Finance* 47(2) (1992), 427–466.

Fayyad, U. M. Editorial. *Data Mining and Knowledge Discovery* 1 (1997), 5–10.

Feynman, Richard P. "Cornell University Lectures." 1964, *NOVA—The Best Mind Since Einstein*, videotape, BBC/WGBH, Boston, 1993.

Fishburn, Peter C. "Mean-Risk Analysis with Risk Associated with Below-Target Returns." *American Economic Review* 67(2) (1977), 116–126.

Fisher, R.A. *The Statistical Utilization of Multiple Measurements. Annals of Eugenics* 8 (1938), 376–386.

Glymour, C., et al. "Statistical Themes and Lessons for Data Mining," *Data Mining and Knowledge Discovery*, 1 (1997), 11–28.

Goldberg, D. E. *Genetic Algorithms in Search, Optimization and Machine Learning*. Addison-Wesley, 1989.

Goodman, R. M., and P. Smyth. *An Information-Theoretic Model for Rule-based Expert Systems*. 1988 International Symposium in Information Theory, Kobe, Japan, 1988.

Hai, A., and G. J. Klir. "An Empirical Investigation of Reconstructability Analysis: Probabilistic System." *International Journal of Man-Machine Studies* 22 (1985), 163–192.

Han, J. *Data Mining Techniques and Applications.* UCLA short class, February 2–5, 1998.

Harlow, W. V., and Ramesh K.S. Rao. "Asset Pricing in a Generalized Mean-Lower Partial Moment Framework: Theory and Evidence." *Journal of Financial and Quantitative Analysis* 24(3) (1989), 285–311.

Harlow, W. V. "Asset Allocation in a Downside-Risk Framework." *Financial Analyst Journal* 47(5) (1991), 28–40.

Hartley, R. V. L. "Transmission of Information." *Bell Systems Technical Journal* 7 (1928), 535.

Haugen, Robert A. "Building a Better Index: Cap-Weighted Benchmarks Are Inefficient Vehicles." *Pensions and Investments,* October 1, 1990.

Hogan, William W., and James M. Warren. "Computation of the Efficient Boundary in the E-S Portfolio Selection Model." *Journal of Financial and Quantitative Analysis* 7(4) (1972), 1881–1896.

Hogan, William W., and James M. Warren. "Toward the Development of an Equilibrium Capital-Market Model Based on Semivariance." *Journal of Financial and Quantitative Analysis* 9(1) (1974), 1–11.

Hosmer, D. W., and S. Lemeshow. *Applied Logistic Regression.* New York: Wiley, 1989.

Ibbotson, Roger G., and Paul D. Kaplan. "Does Asset Allocation Policy Explain 40, 90, or 100 Percent of Performance?" Yale ICF Working Paper No. 00-54, *Financial Analysts Journal* 56(1) (2000), 26–33.

Iverson, G. R., and H. Norpot. *Analysis of Variance.* Beverly Hills, CA: Sage Publications, 1976.

Jahnke, William, W. "The Asset Allocation Hoax." *Journal of Financial Planning,* February 1997, 109–113.

Johnson, R. A., and D.W. Wichern. *Applied Multivariate Statistical Analysis.* Englewood Cliffs, NJ: Prentice Hall, 1988.

Jones, B. "K-systems versus Classical Multivariate Systems." *International Journal of General Systems* 12 (1986), 1–6.

Jones, B., and D. Gouw. "The Interaction Concept of K-Systems Theory," *International Journal of General Systems,* 24 (1996), 163–169.

Joslyn, C. *Towards General Information Theoretical Representations of Database Problems.* Proceedings of 1997 Conference of the IEEE Society for Systems, Man, and Cybernetics, 1997.

Joslyn, C. *Data Exploration through Extension and Projection*. Unpublished technical report, 1998.

Kaplan, Paul D. *CFA Asset Allocation Using the Markowitz Approach*. 1998.

Kaplan, Paul D., and Laurence B. Siegel. "Portfolio Theory Is Alive and Well." *Journal of Investing* 3(3) (1994a), 18–23, 45–46.

Klemkosky, Robert C. "The Bias in Composite Performance Measures." *Journal of Financial and Quantitative Analysis* 8(3) (1973), 505–514.

Klir, G. J. "On Systems Methodology and Inductive Reasoning: The Issue of Parts and Wholes." *General Systems Yearbook* 26, 29–38.

Klir, G. J. *Architecture of System Problem Solving*. New York: Plenum Press, 1985.

Klir, G. J., and B. Parvi. "General Reconstruction Characteristics of Probabilistic and Possibilistic Systems." *International Journal of Man-Machine Studies* 25 (1986), 367–397.

Klir, G. J., and T. Folger. *Fuzzy Sets, Uncertainty, and Information*. Englewood Cliffs, NJ: Prentice Hall, 1988.

Klir, G. J., and B. Yuan. *Fuzzy Sets and Fuzzy Logic: Theory and Applications*. Upper Saddle River, NJ: Prentice Hall, 1995.

Knoke, D., and P.J. Burke. *Log-Linear Models*. Sage University Paper Series on Quantitative Applications in the Social Sciences, series no. 07-020. Beverly Hills and London: Sage Publications, 1980.

Kroll, Yoram, Haim Levy, and Harry M. Markowitz. "Mean-Variance Versus Direct Utility Maximization." *Journal of Finance* 39(1) (1984), 47–62.

Laughhunn, D. J., J. W. Payne, and R. Crum. "Managerial Risk Preferences for Below-Target Returns." *Management Science* 26 (1980), 1238–1249.

Levy, Haim, and Harry M. Markowitz. "Approximating Expected Utility by a Function of Mean and Variance." *American Economic Review* 69(3) (1979), 308–317.

Lin, T. Y., and N. Cercone. *Rough Sets and Data Mining*. Norwell, MA: Kluver, 1997.

Lintner, J. "The Valuation of Risk Assets and the Selection of Risky Investments in Stock Portfolios and Capital Budgets." *The Review of Economics and Statistics* 47(1) (1965), 13–37.

Lummer, Scott L., Mark W. Riepe, and Laurence B. Siegel. "Taming Your Optimizer: A Guide Through the Pitfalls of Mean-Variance Optimization." *Global Asset Allocation: Techniques for Optimizing Portfolio Management*. J. Lederman and R. Klein, eds. New York: Wiley, 1994.

Lummer, Scott L. and Mark W. Riepe. "The Role of Asset Allocation in Portfolio Management." *Global Asset Allocation: Techniques for Optimizing Portfolio Management*. J. Lederman and R. Klein, eds. New York: Wiley, 1994.

Mao, James C. T. "Models of Capital Budgeting, E-V vs. E-S." *Journal of Financial and Quantitative Analysis* 5(5) (1970), 657–676.

Markowitz, Harry M. "Portfolio Selection." *Journal of Finance* 7(1) (1952), 77–91.

Markowitz, Harry M. "The Optimization of a Quadratic Function Subject to Linear Constraints." *Naval Research Logistics Quarterly* 3 (1956), 111–133.

Markowitz, Harry M. *Portfolio Selection*, 1st ed. New York: John Wiley, 1959.

Markowitz, Harry M. *Portfolio Selection*, 2nd ed. Cambridge, MA: Basil Blackwell, 1991.

Markowitz, Harry M. *Mean-Variance Analysis in Portfolio Choice and Capital Markets*. Cambridge, MA: Basil Blackwell, 1987.

Markowitz, Harry M. "The Early History of Portfolio Theory: 1600–1960." *Financial Analysts Journal* 55(4) (1999), 5–16.

Martin, J. K. "An Exact Probability Metric for Decision Tree Splitting and Stopping." *Machine Learning* 28 (1997), 257–291.

McCulloch, W. S. and W. Pitts. "A Logical Calculus of the Ideas Immanent in Neuron Activity." *Bulletin of Mathematical Biophysics*, 5 (1943), 115–133.

Miller, I., J. E. Freund, and R. A. Johnson. *Probability and Statistics for Engineers*, 4th ed. Englewood Cliffs, NJ: Prentice Hall, 1990.

Mitchell, M. *An Introduction to Genetic Algorithms*. Boston: MIT Press, 1996.

Mossin, Jan. "Equilibrium in a Capital Asset Market." *Econometrica* 34 (1966), 768–783.

Motwani, R., S. Brin, and C. Silverstein. *Beyond Market Baskets: Generalizing Association Rules to Correlation*, 1997 ACM SIGMOD Conference on Management of Data, 1997, pp. 265–276.

Nantell, Timothy J., and Barbara Price. "An Analytical Comparison of Variance and Semivariance Capital Market Theories." *Journal of Financial and Quantitative Analysis* 14(2) (1979), 221–242.

Nawrocki, David. "A Comparison of Risk Measures When Used in a Simple Portfolio Selection Heuristic." *Journal of Business Finance and Accounting* 10(2) (1983), 183–194.

Nawrocki, David, and Katharine Staples. "A Customized LPM Risk Measure for Portfolio Analysis." *Applied Economics* 21(2) (1989), 205–218.

Nawrocki, David. "Tailoring Asset Allocation to the Individual Investor." *International Review of Economics and Business* 38(10–11) (1990), 977–990.

Nawrocki, David N. "Optimal Algorithms and Lower Partial Moment: Ex Post Results." *Applied Economics* 23(3) (1991), 465–470.

Nawrocki, David N. "The Characteristics of Portfolios Selected by n-Degree Lower Partial Moment." *International Review of Financial Analysis* 1(3) (1992), 195–210.

Nilsson, N. J. *Learning Machines: Foundations of Trainable Pattern-Classifying Systems.* New York: McGraw-Hill, 1965.

Pandya, A. S., and R. B. Macy. *Pattern Recognition with Neural Networks in C++.* Boca Raton, FL: CRC-Press, 1996.

Philippatos, George C. "Computer Programs for Implementing Portfolio Theory." Unpublished Software, Pennsylvania State University, 1971.

Piatetsky-Shapiro, G., and W.J. Frawley, eds. *Knowledge Discovery in Databases.* Menlo Park, CA: AAAI Press/ MIT Press, 1991.

Pittarelli, M. "A Note on Probability Estimation Using Reconstructability Analysis." *International Journal of General Systems* 18 (1990), 11–21.

Pittarelli, M. "An Algebra for Probabilistic Databases." *IEEE Transactions on Knowledge and Data Engineering* 6 (1994), 293–303.

Popper, K. R. *The Logic of Scientific Discovery.* New York, 1959.

Porter, R. Burr, James R. Wart, and Donald L. Ferguson. "Efficient Algorithms for Conducting Stochastic Dominance Tests on Large Numbers of Portfolios." *Journal of Financial and Quantitative Analysis* 8(1) (1973), 71–81.

Porter, R. Burr. "Semivariance and Stochastic Dominance: A Comparison." *American Economic Review* 64(1) (1974), 200–204.

Porter, R. Burr, and Roger P. Bey. "An Evaluation of the Empirical Significance of Optimal Seeking Algorithms in Portfolio Selection." *Journal of Finance* 29(5) (1974), 1479–1490.

Quinlan, J. R. "Induction of Decision Trees." *Machine Learning* 1, 81–106.

Quirk, J. P., and R. Saposnik. "Admissability and Measurable Utility Functions." *Review of Economic Studies* 29 (1962).

Rom, Brian M., and Kathleen W. Ferguson. "Post-Modern Portfolio Theory Comes of Age," *Journal of Investing* 3(3) (1994a), 11–17.

Rom, Brian M., and Kathleen W. Ferguson. "Portfolio Theory Is Alive and Well: A Response." *Journal of Investing* 3(3) (1994b), 24–44.

Rom, Brian M., and Kathleen W. Ferguson. "Using Post-Modern Portfolio Theory to Improve Investment Performance Measurement." *Journal of Performance Measurement* 2(2) (1997/1998), 5–13.

Ross, Stephen A. "The Capital Asset Pricing Model (CAPM), Short-Sale Restrictions and Related Issues." *Journal of Finance* 32 (1977), 177–183.

Roy, A.D. "Safety First and the Holding of Assets." *Econometrica* 20(3) (1952), 431–449.

Shannon, C. E. "A Mathematical Theory of Communication." *The Bell Systems Technical Journal* 27 (1948), 379–423.

Sharpe, William F. "Mutual Fund Performance." *Journal of Business* 39(1) (1966), 119–138.

Sharpe, William F. "A Linear Programming Algorithm for Mutual Fund Portfolio Selection." *Management Science* 13(7) (1967), 499–510.

Sharpe, William F. "Capital Asset Prices: A Theory of Market Equilibrium under Conditions of Risk." *Journal of Finance* 19(3) (1964), 425–442.

Sharpe, William F., and Gordon J. Alexander. *Investments*, 4th ed. Englewood Cliffs, NJ: Prentice Hall, 1990.

Shen, Wei-Min, et al. "An Overview of Database Mining Techniques." http://www.isi.edu/~shen/Tsur.ps.

Silver, Lloyd. "Risk Assessment for Security Analysis." *Technical Analysis of Stocks and Commodities*. January 1993, 74–79.

Simon, Herbert A. "A Behavioral Model of Rational Choice." *Quarterly Journal of Economics* 69(1) (1955), 99–118.

Smyth, P., and Goodman, R. M. "An Information Theoretic Approach to Rule Induction from Databases." *IEEE Transactions on Knowledge and Data Engineering* 4 (1992), 301–316.

Sortino, Frank A., and Robert Van Der Meer. "Downside Risk." *Journal of Portfolio Management* 17(4) (1991), 27–32.

Sortino, Frank A., and Lee N. Price. "Performance Measurement in a Downside Risk Framework." *Journal of Investing* 3(3) (1994), 59–64.

Sortino, Frank A., and Hal J. Forsey. "On the Use and Misuse of Downside Risk." *Journal of Portfolio Management* 22(2) (1996), 35–42.

Srikant, R., and R. Agrawal. *Mining Generalized Association Rules.* Proceedings of the 21st VLDB Conference, Zurich, Switzerland, 1995.

Surz, Ronald J., Dale H. Stevens, and Mark E. Wimer. "The Importance of Investment Policy." *Journal of Investing* 8(4) (1999).

Swalm, Ralph O. "Utility Theory—Insights Into Risk Taking." *Harvard Business Review* 44(6) (1966), 123–138.

Tobin, James. "Liquidity Preference as Behavior Towards Risk." *The Review of Economic Studies* 25(2) (1958), 65–86.

The Vanguard Group Inc. "Sources of Portfolio Performance: The Enduring Importance of Asset Allocation." July 2003.

Veelentwurf, L. P. J. *Analysis and Applications of Artificial Neural Networks.* Hertfordshire, UK: Prentice Hall, 1995.

von Neumann, J., and O. Morgenstern. *Theory of Games and Economic Behavior.* Princeton, NJ: Princeton University Press, 1944.

Wasserman, P. D. *Advanced Methods in Neural Computing.* New York: Van Nostrand Reinhold, 1993.

Zwick, M., H. Shu, and R. Koch. "Information-Theoretic Mask Analysis of Rainfall Time Series Data." *Advances in System Science and Application* 1 (1995), 154–159.

About the Author

Acclaimed Financial Advisor

Barron's has four times (2004–2007) ranked Ric Edelman among America's 100 top financial advisors. In 2004, Ric was inducted into the Financial Advisor Hall of Fame, ranked the #1 advisor in the nation by *Research Magazine* for his focus on the individual client and ranked #42 on *Registered Rep* magazine's list of "America's Top 50 Advisors." *Inc.* magazine three times named the firm the fastest-growing privately-held financial planning firm in the country. Ric received an honorary doctorate from Rowan University in 1999 and in 2007 was inducted into the Rowan University Public Relations Student Society of America Hall of Fame.

Best-selling Author

Ric is a #1 *New York Times* best-selling author. His five books on personal finance include *Ordinary People, Extraordinary Wealth*; *The New Rules of Money*; *Discover the Wealth Within You; What You Need to Do Now*; the personal finance classic, *The Truth About Money* and his latest, *The Lies About Money*. Ric's books have been translated into several languages, and have educated countless people worldwide.

National Radio Show Host and Educator

The Ric Edelman Show, broadcast on the ABC Radio Networks, can be heard on radio stations throughout the country. The live call-in advice program has been on the air for more than 15 years and earned Ric the A.I.R. Award for Best Talk Show Host in Washington D.C. (1993). His newspaper column is nationally syndicated by United Media. He also publishes a monthly newsletter, has built one of the most comprehensive and free online educational resources about personal finance at RicEdelman.com, and is the author of video and audio educational systems that help people achieve their financial goals.

Philanthropic Activities

Ric and Jean have donated $1 million to Rowan University, which named its new planetarium in their honor. They also funded the Edelman Nursing Career Development Center at Inova Health System Foundation.

Ric served five years on the board of the United Way of the National Capital Area and in 2007 completed his two-year term as chairman of the board. He also serves on the boards of The Boys & Girls Clubs of Greater Washington, D.C., and its foundation. Ric is also a full partner of the American Savings Education Council and the Jump$tart Coalition for Personal Financial Literacy. He is a former board member of Junior Achievement of the National Capital Area and served for three years on the Grants Committee of the Foundation for Financial Planning, where he remains a major donor. Ric and Jean also actively support HEROES Inc., Make-a-Wish Foundation, The Leukemia & Lymphoma Society, and many other charities.

How to Give Your Child or Grandchild as Much as
$2,451,854 for Only $5,000*

A small amount of money can grow into a small fortune, thanks to compound interest. But as simple and effective as it is, few people take as much advantage of this concept as they can. For example, few begin saving for college as soon as a child is born. And even if you were to set aside $5,000 for a newborn, it would grow over 18 years to just $27,800 (assuming 10% per year). That's hardly enough to pay for college today, let alone 18 years from now.

But imagine saving that same $5,000 for the child's retirement rather than college. With 65 years on which to compound the interest, again assuming a 10% annual return, the account would be worth not just $27,800 but more than $2.4 million!*

Although easy to understand, the tax, legal, and economic obstacles prevented most of us from creating an account that could let money grow like this. But now you can do this for the benefit of your loved ones!

Introducing the Retirement InCome — for Everyone Trust® So Innovative, It's Patented!

Your kids don't need a lot of money, and they don't need an astronomically high rate of return. All they need is a little money and an opportunity to obtain a competitive return — because time does the rest.

Through the RIC-E Trust®, you can put the power of compound interest to work for your children and grandchildren. You can establish a RIC-E Trust® for any child of any age. You don't have to be the child's parent or grandparent, and the child even can be an adult. It's perfect for newlyweds and recent graduates! You can contribute as little as $5,000 (more if you like) and the money can grow undisturbed until the child reaches retirement age (you designate the age, at least 59).

Best of all, with the RIC-E Trust®, there are no trustee fees, no investment advisory fees — and no annual income taxes for the life of the trust! Thus, all of the Trust's earnings grow tax-deferred for the benefit of the child — giving the trust the opportunity to grow to millions of dollars over the course of the child's life.

The RIC-E Trust® offers you a truly revolutionary way to help you secure the retirement future of a child you love. It's so innovative, a patent application has been filed for it.

I invite you now to learn how you can put the RIC-E Trust® to work for the important children in your life.

the
Retirement InCome
– for Everyone® trust

Get all the information at
ricetrust.com
No Web access?
Call us at **888-752-6742**

More from Ric Edelman

Talk to Ric live at 888-PLAN-RIC

Tune In Nationwide to Ric's Radio Show

Every week, Ric shares his vast financial expertise giving you the information you need to stretch your dollars farther and increase your wealth faster — without the hype and hoopla often seen elsewhere. Tune in for the answers to those tough financial questions, such as how to get out of debt; how to lower your taxes; whether to buy or lease your next car; when to refinance; how to pay for college for your kids or grandkids; how to tell if you have the right kind and amount of insurance; what to look for when choosing a financial advisor; how to help family and loved-ones when setting up wills and trusts; and the ever popular question, how to invest more successfully and safely. Visit RicEdelman to find your local listing.

43% savings
off the regular price
One-Year Subscription: $39.95

Subscribe to Ric's Award-Winning 12-Page Monthly Newsletter, *Inside Personal Finance*

You'll get the latest on investments, taxes, insurance, estate planning, retirement, elder care, your IRA, 401(k), 403(b) and Thrift plans, mortgages, home ownership, and much more delivered straight to your home every month. It's the most comprehensive source you'll find on the topic of personal finance — explained in plain English — no gobbledygook.

Order online at RicEdelman.com or call toll-free 888-987-7526.

Explore RicEdelman.com

Ric offers one of the most comprehensive and free online educational resources available today — free articles, audio, video — all at your fingertips. If you think you know everything you need to know about personal finance, you haven't been to RicEdelman.com.

Also available in bookstores everywhere

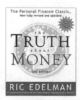 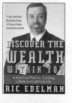 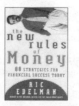 

Index

A. B. Watley Direct, 150
A. G. Edwards, 68, 131, 136, 139, 145, 148, 152, 159, 162
Ableson, Alan, 76
academic approach: as basis of Edelman approach, 40, 41–82; as basis for portfolio construction, 4, 67; and institutional funds, 171; as source of analysis, 4
accumulation accounts, 259, 259n, 261n, 263
active selection, 174–78
actual return, 42, 43
ADP, 147
Advisor's Edge, 279
AEGON, 279
AGF funds, 147
AIG, 133
AIM funds, 126, 129, 131, 138
Alger Funds, 147
Allegiant Asset Management, 156
Alliance Capital Management, 141, 148, 149
Alliance Funds, 121, 138
AllianceBernstein, 60, 161, 208, 214, 215, 223
Allstate, 159
American Council of Life Insurers, 252
American Express, 126, 141
American Express Financial Advisors. See Ameriprise Financial
American Funds, 103–4, 104n, 133, 135, 136, 137, 145, 146, 147, 153, 160
American General, 150
Americans for Secure Retirement, 246

Ameriprise Financial, 94, 138, 139, 140, 141, 145, 146, 158, 171, 280
AmSouth, 133
Amvescap, 129
Analysis Group, 112
analysts, market, 70–72, 86
annual expense ratio, 109–10, 179
annual reports, 85
annual returns, 50–51, 52, 56, 59
annuities: distributions from, 276; and Edelman investment strategy, 4, 269–81, 291–92; fees/commissions for, 271, 272, 273, 278, 280; getting rid of, 281; income from, 272; and mutual fund scandal, 121, 125–28, 134–37, 139, 140, 148, 149, 155; and mutual funds, 271, 272; Pre-TEFRA, 276n; rebalancing of, 39; and retirement plans, 280; and taxes, 264n; variable, 91, 121, 125, 127, 128, 134, 135, 136, 137, 139, 140, 148, 149, 269–81; withdrawals from, 272, 275, 276, 277
arithmetic mean, 45–46, 67
arithmetic returns, 47
asset allocation, 59–60, 61, 67, 69, 79, 170–72, 174, 185, 231–32
asset classes, 25, 33–38, 61, 66, 171, 197, 210, 211, 231–32, 289. See also rebalancing
average returns, 26, 42, 44–46, 47–48, 50, 106

AXA Equitable Life Insurance Company, 149
AXA Financial, 123

baby-boomer generation, 283–88, 292
BabyMint, 226
Bag Lady Syndrome, 285
Banc of America Securities, 145
Bank of America, 123, 136, 137, 143
Bank of Hawaii, 144
Bank of New York, 137
Bank One, 127, 135, 139
Barclays Bank, 180
Barclays Global Investors, 181
Beacon Rock Capital, 161
Bear Stearns, 68, 127, 131, 132, 136, 137, 139, 140, 141, 147, 149, 153
"beating the market" mantra, 7
Bechtel Group, 153
Beebower, Gilbert, 42, 58–60
Berkshire Hathaway, 59, 113
best performing stocks, 35, 65
Bianca Research, 75
Biggs, John, 269
Bing, Stanley, 76
BISYS, 139, 154, 156
bloating, 103–5, 175
Block, Sandra, 76
"blue-sky laws," 85
boards of directors, 86, 133, 147
Bogle, John, 47–48, 94, 115, 180
bonds, 58, 90, 231, 234, 236–37, 238, 253, 255, 264n
bonuses, 124, 127, 133
Boston Capital Securities, 149

Boston College, Center for Retirement Research at, 244
bracket creep, 97–98, 174, 176, 197
brain damage, 20
Brean Murray, 136, 137
Bridgeway Capital Management, 130
Brinson, Gary, 42, 58–60, 61, 66, 171
brokers/brokerage firms: advisors differentiated from, 68–69. *See also specific firm or topic*
Buffett, Warren, 62*n*, 97, 113
Bush, George W., 86
buy low, sell high, 31–33, 47
buy-and-hold approach. *See* long-term investing

Calendar Rules, 77–78, 79
California Public Employees Retirement System (CalPERS), 122, 170
Canada, 125, 133, 134, 135, 137, 142, 147, 160
Canadian Bank of Commerce, 122
Canary Capital Partners, 148
Capital Analysts, 138
Capital Asset Pricing Model, 41, 57–58, 67, 79–80
capital gains, 37–38, 39, 179, 201, 235, 274, 276
Capital Research and Management, 104
Carnegie Mellon University, 20
Carpenter Analytical Services, 99
cash, 10, 38, 99–100, 120, 174, 192, 258–68
Caterpillar, 153
CCO Investment Services, 155
CDs (certificates of deposit), 12, 50–51, 90, 231–34, 231*n*, 254, 255, 291

Celent, 181–82
Center for American Progress, 206*n*
Center for Research in Security Prices, 107
CFA Institute, 70, 107
Charles Schwab & Co., 130, 136
Chartered Financial Analyst, 70
Chase Investment Services, 147
Chatzky, Jean, 76
"cherry picking," 94–95
CI Mutual Funds, 147
CIBC, 122, 129, 160
Citigroup, 132, 138, 140, 142, 152
Citizens Bank, 155
Clements, Jonathan, 278–79
cloning, 105, 174–75, 271
closet indexing, 98, 101, 175
College Board, 227
college savings: and debt, 10*n*, 225–26; and Edelman investment strategy, 4, 221–30; as financial goal, 8; by grandparents, 228–30, 291; and mutual fund scandal, 123, 141, 145, 155, 156; not saving for, 223–28; popularity of, 2; portfolios for, 222, 291; and postgraduate degrees, 225; and retirement plans, 221*n*; and taxes, 222, 230, 264*n*. *See also* Section 529 College Savings Plan
College of William and Mary, 95
Columbia Mutual Funds, 136
commissions. *See* fees/commissions
Commonwealth Financial Network, 144
compensation, brokers, 145, 159
compounding, long-term, 37

Conseco, 121, 128
Constantides, George M., 177
Consumer Federation of America, 124
Cornell University, 10, 33
Cornerstone Equity Advisors, 154
Corporate Insight, 60
costs: and demise of retail mutual funds industry, 100, 110, 113, 116; of ETFs, 179; of index funds, 179; and institutional funds, 175; of L-funds, 212; of life insurance, 263, 265; and mutual fund scandal, 123, 125; of mutual funds, 179; rising, 113, 175; variable, 110. *See also* dollar cost averaging; expenses; fees/commissions
covariance, 52–54, 56
Coverdell Education Savings Account, 228
Cramer, Jim, 73–74, 74*n*, 190
creation bias, 107, 175
credit cards, 10, 10*n*, 192
Cronqvist, Henrik, 76

Dalbar, 47
data mining, 72–74, 78
Davenport, 126
David Lerner Associates, 125
Deutsche Bank, 148, 155, 158
Dimensional Fund Advisors (DFA), 176–78, 187, 197, 222, 279
DiMeo Schneider & Associates, 21
disclosure, 85–87, 109–11, 117, 145, 147
discounts, 113–15, 122, 126, 140, 141, 148, 160
distributions, 232, 274, 276, 277, 286
diversification: and academic

advice, 61, 69; and creating right portfolio, 197; and dividends and capital gains, 37; and employer retirement funds, 210, 211–14, 290; and ETFs, 180; example of, 27; and expert behavior, 75; and financial goals, 8, 40; importance of, 3, 81, 289; and income investing, 231, 233, 234, 291; and institutional funds, 176; and money management firms, 168; and mutual funds, 69, 88; need for full, 28–30; reasons for, 25–33; and rebalancing, 35, 36; and risk, 61, 290; Shakespeare's knowledge of, 56; and terminal wealth dispersion, 62, 66; and where to invest, 26

Diversified Investment Advisors, 137

dividends, 37–38, 235, 274, 286

Dodd, David, 80

"Dogs of the Dow" strategy, 72–73, 72n

dollar-cost averaging (DCA), 209, 210, 211, 216

dollar-weighted performance, 48

Dow Jones & Company, 172

Dow Jones Industrial Average, 11, 14, 70, 78, 209

Dow Jones Wilshire Real Estate Securities Index, 232

Dreyfus Funds, 150, 153

Dunham & Associates Investment Counsel, 154

Economic Policy Institute, 243

economies of scale, 113, 115, 175

Edelman Financial, 3, 5, 41

Edelman Guide to Portfolio Selection, 4, 42, 192–97. *See also specific topic*

Edelman, Jean, 1, 3, 5, 29–30, 41, 165, 168

Edelman Managed Asset Program, 4, 186

Edward D. Jones & Co., 124, 134, 135, 137, 138, 143, 146, 149, 151, 153, 158, 162

Efficient Frontier, 56, 67

Eleventh Commandment, 285

emotions, 20, 36

Empire Financial, 126, 127

Employee Benefit Research Institute, 216, 242, 243, 250

equities, examples of, 90, 91

Equity Index Universal Life Insurance, 262–63

Evergreen Investments, 128, 145, 159

Exchange-Traded Funds (ETFs), 179–84, 186, 187, 192, 197, 206, 222, 266, 279, 281, 290, 291

Exelon, 153

expense ratios, 109–10, 113, 179, 212

expenses, 109–10, 120, 124, 179, 261n, 292. *See also* commissions; expense ratios; fees/commissions

experts, 73–77

Fair Labor Standards Act, 68

Fama, Eugene F., 42, 58, 61, 177. *See also* Fama-French Three-Factor Model

Fama-French Three-Factor Model, 42, 58, 61, 66, 67

Federal Reserve, 121

Federated Investments, 124, 128, 135, 146, 153

fees/commissions: for

annuities, 271, 272, 273, 278, 280; and college savings, 222; and demise of retail mutual funds industry, 93, 94, 97, 98, 101, 109–11, 113, 114; on ETFs, 181; of financial advisors, 68, 111, 188–91, 197; for 401(k) plans, 153, 206n; for hedge funds, 94; hidden, 109–11, 111n, 122, 153, 167, 175; and insights for success, 202, 292; and institutional funds, 175, 176; for life insurance, 261n, 265, 266; of money management firms, 168; and mutual fund scandal, 120, 122, 123, 125, 126, 127, 129, 130, 131, 134, 136, 137, 141, 143, 151–52, 153, 156, 158, 159, 160, 161, 167; for mutual funds, 90, 151, 181, 202, 212, 271; and rebalancing, 39; and retail mutual funds, 110; for retirement plans, 110, 215

Fidelity: and mutual fund scandal, 123, 128, 129, 134, 135, 138, 139, 141, 142, 145, 147, 157–58, 160, 161, 162; and retirement plans, 208

Fidelity Magellan, 97–98, 98n, 104, 104n, 105n

financial advisors: and baby-boomer generation, 284, 285; books as replacing, 188–97; brokers differentiated from, 68–69; and college savings, 221; and creating the right portfolio, 67, 186, 187, 188–91, 197; and demise of retail mutual funds industry, 109;

financial advisors *(cont.)*
fees/commissions for, 68,
111, 188–91, 197, 266;
functions of, 68, 189*n*,
190; importance of, 188;
and institutional funds,
186; insurance agents as,
265–66; and L-funds, 214;
and life insurance, 266,
267, 291; and mutual fund
scandal, 120, 164;
registration of, 68, 85;
and retirement plans, 214;
selecting, 191; shelf-space
payments to, 120; and
variable annuities, 279
Financial Network Investment
Corporation, 152
financial plans: and college
savings, 223; insights for,
199–203, 241–55, 292; lack
of, 226–27
Financial Research
Corporation, 104, 104*n*
Financial Well-Being Index,
244
First Allied Securities, 144
First Command, 134
First Western, 161
1st Global Capital
Corp., 156
Fiserv, 139, 140, 152
529 plans. *See* college
savings
Fleet Boston, 122, 123
Florida International
University, 65
FMI Mutual Funds, 132
401(k) plans: and bear
market of 2002–2002, 216;
choice of mutual funds in,
280; and demise of retail
mutual funds industry, 103,
110; and estimating needs
for retirement, 248; fees
for, 153, 206*n*; and
Generation Y, 208; and L-

funds, 214; and life
insurance, 266; and mutual
fund scandal, 124, 125, 127,
138, 142, 153, 156; as type
of retirement plan, 205;
withdrawals from, 216, 217.
See also retirement plans
403(b) plans, 205, 280
457 plans, 205
Franklin Resources, 113–14
Franklin Templeton, 115, 122,
126, 128, 129, 130, 132,
133, 137, 147, 157
Fred Alger & Co., 121, 160
Fremont Investment Advisors,
127, 132
French, Kenneth R., 42, 58,
61, 177. *See also* Fama-
French Three-Factor Model
futures contracts, 181

Gabelli, Mario, 131, 149, 151
GAO study, 287
Gartmore, 131, 153
Gemstar, 132
gender, and stock picking, 22
General Dynamics, 153
Genworth Financial, 252
geometric mean, 46, 67
geometric returns, 47
Georgia Institute of
Technology, 78
goals, financial: evaluation
of investments in terms of,
7–8; and life insurance,
259; profits as, 259; steps
for achieving, 8–40
Gold Index, 232
Goldman Sachs, 127, 135, 153
Google, 170
Gould, John P., 177
Government Accountability
Office, U.S., 110, 156
GPS, 185–88, 193–96
Graham, Benjamin, 61, 62*n*, 63,
64, 80
Greenwich Associates, 95, 110

Growth Fund of America, 103–4
growth stocks, 58, 232
guarantees: and annuities,
271, 272–74, 277, 280, 281;
and life insurance, 260,
263–64, 265, 266; and
mutual fund scandal, 127;
and pensions, 237
Guardian Life Insurance
Company of America, 241

H&R Block, 134
Haaga, Paul Jr., 104
Haldeman, Charles E., 145
Hamilton, Alexander, 4, 83–84,
83*n*
Hamilton, Martha, 77
Hamilton Funds, 137
Hantz Financial Services, 142
Hartford Financial Services
Group, 60, 121, 135, 150,
153, 156
Harvard University, 90, 111,
112, 133, 170
hedge funds: Cramer's
statement about, 74*n*; and
ETFs, 181; and mutual fund
scandal, 122, 132, 134, 138,
142, 144, 147, 149, 150,
151, 155, 157, 159, 160,
161, 162; mutual funds
compared with, 94–95;
regulation of, 86, 91
Hewitt Associates, 208, 209
HighMark Funds, 156
Hinden, Stan, 74–75
Hood, Randolph, 42, 58–60
hot tips, 65, 70, 76, 290
HSBC Securities, 142
Hulbert, Mark, 76

Ibbotson, Roger G., 60, 177
Ibbotson Associates, 14, 231,
232, 253
IG Investment Management,
147
income: from annuities, 272;

Edelman strategy when investing for, 231–39, 291; estimating retirement, 242–55, 292; from mutual funds, 274. *See also* dividends

incubation strategy, 107–8

index arbitrage trading, 149

index funds, 171–72, 179

indexes: examples of, 10*n*; mutual funds as replicas of, 10*n*, 65*n*, 101, 103. *See also specific index*

inflation, 38, 233, 236, 238, 245, 248, 251, 272*n*, 291

information, 84–85, 95. *See also* insider trading

ING, 129, 132, 144, 151, 152, 155, 159, 162

initial public offerings (IPOs), 83, 85, 108, 125

insider trading, 83*n*, 86, 150, 151

insights, for investment success, 199–203, 241–55, 292

institution class shares, 176, 266

institutional funds: and creating the right portfolio, 186, 187, 197, 290; Edelman's decision to invest in, 169–78; and employer retirement funds, 206, 291; retail mutual funds compared with, 170–76; and size of investment, 170–71; as type of mutual fund, 169; and variable annuities, 281

institutional investors, 181, 254

insurance. *See* life insurance

International Paper, 153

international stocks, 232

Internet, 71, 268

Invesco Funds, 121, 127, 128, 129, 131

Invest Financial, 144

Investment Advisers Act (1940), 85

Investment Centers of America, 144

Investment Company Act (1940), 90, 91

Investment Company Institute (ICI), 32, 95, 116, 143, 189*n*, 202, 216

Investment Funds Institute of Canada, 142

IRA accounts, 2, 39, 163, 192, 205, 215–17, 278, 278*n*, 280, 286, 291

James River Capital, 155

Janney Montgomery Scott, 144

Janus, 124, 125, 126, 128, 133, 138, 152, 161

JB Oxford Holdings, 129, 148

Jefferies & Company, 141, 157–58, 161

Jefferson National Life Insurance Co., 125, 128

Jefferson Pilot, 138

Jenna, xiv

Jill, xiv

John Hancock, 206, 251

JPMorgan Chase, 131, 134, 156, 253, 254

Kaplan, Paul, 60

Kelm, Donald B., 177

Kelmoore Investments, 160

Kensington, 153

KPMG, 132

L-funds, 211–14, 222

Lange, Harry, 98

Lasser, Lawrence, 159

late trading: and demise of retail mutual fund industry, 116, 117; and institutional funds, 175; as key abuse, 120; and mutual fund scandal, 120–22, 124, 126, 129, 130, 132, 134–37, 139–43, 145–55, 158–60, 167

Latino Coalition, 246

Legg Mason, 132, 143

Lehman Brothers, 131, 142, 150, 172, 231

Liberty Ridge Capital, 131

life insurance, 4, 91, 158, 159, 257–68, 291

Lincoln Financial Advisors Corp., 121, 144

Linsco/Private Ledger, 136, 147

Lipper Analytical Services, 35, 66, 93, 102, 106

liquidity, 201

load and no-load funds, 108–9

Lockheed Martin, 153

long-term investing: and demise of mutual funds industry, 114; and "dogs of the Dow" strategy, 73; and Edelman investment strategy, 3; and employer retirement funds, 210–11, 216; and financial goals, 8, 40; importance of, 8, 30, 289; and institutional funds, 176; reasons for, 10–24; and rebalancing, 38; and successful investment strategies, 30, 81

Lord Abbett Funds, 135, 144, 153

lower partial moment (LPM), 58*n*

McKinsey & Company, 250

MainStay Funds, 127

management, active versus passive, 173–78

managers: changes in, 93–94, 174, 176; compensation of, 136; moonlighting by, 94–95, 174; personal trading by portfolio, 116, 117, 121, 130, 162, 175

Manulife Securities, 144
Mao, J.C.T., 56
margin, 99–100, 174
market sectors, 33–38, 61, 66, 171, 197, 210, 211, 231–32, 289. *See also* rebalancing
market timing: and asset allocation, 60; buy-and-hold approach versus, 11–19, 21–24; and demise of mutual fund industry, 115–16, 117; as illegal, 115–16; and institutional funds, 175; as key abuse, 120; and mutual fund scandal, 120–48, 150–55, 157–62, 167
Markowitz, Harry, 41, 55–57, 60, 80
Marsh & McLennan Companies, 133
Massachusetts Mutual Life Insurance Company, 146
MassMutual Financial Group, 140, 142
MBA students: cheating by, 116; and disclosure, 110
media, 3, 73, 75–77, 171
mergers, 106–7
Merrill Lynch: and brokers-advisors debate, 68–69; and mutual fund scandal, 137, 138, 142, 147, 149, 150, 159, 160, 161; and picking stocks/mutual funds, 171, 172
Merton, Robert C., 177
MetLife Securities, 123, 126, 153–54, 156, 159
MFS, 121, 122, 124, 148
Michigan State University, 10
Microsoft, 113, 170
Millennium Partners, 145, 146, 155, 159
Modern Portfolio Theory, 41, 67, 80
momentum investing, 70–72
Monarch International

Holdings, 149
money management firms, 168
money market funds, 37–38, 90
Morgan Keegan, 149
Morgan Stanley, 123, 124, 134, 135, 136, 142, 145, 150, 151, 158, 172, 232
Morgenson, Gretchen, 76
Morningstar: and buy-and-hold approach, 21; categorization of mutual funds by, 66; and demise of retail mutual funds industry, 102, 103, 104, 107, 107n, 109, 110, 114; dollar-weighted performance data from, 48; and ETFs, 179; and fees, 202; and manager moonlighting, 94; and mutual fund scandal, 128; and number of mutual funds, 202; and power of mutual funds, 87; ratings of mutual funds by, 28, 103, 107–8, 107n; and Sharpe ratio, 57n; and style drift and bracket creep, 97; and turnover, 95
Motley Fool, 72–73
MSNMoney, 104
Multi-Financial Securities, 152
mutual funds: advertising by, 76; as basis for Edelman approach, 40; benefits of, 169; "best," 35, 66, 111; as best way to invest, 167; closing of, 174–75; Edelman's decision to invest in, 41; evolution of, 83–91; individual stocks versus, 87–88; as "investment companies," 90; as long-term investments, 192; names of, 100–101, 131; number of, 202; objectives of, 67; past

performance of, 28–29, 31, 46, 66; power of, 87–88; ratings of, 28, 31; reasons for using, 83–92; registration of, 154; reopening of, 174–75; as replicas of indexes, 10n, 65n, 101, 103; S&P Index compared with cash flows of, 32–33; size of, 103–5. *See also specific topic*
mutual funds industry: beating the retail, 167–78; business practices of, 93–118; Edelman decides to leave retail, 167–69; failure of, 165; outrage concerning, 165; and restitution in retail mutual fund scandal, 163; types of, 169. *See also* retail mutual fund scandal; retail mutual funds
Mutual Service Corporation, 144

names, misleading/changes in, 100–101, 131, 145, 174–75
NASD, and variable annuities, 269–70
National Alliance for Caregiving, 251
National Association of Stock Dealers (NASD), 122, 123, 125, 126, 128, 129, 131–42, 144–50, 152, 153–63
National Association of Variable Annuities, 280
National Bureau of Economic Research, 9
National Clearing Corporation, 129, 146
National Endowment for Financial Education, 225
National Financial Services, 160
National Investment Company

Service Association, 104

National Planning Corporation, 144

Nationwide, 94

Nawrocki, David, 56

net asset value (NAV), 112, 120

New England Securities, 153–54

New York Stock Exchange (NYSE): creation of, 83–84; and insider trading, 86; and mutual fund scandal, 135, 137, 141, 142, 147, 148, 149, 152, 159, 163

Norbourg Asset Management, 142

Northwestern University, 97, 100

Numeric, 153

Nuveen funds, 137

Odean, Terrance, 22

Ohio State University, 9–10, 76

Old Mutual, 145

Olympic Cascade, 128

One Group Funds, 156

130/30 funds, 99

Ontario Securities Commission, 125, 130, 144

Oppenheimer, 132, 140, 141, 142, 148, 155

Orman, Suze, 75

overweight people, 9–10, 10n

past performance, 28–29, 31, 46, 66, 73, 104, 108, 234

Paulson Investment Company, 140

Pax World funds, 136

PBHG funds, 145

Pearson, Karl, 41, 49n, 60

Pennsylvania Securities Commission, 270

Pension Benefit Guaranty Corporation, 238

Pension Protection Act (2006), 208, 217n

pensions, 235–39, 248, 291

Peoples Benefit Life Insurance Company, 279

personal finance, overview about, 1–5

Pew Research Center, 242

picks, stock: and active versus passive management, 173–78; and BHB studies, 59, 60; and comparison of retail and institutional funds, 171; and Edelman's decision to leave retail funds, 168; and ETFs, 180; and gender, 22; and index funds, 172; and past performance, 46; and terminal wealth dispersion, 65; ways to do, 69–81

Pilgrim Baxter, 127, 131, 132, 133

PIMCO, 122, 125, 129, 130, 151, 155, 162

Pioneer, 94

Piper Jaffray, 128, 137

portfolio: for college savings, 222; as consistent with current circumstances, 203, 290, 292; creating the right, 185–97, 290; implementing model of, 197; liquidation of, 284–85; maintenance of, 197, 292; pension influence on, 235–39; suitability determination for, 192, 292. See also rebalancing

Portus Alternative Asset Management, 144

Pottruck, David, 126–27

Power Financial Corp., 160

precious metals, 232

predictions, 70–72, 73–78

prime rate, 85

PrimeVest Financial Services, 152

principal, preservation of, 231, 285, 286

Principal Financial Group, 121, 157, 244

prospectus, 94, 98, 100, 109, 110, 111, 120, 133, 142, 144, 222

Prudential Securities, 128, 141, 143, 147, 152–53, 157, 158, 243

Publicly held mutual funds, 113, 114

Purdue University, 100–101

Putnam Investments: and demise of retail mutual fund industry, 117–18; and mutual fund scandal, 121, 123–27, 129, 131, 133–35, 137–39, 141, 143, 145, 148, 153, 159, 160, 167

questionnaire, for Edelman Guide to Portfolio Selection, 194–95

Quick & Reilly, 137

Quinn, Jane Bryant, 269

Quirk, James, 56

rate of return, 12, 42, 43, 44

ratings, 28, 29, 31

Ray, A. D., 55

Raymond James Financial Services, 131, 139, 143

RBC Dain Rauscher, 158

real estate, 91, 232

rebalancing: calendar, 39, 40; and college savings, 222; and creating the right portfolio, 197; and dividends and capital gains, 37–38, 39; and financial goals, 8, 40; and goals, 38; importance of, 4, 289; and mutual funds, 35; percentage, 39–40; periodic, 8, 33–37, 81; reasons for, 33–37; and retirement plans, 214–15, 290; and successful

rebalancing *(cont.)*
investment strategies, 81,
203; and taxes, 39; when to
do, 39–40; and withdrawals,
37
Registered Investment
Advisors, 69, 176
registration: of financial
advisors, 68, 69, 85; of
mutual funds, 154; of
securities, 85, 144
regulation, 84, 90, 104, 116–
17, 127, 157, 163, 265,
280. *See also specific
agency or organization*
Regulation Fair Disclosure, 86
retail mutual funds:
alternatives to, 289;
closing of, 101–3, 105, 106–
7; demise of, 93–118; help
for investors from, 60;
information for, 95;
institutional funds
compared with, 170–76; lies
about, 2, 3; life insurance
compared with, 259, 266;
management of, 93–95;
mergers of, 106–7; as
mimicking S&P 500 Stock
Index, 98, 101; need to
abandon, 3, 5; objectives
of, 98, 105; popularity of,
2; ratings of, 107–8, 107*n*;
reopened, 101–3; selling
holdings in, 165, 290; size
of, 102–3; as type of
mutual fund, 169;
volatility of, 99–100. *See
also* mutual funds; retail
mutual funds scandal;
specific topic
retail mutual funds scandal:
in 2003, 121; in 2004,
121–34; in 2005, 134–47;
in 2006, 148–59; in
2007, 159–62; brokers' and
financial advisors' views

about, 164; next big, 162;
onset of, 117–18, 120–21;
outrage concerning, 165;
restitution in, 163
retirement: and baby-boomer
generation, 283–88, 292;
estimating funds needed for,
242–55, 292; as financial
goal, 8; and mutual fund
scandal, 142; not saving
for, 208, 217–19; planning
for, 74–75, 241–55; sources
of income for, 246. *See
also* retirement plans
Retirement Confidence Survey,
242, 243–44, 247
retirement plans: applying
Edelman strategy to
employer, 205–19; and baby-
boomer generation, 286; and
college savings, 221*n*;
contributions to, 206, 290;
and creating the right
portfolio, 192, 206–11, 290,
291; and date of retirement,
207; and diversification,
210, 211–14, 290;
employer's contribution to,
218, 219; fees for, 110,
215; and L-plans, 211–14;
and leaving employers, 209,
215–17, 291; and mutual
fund scandal, 121, 124, 125,
147, 159; offerings in, 206,
291; participation in, 243;
rebalancing of, 39, 214–15,
290; and restitution in
retail mutual fund scandal,
163; and taxes, 206, 215,
216, 217, 217*n*, 290; types
of, 205; variable annuities
in, 280; withdrawals from,
207, 209, 211, 216–17. *See
also type of plan*
returns: arithmetic and
geometric, 47; from bonds,
253, 255; cash flow data

about, 48; from CDs, 255;
and demise of retail mutual
funds industry, 93; and
employer retirement plans,
207; importance of
considering, 51, 55, 56;
from life insurance, 261,
262, 263–64, 265, 266; of
money management firms,
168; and mutual fund
scandal, 120; from mutual
funds, 46, 47–48, 76, 88,
106, 165; for mutual funds
versus individual stocks,
88; overestimation of, 253–
55; and past performance,
46; randomness of, 25; and
risk, 47–61, 290; and small
versus large stocks, 58;
and successful investment
strategy, 81; and terminal
wealth dispersion, 62, 63,
64–65, 66. *See also* actual
return; average returns;
rate of return
revenue sharing. *See* shelf-
space payments
reverse load fund, 108
risk: alpha, 57, 58, 64, 67;
and asset allocation, 61;
and benefits of mutual
funds, 169; beta, 57, 58,
64, 67; comparing, 42, 52–
55; and demise of retail
mutual funds industry, 97,
100, 101; and disclosure,
87; and diversification, 61,
290; as fundamental concept,
42; importance of
considering, 51, 55–61, 201,
202, 290; information as
means for reducing, 84–85;
measuring, 42, 49–52, 60;
and mutual funds, 84–85,
88; and rebalancing, 289;
and returns, 47–61, 290;
and successful investment

strategy, 81; systematic and unsystematic, 57, 57*n*; and terminal wealth dispersion, 62–63, 64–65. *See also type of risk*

Royal Alliance Associates, 158

RS Investment Management, 123, 124, 131

Russell Investment Group, 172

Ryan Beck, 68

S&P 500 Stock Index: and buy-and-hold approach, 10, 11–19; and Calendar Rules, 78; and ETFs, 181; and income investing, 238; loss of value in, 216, 242*n*; and market timing, 12–19; mutual funds cash flows compared with, 32–33; mutual funds as mimics of, 65*n*, 98, 101, 103; and performance of mutual funds, 31, 172; and retirements plans, 216; returns from, 26, 44–45, 46, 47, 50–51, 52, 253, 254, 261, 262, 263–64; and risk, 63; and terminal wealth dispersion, 63, 64–65

S&P/BARRA 500 Growth Index, 232

S&P/BARRA 500 Value Index, 232

Salomon Brothers, 127, 128

Sanford C. Bernstein, 149

Saposnik, Rubin, 56

Sarbanes-Oxley Act (2002), 86

savings: importance of regular, 2, 8–10, 289; and not saving for retirement, 208, 217–19; ways to achieve, 9–10. *See also type of savings*

Scholes, Myron S., 177

Scotland, 4, 89

Scudder funds, 124, 148, 155

securities: and how many should you own, 61, 62–66; registration of, 144

Securities Act (1933), 85

Securities America, 158

Securities Exchange Act (1934), 85

Securities and Exchange Commission (SEC): and broker-advisor debate, 69; Cramer's statement about, 74*n*; and demise of mutual fund industry, 98, 105, 117; and disclosure rules, 85, 86; and hedge funds, 86; and L–funds, 212; and mutual fund scandal, 122, 124–43, 145–48, 150–62, 163; as regulatory agency, 91–92

Securities Investor Protection Corporation (SIPC), 86

Security Brokerage, 148

Security Trust Company, 142–43

seeding, 94, 108, 175

Seligman Funds, 125, 144, 154

semicovariance, 56

semivariance, 53, 56

Sentinel Funds, 131

September 11, 2001, 158

Seton Hall University, 65

share classes: confusing, 108–9, 175; and mutual fund scandal, 156

shareholders, voting rights of, 85

Sharpe, William, 41, 57–58, 57*n*, 61, 64, 79–80

shelf-space payments: and demise of retail mutual fund industry, 116–18; and institutional funds, 175; as key abuse, 120; and mutual fund scandal, 120, 122, 124, 126, 127, 129, 130, 133–36, 138, 142, 145–

49, 151, 153, 155–60

shorting stocks, 99, 141

SII Investment, 144

Singer, Brian, 60

Singletary, Michelle, 77

Skifter Ajro, 141

Sloan, Allan, 76

Smith, Abbie J., 177

Smith Barney, 117, 127, 128, 140, 154, 171

Social Security, 241, 243, 245–47, 276

Southwest Securities, 135

stale pricing, 112, 112*n*, 175

Standard & Poor's, 66, 172. *See also* S&P 500 Stock Index

Standard & Poor's Mutual Fund Persistence Scorecard, 165

standard deviation, 41, 49–50, 49*n*, 51, 52, 67

Stanford University, 20

Stansky, Robert, 97–98

State Street, 122

State University of New York, 98

Statement of Additional Information, 110, 111

steering business, 116

Stevens, Tom, 191

strategies, investment: as evolutionary process, 79–81; fundamental concepts used for evaluation of, 42; ideal, 79; most proven, successful, 7–40. *See also* Edelman Guide to Portfolio Selection

Strong Funds, 123, 126, 132, 136

Struck, Patricia, 270

style drift, 94, 97–98, 174, 176, 197

subaccounts, 271, 272, 275

suitability, 139, 192, 292

Sun Life Financial, 241

SunTrust Securities, 140

survivorship bias, 106–7, 175

Swensen, David, 165, 170, 171, 174

T+1 accounting, 112
T. Rowe Price, 127
tattoo metaphor, 210–11
taxes: and annuities, 264n, 281; and baby-boomer generation, 286, 287; and bonds, 264n; and buy-and-hold approach, 21; capital gains, 201; and cash, 38; and college savings, 222, 230, 264n; deferral of, 274–79, 281; and demise of retail mutual funds industry, 93, 97, 106, 114; and ETFs, 179–80; and income investing, 235; and insights for success, 199–201, 292; and IRAs, 280; and life insurance, 263, 264, 264n, 265, 266; and mutual fund scandal, 161; on mutual funds, 274, 275, 276, 277; and rebalancing, 39; and restitution in retail mutual fund scandal, 163; and retirement plans, 206, 215, 216, 217, 217n, 290; and types of investment accounts, 189
TD Waterhouse, 130
term insurance, 267–68
terminal wealth dispersion, 42, 62–66
TheStreet.com, 73, 74n
Thrift Savings Board, 213–14
Thrift Savings Plan, 205, 214, 215
TIAA-CREF, 147
time-weighted performance, 48
transaction costs, 21, 38, 39
transparency, 86, 87, 125. *See also* disclosure
Trautman Wasserman, 140, 153

trend analysis, 70–72
turnover, stock, 95–97, 100, 174, 176, 179–80, 197, 274n, 277
UBS Financial Services, 68, 148, 158, 159, 171
Uniform Transfer to Minors Act, 228
Union Bank of California, 156
unit investment trusts (UITs), 91
United Technologies, 153
University of California, Berkeley, 22
University of California, Davis, 70
University of Florida, 110
University of Iowa, 20
University of Missouri, 87, 97
University of Pennsylvania, 95, 111
University of Texas at Austin, 33
Upromise, 226
U.S. Department of Health and Human Services, 252
U.S. Justice Department, 131, 149, 151, 161
U.S. Labor Department, 68, 125, 142, 208

value stocks, 58, 232
Van Eck, 128
Van Kampen, 135, 153
Van Wagoner Funds, 129
Vanguard Funds, 94, 104, 104n, 122, 126, 129, 147, 214
variance, 49, 51–54, 56, 59, 67
Veras Investment Partners, 161
Vinik, Jeffrey, 97–98
volatility: and asset allocation, 59; and BHB studies, 58–60; causes of, 42, 58–60, 171; and creating the right portfolio, 197; and demise

of retail mutual funds industry, 99–100, 116; downside, 53; and income investing, 231n, 233n; and mutual fund scandal, 120; and retirement funds, 206, 206n, 209, 211; and risk, 56

Wachovia Securities, 68, 130, 159
Waddell & Reed, 139, 140, 151–52, 161
Wake Forest University, 110
Wall Street Access, 155
Walnut Street Securities, 153–54
Washburn University, 73
Weiss, Gary, 71, 117, 165
Wellington, 126
Wells Fargo Investments, 147
White, Halbert, 78
Wilshire Associates, 172
window dressing, 100, 174–75, 180
withdrawals: from annuities, 272, 275, 276, 277; and creating the right portfolio, 192; and income investing, 232, 233n, 234, 291; from life insurance, 263, 265; and mutual fund scandal, 120; and rebalancing, 37; from retirement plans, 207, 209, 216–17
WWW Internet Fund, 131
Wyderko, Susan, 95

Yale University, 100, 101, 111, 165, 170

Zero Alpha Group, 110
Zonis, Marvin, 177
Zurich Capital, 162
Zweig, Jason, 76